The Works of Jonathan Swift
by Jonathan Swift

NCF
with

THE

WORKS

OF

JONATHAN SWIFT, D.D.

DEAN OF ST PATRICK'S, DUBLIN;

CONTAINING

ADDITIONAL LETTERS, TRACTS, AND POEMS,

NOT HITHERTO PUBLISHED;

WITH

NOTES,

AND

A LIFE OF THE AUTHOR,

BY

WALTER SCOTT, ESQ.

VOLUME XIX.

EDINBURGH:

PRINTED FOR ARCHIBALD CONSTABLE AND CO. EDINBURGH;
WHITE, COCHRANE, AND CO. AND GALE, CURTIS, AND FENNER,
LONDON; AND JOHN CUMMING, DUBLIN.

1814.

CONTENTS

OF

VOLUME NINETEENTH.

SWIFT'S
EPISTOLARY CORRESPONDENCE.

LETTERS
FROM JANUARY 1735-6 TO JANUARY 1746.

VOL. XIX.   A

LETTERS

FROM THE EARL OF ORRERY.

January 3, 1735-6.

DEAR SIR,

I HAVE thought it more than a century since I saw you. I crawled out to you on Saturday, but was forced to come from your house and go to bed; since which time I have not stirred out of my chamber. My cold continues still bad; and has been hanging upon me now for above a fortnight. Pray tell me when I may hope to see you again: *et notas audire et reddere voces.* I dine at home to-morrow: will you share a fowl with me? I am scarce able to hold up my head; but the sight of you will go a great way toward recovering

Your ever obliged and faithful servant,

ORRERY.

FROM MRS PENDARVES.

Bath, Jan. 1735-6.

SIR,

I AM told you have some thoughts of coming here in the spring. I do not think it proper to tell you how well pleased I am with that faint prospect: for such I must call it till the report is confirmed with your own hand. I write all in haste to know if you really have any such design; for if you have, I shall order my affairs accordingly, that I may be able to meet you here. The good old custom of wishing a happy new year to one's friends is now exploded amongst our refined people of the present age; but I hope you will give me leave to tell you, without being offended, that I wish you many years of happiness. The physicians have at last advised my sister to the Bath waters. We have been here a fortnight: they do not disagree with her; this is all can be said of them at present. I wrote to you from Paradise, and hope there is a letter of yours travelling towards me: I think I have used you to a bad custom of late, that of writing two letters for one of yours. I am often told I have great assurance in writing to you at all; and to be sure I must do it with great fear and trembling. I am not believed when I affirm I write to you with as much ease as to any correspondent I have; for I know you are as much above criticising a letter of mine, as I should be below your notice, if I gave myself any affected airs: you have encouraged my correspondence, and I should be a brute if I did not make the best of such an opportunity.

Bath is full of people, such as they are; none

worth giving you any account of: my solace is Mrs Barber, whose spirit and good countenance cheers me whenever I hear or see her; she is at present pretty well.

Company is this moment coming up stairs, and I can only add that I am, Sir,

your most faithful humble servant,

M. PENDARVES.

TO MR FAULKNER.

January 8, 1735-6.

MR FAULKNER,

I AM answering a letter I had from Mr Pope, when I was at Cavan. My absence and sickness, since I retired, have hindered me from writing to him. He complains of his unluckiness that you could never find him at home, which, he says, since his mother's death, he is often absent from. I here will transcribe a paragraph which relates to you, and I desire you will return an answer to it, time enough for me to send a letter to-night, and I will insert the sum of it.

" As to his (Mr Faulkner's) design about my works, I beg you will desire him to postpone it, until he sees the duodecimo edition of them here, with the first volume, published by Lintot: for that, joined to the rest by Gillever, * will make the completest hitherto extant, and is revised by me. I guess they will be out at Christmas."

---

* Lawton Gillever, a bookseller.—H.

Pray, let me know what answer I shall make to Mr Pope : write it down and send it by any messenger, the sooner the better, for I am an ill writer at night.

I am yours, &c.

JON. SWIFT.

I think you may send your answer by the bearer, for it need not take above two lines.

FROM DR SHERIDAN.

Cavan, Jan. 17, 1735-6.

DEAR SIR,

I RECEIVED your letter of reproaches with pleasure ; and as I know you hate excuses, I shall make none. Whoever has informed you that I was not in my school at the right time appointed, has not done me justice ; for whatever else I may disappoint, that shall be inviolably and punctually observed by me. * * * * * * * *

As for my *quondam* friends, as you style them, *quon-dam* them all. It is the most decent way I can curse them ; for they lulled me asleep till they stole my school into the hands of a blockhead, and have driven me toward the latter end of my life to a disagreeable solitude, where I have the misery to reflect upon my folly in making such a perfidious choice, at a time when it was not in my nature to suspect any soul upon earth. * * * * * * *

Now to think a little for myself. The Duke of Dorset does certainly owe me a small living, for the

expensive entertainment I gave him from Terence.*
I only want a proper person to dun him; and I
know it will be done if my Lord Orrery will undertake it.   Do not think me sanguine in this; for
more unlikely and less reasonable favours have been
granted.   God knows whether, during my life, we
shall have another scholar sent us for a lord lieutenant.   *   *   *   *   *   *   *   *   *   *   *   *

I wish you as much happiness as I have plague,
which is enough for any honest man.   I am, dear Sir,
   Your most obedient very humble servant,
              THOMAS SHERIDAN.

TO MR POPE.

February 7, 1735-6.

IT is some time since I dined at the Bishop of
Derry's, where Mr Secretary Cary told me, with
great concern, that you were taken very ill.   I have
heard nothing since, only I have continued in great
pain of mind, yet for my own sake and the world's
more than for yours; because I well know how little
you value life, both as a philosopher, and a Christian; particularly the latter, wherein hardly one in
a million of us heretics can equal you.   If you are
well recovered, you ought to be reproached for not
putting me especially out of pain, who could not
bear the loss of you; although we must be for ever
distant as much as if I were in the grave, for which
my years and continual indisposition are preparing
me every season.   I have staid too long from pres-

---

* This was a play of Terence, acted by the Doctor's scholars
for the entertainment of the duke.—D. S.

sing you to give me some ease by an account of
your health; pray do not use me so ill any more.
I look upon you as an estate from which I receive
my best annual-rents, although I am never to see it.
Mr Tickel was at the same meeting under the same
real concern; and so were a hundred others of this
town who had never seen you.

I read to the Bishop of Derry the paragraph in
your letter which concerned him, and his lordship
expressed his thankfulness in a manner that became
him. He is esteemed here as a person of learning,
and conversation, and humanity, but he is beloved
by all people.

I have nobody now left but you: pray be so kind
as to outlive me, and then die as soon as you please,
but without pain, and let us meet in a better place,
if my religion will permit, but rather my virtue, although much unequal to yours. Pray let my Lord
Bathurst know how much I love him; I still insist
on his remembering me, although he is too much
in the world to honour an absent friend with his
letters. My state of health is not to boast of;
my giddiness is more or less too constant; I sleep
ill, and have a poor appetite. I can as easily write
a poem in the Chinese language as my own: I am
as fit for matrimony as invention; and yet I have
daily schemes for innumerable essays in prose, and
proceed sometimes to no less than half a dozen
lines, which the next morning become waste paper. What vexes me most is, that my female
friends, who could bear me very well a dozen years
ago, have now forsaken me, although I am not so
old in proportion to them, as I formerly was: which
I can prove by arithmetic, for then I was double
their age, which now I am not. Pray put me out
of fear as soon as you can, about that ugly report

of your illness; and let me know who this Che-selden * is, that has so lately sprung up in your favour. Give me also some account of your neigh-bour † who writ to me from Bath : I hear he resolves to be strenuous for taking off the test; which grieves me extremely, from all the unprejudiced reasons I ever was able to form, and against the maxims of all wise Christian governments, which always had some established religion, leaving at best a tolera-tion to others.

Farewell my dearest friend; ever, and upon eve-ry account that can create friendship and esteem.

JON. SWIFT.

FROM LADY BETTY GERMAIN.

February 10, 1735-6.

I AM sorry to hear your complaints still of gid-diness. I was in hopes you would have mended, like my purblind eyes, with old age. According to the custom of all old women, I must recommend to you a medicine, which is certainly a very inno-cent one, and they say does great good to that dis-temper, which is only wearing oil-cloth the breadth of your feet, and next to your skin. I have often found it to do me good for the headach.

I do not know what offences the Duke of Dorset's club, as you call them, commits in your eyes; but, to my apprehension, the parliament cannot but

---

* The celebrated surgeon and anatomist.—BOWLES.
† Mr Pulteney.

behave well, since they let him have such a quiet session. And as to all sorts of politics, they are now my utter aversion, and I will leave them to be discussed by those who have a better skill in them.

If my niece has been humbled by being nine years older, her late inherited great fortune will beautify her in the eyes of a great many people; so she may grow proud again upon that. The Countess of Suffolk is your humble servant. Mr Pope and she appear to have a true value for one another, so I suppose there is no doubt of it; I will answer for my friend's sincerity, and I do not question Mr Pope's. Why, pray, do you fancy I do not desire to cultivate Mr Pope's acquaintance? But perhaps, if I seek it too much, I might meet with a rebuff, as you say her M. did. However, we do often dine together at third places; and as to my own house, though he would be extremely welcome, he has too numerous friends and acquaintance already to spare me a day, unless you will come to England and then he might be induced to meet you here. Mrs Biddy Floyd has passed thus far of the winter in better health than usual, though her cough will not forsake her. She is much your humble servant, and so is most sincerely your old friend,   E. GERMAIN.

TO MRS WHITEWAY.

February 18, 1735-6.

My DEAR MADAM,
I PITY you and your family, and I heartily pray for both: I pity myself, and my prayers are not

wanting : but I pity not him. *   I count already
that you and I and the world must lose him : but
do not lose yourself.   I was born to a million of
disappointments ; I had set my heart very much
upon that young man ; but I find he has no business in so corrupt a world.   Therefore pray take
courage from Christianity, which will assist you
when humanity fails : I wish I were in his condition, with his virtues.   I am a little mending, to
my shame be it spoken.   I shall also lose a sort of
a son as well as you ; only our cases are different ;
for you have more, and it is your duty to preserve
yourself for them.   I am ever your most affectionate
and obedient, &c.

JON. SWIFT.

FROM THE BISHOP OF KILMORE. †

February 23, 1735-6.

REVEREND SIR,
I send you the whole piece, ‡ such as it is : I
fear you will find the addition, pursuant to your
hint, heavy ; for I could not get my imagination
warmed to the same degree as in the former part.
I hope you will supply what shall be wanting of

---

* Theophilus Harrison, Esq. a young gentleman of three-and-
twenty, who was then upon his death-bed.—D. S.
  † Dr Josiah Hort, afterward Archbishop of Tuam.—N.
  ‡ A satire on Quadrille, for which Mr Faulkner the printer,
fell under the lash of government, and was imprisoned.   The
Dean was very indignant at the bishop's backwardness in not
standing forth to save Faulkner.   See his letter of 12th May 1736.

spirit; and when you have pruned the rough feathers, the ands and thats, &c. you will send the Kite to the Faulconer, to set it a flying.
I am your very faithful and
obedient servant,

J. H.

May not I claim three or four copies when printed?

TO MISS HARRISON.

Feb. 23, 1735-6.

DEAR MISS HARRISON,
I AM in all possible concern for your present situation : I heartily wish you could prevail on your mother to remove immediately to some friend or neigbbour's house, that she may be out of the sight and hearing of what must be done to-day. I wish your eldest brother Whiteway would take care to carry her to some part of the town where she might continue until your house may be put in order, and every thing that might renew the memory of melancholy objects be removed. Let your brother Whiteway write to me, that I may know how you all are, particularly your poor mother.
I am ever, &c.
JON. SWIFT.

FROM DR SHERIDAN.

February 23, 1735-6.

DEAR SIR,

I AM extremely concerned to find your old disorder has got hold of you again, which would not have happened if you had taken my advice to continue here where you were well. I cannot help retorting, that I never knew any person so unadvisable as you are, especially when it comes from me, who am famous for giving the best advice, and following the worst. Surely Mr —— cannot be so unjust as to let me be above —— pounds a sufferer for that profligate brute he shaked-off upon me : if he does persevere in it, I will let all mankind know, that he acts rather like a little rascally Irish solicitor than a man of honour. I have already almost finished a dialogue between Lady Betty Tattle and John Solemn (if my money be not paid, necessity must make me write for bread) upon a subject they will not much like ; which I vow to God shall be published. As I do not wear a sword, I must have recourse to the weapon in my hand. It is a better method than a lawsuit. My school only supplies me with present food, without which I cannot live. I hope, if I have any friends left, it may increase, and once more put me out of a miserable dependence upon the caprice of friendship. This year has been to me like steering through the Cyclades in a storm without a rudder ; I hope to have a less dangerous and more open sea the next ; and as you are out of all danger to feel the like sufferings, I pray God you may never feel a dun to the end of your life ; for it is too shocking to an honest heart.   It grieves me much to hear poor Mr Harrison is in such a dangerous way.   I pray God preserve him, not only for his poor mother's sake, but the good of mankind; for I think I never knew so valuable a young man.   I beseech you to let me know, by the next post, how he is.   I fear the worst of that horrid treacherous distemper.   I am, dear Sir, with all respect,

Your most obedient and
very humble servant,
THOMAS SHERIDAN.

I lost sixty-six pounds by a rogue who run off to Drumcor last year.

TO MRS WHITEWAY.

Feb. 25, 1735-6.

DEAR MADAM,

IN the midst of your grief and my own for the same misfortune, I cannot forbear complaining of your conduct through the whole course of your affliction, which made you not only neglect yourself, but the greater part of those who are left, and, by the same law of nature, have an equal title to your care.   I writ on Monday to Miss Harrison, that she would beg you, in my name, to remove some hours to a neighbour, that your ears might not be harassed with the preparations for what was then to be done.   She told me you would not yield; and, at the same time, she much feared she must lose you too.   Some degree of wisdom is required in the greatest calamity, because God requires it; because he knows what is best for us because he never intended any thing like perfect happiness in the present life; and, because it is our duty, as well as interest, to submit. I will make you another proposal, and shall take it very unkindly if you do not comply. It is, that you would come hither this day immediately, where you will have a convenient apartment, and leave the scene that will be always putting you in mind of your loss. Your daughter can manage the house, and sometimes step to see you. All care should be taken of you, and Dr Robinson will visit you with more ease, if you have occasion for him. Mrs Ridgeway shall attend you, and I will be your companion. Let Miss Harrison return me an answer, and things shall be ready for you. I am ever, with true esteem and affection, dear Madam,

Your most obedient servant and cousin,

JON. SWIFT.

FROM DR SHERIDAN.

Feb. 29, 1735-6.

DEAR SIR,

I SINCERELY condole with you for the unspeakable loss of Mr Harrison, which cannot be repaired in any other of his age in this world. It wounds my heart every moment I recollect him. I do verily believe no man living has met with such severe trials in losses of this kind as you have; and for this last, I must own, that I have great compassion for you, as he was every day growing more and more into a friend and companion; especially at a time of life which requires such a comfort: God Almighty support his poor mother; for none else can give her consolation under such a dreadful affliction.

Poor old Mr Price cannot hold out a fortnight; and his son claims your promise of getting him something from the Concordatum; if it overtakes him alive, it may be a legacy for a worthy suffering person, who has fallen a sacrifice to his principles. I am, dear Sir, with all respect,

Your most obedient and
very humble servant,
THOMAS SHERIDAN.

FROM MR CARTER. *

Henrietta Street, March 15, 1735-6.

SIR,

I WOULD have waited on you, when I sent my servant with a message, but was informed you did not see company.

I have no doubt the printer will have occasion for a great many cargoes from our friend Mr Jervas. †

I am very glad I had an opportunity of doing any thing agreeable to you. I have long wished

---

* Mr Carter was Master of the Rolls in Ireland.—D. S.

+ A fine print of the Dean, engraved by Fourdrinier, from an original picture painted by Jervas, which was afterward purchased by the Earl of Chesterfield, and placed in his elegant library at May Fair, in the collection of English authors.—D. S.

for some instance of assuring you that I am, with great respect,

Your most obedient and
most humble servant,
THOMAS CARTER.

FROM MR POPE.

March 25, 1736.

IF ever I write more epistles in verse, one of them shall be addressed to you. I have long concerted it and begun it, but I would make what bears your name as finished as my last work ought to be, that is to say, more finished than any of the rest. The subject is large, and will divide into four epistles, which naturally follow the Essay on Man, viz. 1. Of the Extent and Limits of Human Reason and Science: 2. A View of the useful and therefore attainable, and of the unuseful and therefore unattainable, Arts: 3. Of the Nature, Ends, Application, and Use of different Capacities: 4. Of the Use of Learning, of the Science of the World, and of Wit. It will conclude with a Satire against the misapplication of all these, exemplified by pictures, characters, and examples.

But alas! the task is great, and *non sum qualis eram!* My understanding, indeed, such as it is, is extended rather than diminished: I see things more in the whole, more consistent, and more clearly deduced from, and related to each other. But what I gain on the side of philosophy, I lose on the side of poetry: the flowers are gone, when the fruits begin to ripen, and the fruits perhaps will never ripen perfectly. The climate (under our Heaven of a court) is but cold and uncertain; the winds rise, and the winter comes on. I find myself but little disposed to build a new house; I have nothing left but to gather up the relicks of a wreck, and look about me to see how few friends I have left. Pray whose esteem or admiration should I desire now to procure by my writing? whose friendship or conversation to obtain by them? I am a man of desperate fortunes, that is, a man whose friends are dead, for I never aimed at any other fortune than in friends. As soon as I had sent my last letter, I received a most kind one from you, expressing great pain for my late illness at Mr Cheselden's. I conclude you was eased of that friendly apprehension in a few days after you had dispatched yours, for mine must have reached you then. I wondered a little at your quere who Cheselden was? it shows that the truest merit does not travel so far any way as on the wings of poetry; he is the most noted, and most deserving man in the whole profession of chirurgery; and has saved the lives of thousands by his manner of cutting for the stone. I am now well, or what I must call so.

I have lately seen some writings of Lord Bolingbroke's, since he went to France. Nothing can depress his genius: whatever befals him, he will still be the greatest man in the world, either in his own time, or with posterity.

Every man you know or care for here, inquires of you, and pays you the only devoir he can, that of drinking your health. I wish you had any motive to see this kingdom. I could keep you, for I am rich; that is, I have more than I want. I can

afford room for yourself and two servants; I have
indeed room enough; nothing but myself at home:
the kind and hearty housewife is dead; the agreeable and instructive neighbour is gone; yet my
house is enlarged, and the gardens extend and
flourish, as knowing nothing of the guest they have
lost. I have more fruit-trees and kitchen garden
than you have any thought of; nay I have good
melons and pine-apples of my own growth. I am
as much a better gardener, as I am a worse poet,
than when you saw me: but gardening is near akin
to philosophy, for Tully says, *agricultura proxima
sapientiæ*. For God's sake, why should not you
(that are a step higher than a philosopher, a divine,
yet have more grace and wit than to be a bishop)
even give all you have to the poor of Ireland (for
whom you have already done every thing else)
so quit the place, and live and die with me? And
let *tales animæ concordes* be our motto and our
epitaph.

FROM DR SHERIDAN.

March 27, 1736.

DEAR SIR,

I HAD a pleasure and grief at once in your letter,
to find you had not forgotten me, and to find you
uneasy at a thing which God only can mend. The
dream, which I had before the receipt of yours, was
so odd and out of the way, that if Artemidorus were
living, he would confess it to be out of all methods
of interpretation; yet I cannot avoid imparting it

to you, because if you be not much changed, no man ever could sift a matter to the truth beyond you.   Thus it was ;

Imprimis, I fell asleep (or I could not dream) and what was the first thing I saw, but honest Cato in a cockboat by himself, engaging not only a large fleet of foreigners, but now and then obliged to tack about against some dirty shattered floats, filled with his own countrymen.   All were his enemies, except a very few, who were pressed and carried on against their will by the arbitrary power of the, rowers.   I would give a shilling, as low as money is reduced, to know the meaning of it.

* * * * * * * * * * * *
* * * * * * * * * * * *

DR SHERIDAN TO MRS ALBA VIA.

DEAR MADAM,

I THANK my dear friend the Dean and you for your kind warning against a cold, which, I thank God, is not among us, as I told you in my last. Whisky, of which I take half a pint in the twenty-four hours, with an agreeable mixture of garlick, bitter orange, gentian-root, snake-root, wormwood, &c. hath preserved me from the asthma for three weeks past to any violent degree.   I am happy when my gaspings are no quicker than those of a very quick walker.   So much for myself.

Now for your jewel of a son.   I never met with any boy of his age of such thorough good sense, and so great a thirst for improving himself. I thank God, he is as you and I could wish. The Dean will have pleasure to examine him. Adieu.

FROM DR SHERIDAN.

April 3, 1736.

Dear Sir,

I would have written last post, but I had such a violent headach, that I could no more think than a cabbage. And now all the business I have is to make you a paper visit, only to ask you, how you do? You may think me impertinent for the question; but when I tell you, that I have not above three friends, you will not wonder that I should be afraid of losing one of them; and therefore I must give you some rules of regimen.

1. Walk little and moderately.
2. Ride slow and often.
3. Keep your temper even with my friend Mrs Whiteway.
4. Do not strain your voice.
5. Fret not at your servants' blunders.
6. Take a cheerful glass.
7. Study as little as possible.
8. Find out a merry fellow, and be much with him.

Get these precepts by heart, and observe them strictly; and, my life for yours, we shall see better times in the next century.

FROM MRS PENDARVES.

London, April 22, 1736.

Sir,

I am sorry you make use of so many good arguments for not coming to Bath. I was in hopes, you might be prevailed with. And though one of my strongest reasons for wishing you there, was the desire I had of seeing you, I assure you the consideration of your health took place of it. I have heard since I received the favour of your last letter, that you have been much out of order. I believe we sympathised, for I was very ill with a feverish disorder and cough for a month, which obliged me to defer answering your letter till I came to town. I left the Bath last Sunday se'nnight, very full and gay. I think Bath a more comfortable place to live in than London; all the entertainments of the place lie in a small compass, and you are at your liberty to partake of them, or let them alone, just as it suits your humour. This town is grown to such an enormous size, that above half the day must be spent in the streets, going from one place to another. I like it every year less and less. I was grieved at parting with Mrs Barber. I left her pretty well. I had more pleasure in her conversation than from any thing I met with at the Bath. My sister has found the good effect of your kind wishes. She is very much recovered, and in town with me at present; but leaves me in a fortnight to go to my mother.

When I went out of town last autumn, the reigning madness was Farinelli:* I find it now turned

---

* A celebrated Italian singer.

on " Pasquin," a dramatic satire on the times. * It
has had almost as long a run as the Beggar's Opera;
but, in my opinion, not with equal merit, though it
has humour.   Monstrous preparations are making
for the royal wedding. †   Pearl, gold and silver,
embroidered on gold and silver tissues.   I am too
poor and too dull to make one among the fine mul-
titude.   The newspapers say, my Lord Carteret's
youngest daughter is to have the Duke of Bedford. ‡
I hear nothing of it from the family; but think it
not unlikely.   The Duke of Marlborough and his
grandmother are upon bad terms. The Duke of
Bedford, who has also been ill treated by her, has
offered the Duke of Marlborough to supply him
with ten thousand pounds a-year, if he will go to
law and torment the old dowager.   The Duke of
Chandos's marriage has made a great noise ; and the
poor duchess is often reproached with her being
bred up in Bur Street, Wapping. §

Mrs Donnellan, I am afraid, is so well treated in
Ireland, that I must despair of seeing her here: and
how or when I shall be able to come to her, I cannot

---

* This was written by Henry Fielding, Esq.; and was a re-
hearsal of a comedy and a tragedy ; the comedy was called " The
Election," and the tragedy, " The Life and Death of Queen
Common Sense." This and some other dramatic satires, by
the same author, levelled against the administration of the late
Lord Orford, produced an act of parliament for licensing the
stage, and limiting the number of playhouses, which was passed
in 1737.—H.
    † Of Frederick, Prince of Wales.—H.
    ‡ His grace married Miss Gower, daughter of the Lord Gower
by his first wife, on the 1st of April 1737.—H.
    § She was Lady Daval, widow of Sir Thomas Daval, and had
a fortune of 40,000l.—H.

yet determine. She is so good to me in her letters, as always to mention you.

I hope I shall hear from you soon : you owe me that pleasure, for the concern I was under when I heard you were ill. I am, Sir, your faithful and obliged humble servant,

M. PENDARVES.

I beg my compliments to all friends that remember me, but particularly to Dr Delany.

TO MR POPE.

Dublin, April 22, 1736.

My common illness is of that kind which utterly disqualifies me for all conversation ; I mean my deafness; and indeed it is that only which discourages me from all thoughts of going to England ; because I am never sure that it may not return in a week. If it were a good honest gout, I could catch an interval to take a voyage, and in a warm lodging get an easy chair, and be able to hear and roar among my friends.

As to what you say of your letters, since you have many years of life more than I, my resolution is to direct my executors to send you all your letters, well sealed and packetted, along with some legacies mentioned in my will, and leave them entirely to your disposal : those things are all tied up, endorsed and locked in a cabinet, and I have not one servant who can properly be said to write or read: no mortal shall copy them, but you shall surely have them, when I am no more.

I have a little repined at my being hitherto slipped by you in your epistles; not from any other ambition than the title of a friend, and in that sense I expect you shall perform your promise, if your health, and leisure, and inclination will permit. I deny your losing on the side of poetry; I could reason against you a little from experience; you are, and will be some years to come, at the age when invention still keeps its ground, and judgment is at full maturity; but your subjects are much more difficult when confined to verse. I am amazed to see you exhaust the whole science of morali y in so masterly a manner. Sir W. Temple said, that the loss of friends was a tax upon long life: it need not be very long, since you have had so great a share.; but I have not above one left: and in this country I have only a few general companions of good nature, and middling understandings. How should I know Cheselden? On your side, men of fame start up and die before we here (at least I) know any thing of the matter. I am a little comforted with what you say of Lord Bolingbroke's genius still keeping up, and preparing to appear by effects worthy of the author, and useful to the world.—— Common reports have made me very uneasy about your neighbour Mr Pulteney. It is affirmed that he hath been very near death: I love him for being a patriot in most corrupted times, and highly esteem his excellent understanding. Nothing but the perverse nature of my disorders, as I have above described them, and which are absolute disqualifications for converse, could hinder me from waiting on you at Twittenham, and nursing you to Paris. In short my ailments amount to a prohibition; although I am as you describe yourself, what *I must call well;* yet I have not spirits left to ride out, which (excepting walking) was my only diversion. And I must expect to decline every month, like one who lives upon his principal sum which must lessen every day: and indeed I am likewise literally almost in the same case, while every body owes me, and nobody pays me. Instead of a young race of patriots on your side, which gives me some glimpse of joy, here we have the direct contrary; a race of young dunces and atheists, or old villains and monsters, whereof four-fifths are more wicked and stupid than Chartres. Your wants are so few, that you need not be rich to supply them; and my wants are so many, that a king's seven millions of guineas would not support me.

TO DR SHERIDAN. *

April 24, 1736.

I HAVE been very ill for these two months past with giddiness and deafness, which lasted me till about ten days ago, when I gradually recovered, but still am weak and indolent, not thinking any thing worth my thoughts; and although (I forget what I am going to say, so it serves for nothing) I am well enough to ride, yet I will not be at the pains. Your friend Mrs Whiteway, who is upon all occasions so zealous to vindicate, is one whom I desire you to chide; for during my whole sickness, she was perpetually plaguing and sponging on me;

---

* The paragraphs in *Italics* were written by Mrs Whiteway.—H.

and though she would drink no wine herself, yet she
increased the expence by making me force it down
her throat. Some of your eight rules I follow, some
I reject, some I cannot compass, I mean merry fellows. Mr J. R—— never fails; I did within two days
past ring him such a peal in relation to you, that he
must be the d——l not to consider it; I will use him
the same way if he comes to-morrow (which I do
not doubt) for a pint of wine. I like your project
of a satire on Fairbrother, who is an errant rascal in
every circumstance.

Every syllable that is worth reading in this letter,
you are to suppose I writ; the Dean only took the
hints from me, but he has put them so ill together,
that I am forced to tell you this in my own justifi-
cation. Had you been worth hanging, you would
come to town this vacation, and I would have shewn
you a poem on the Legion Club. *I do not doubt*
but that a certain person will pretend he writ it, be-
cause there is a copy of it in hand, lying on his ta-
ble; but do not mind that, for there are some people
in the world will say any thing. I wish you could
give some account of poor Dr Sheridan; *I hear the*
reason he did not come to town this Easter *is, that*
he waited to see a neighbour of his hanged.

Whatever is said in this page by Goody Whiteway, I have not read, nor will read: but assure you,
if it relates to me it is all a lie; for she says you have
taught her that art, and as the world goes, and she
takes you for a wise man, she ought to follow your
practice. To be serious, I am sorry you said so little of your own affairs, and of your health; and
when will you pay me any money? for upon my
conscience you have half starved me.

The plover eggs were admirable, and the worsted

for the Dean's stockings so fine, that not one knitter here can knit them.

We neither of us know what the other hath writ; so one answer will serve, if you write to us both, provided you justly give us both our share, and each of us will read our own part. Pray tell us how you breathe, and whether that disorder be better.

If the Dean should give you any hint about money, you need not mind him, for to my knowledge he borrowed twenty pounds a month ago, to keep himself alive.

I am sorry to tell you, that poor Mrs Whiteway is to be hanged on Tuesday next for stealing a piece of Indian silk out of Bradshaw's shop, and did not set the house on fire, as I advised her. I have writ a very masterly poem on the Legion Club; which, if the printer should be condemned to be hanged for it, you will see in a threepenny book; for it is 240 lines. Mrs Whiteway is to have half the profit and half the hanging.

The Drapier went this day to the Tholsel as a merchant, to sign a petition to the government against lowering the gold, where we hear he made a long speech, for which he will be reckoned a jacobite. God send hanging does not go round.

                    Yours, &c.

TO BISHOP HORT.

                              May 12, 1736.
My Lord,
I have two or three times begun a letter to your lordship, and as often laid it aside; until, by the unasked advice of some friends of yours, and of all

my own, I resolved at last to tell you my thoughts upon the affair of the poor printer who suffered so much upon your lordship's account, confined to a dungeon among common thieves, and others with infectious diseases, to the hazard of his life; beside the expence of above twenty-five pounds, and beside the ignominy to be sent to Newgate like a common malefactor.

His misfortunes do also very highly and personally concern me. For, your lordship declaring your desire to have that paper looked for, he did at my request search his shop, and unfortunately found it; and, although he had absolutely refused before to print it, because my name as the author was fixed to it; which was very legible, notwithstanding there was a scratch through the words; yet, at my desire, he ventured to print it. Neither did Faulkner ever name you as the author, although you sent the paper by a clergyman, one of your dependents: but your friends were the only persons who gave out the report of its having been your performance. I read your lordship's letter written to the printer, wherein you argue, " That he is, in these dealings, the adventurer, and must run the hazard of gain or loss." Indeed, my lord, the case is otherwise. He sells such papers to the running boys for farthings apiece; and is a gainer, by each, less than half a farthing; and it is seldom he sells above a hundred, unless they be of such as only spread by giving offence, and consequently endanger the printer both in loss of money and liberty, as was the case of that very paper: which, although it be written with spirit and humour, yet, if it had not affected Bettesworth, would scarce have cleared above a shilling to Faulkner; neither would he have done it at all but at my urgency, which was the effect of your lordship's commands to me. But, as your lordship has since been universally known for the author, although never named by Faulkner or me; so it is as generally known that you never gave him the least consideration, for his losses, disgraces, and dangers of his life. I have heard this, and more, from every person of my acquaintance whom I see at home or abroad: and particularly from one person too high to name,* who told me all the particulars: and I heartily wished, upon your account, that I could have assured him that the poor man had received the least mark of your justice, or, if you please to call it so, your generosity: which I would gladly inform that great person of before he leave us.

Now, my lord, as God, assisting your own good management of a very ample fortune, has made you extremely rich: I may venture to say, that the printer has a demand, in all conscience, justice, and honour, to be fully refunded, both for his disgraces, his losses, and the apparent danger of his life; and that my opinion ought to be of some weight, because I was an innocent instrument, drawn in by your lordship, against Faulkner's will, to be an occasion of his sufferings. And if you shall please to recompense him in the manner that all people hope or desire, it will be no more in your purse than a drop in the bucket: and as soon as I shall be informed of it, I shall immediately write to that very great person, in such a manner as will be most to the advantage of your character; for which, I am sure, he will rejoice, and so will all your friends;

---

* The Duke of Dorset probably.

or, if you have any enemies, they will be put to silence.

Your lordship has too good an understanding to imagine that my principal regard in this affair is not to your reputation, although it be likewise mingled with pity to the innocent sufferer. And I hope you will consider, that this case is not among those where it is a mark of magnanimity to despise the censure of the world : because all good men will differ from you, and impute your conduct only to a sparing temper, upon an occasion where common justice and humanity required a direct contrary proceeding.

I conclude with assuring your lordship again, that what I have written was chiefly for your lordship's credit and service : because I am, with great truth,

Your Lordship's most, &c.
JON. SWIFT.

FROM DR SHERIDAN TO DR SWIFT AND MRS WHITEWAY.

May 12, 1736.

DEAR SIR,

I send you an encomium upon Fowlbrother enclosed, which I hope you will correct ; and if the world should charge me with flattery, you will be so good as to explain the obligations I lie under to that great and good bookseller.

MADAM,

How the plague can you expect that I should answer two persons at once, except you should think

I had two heads? but this is not the only giddiness you have been guilty of. However I shall not let the Dean know it.

SIR,

I wonder you would trust Mrs Whiteway to write any thing in your letter. You have been always too generous in your confidence. Never was any gentleman so betrayed and abused. She said more of you than I dare commit to this paper.

MADAM,

I have let the Dean know all the kind things you said of him to me, and that he has not such a true friend in the world. I hope you will make him believe the same of me.

SIR,

I wish you would banish her your house, and take my wife in your stead, who loves you dearly, and would take all proper care, if any sickness should seize you. She would as infallibly take as much care of you as ever she did of me; and you know her to be a good-natured, cheerful, agreeable companion, and a very handy woman; whereas Mrs Whiteway is a morose, disagreeable prater, and the most awkward devil about a sick person, and very ill-natured into the bargain.

MADAM,

I believe it will not require any protestations to convince you, that you have not a more sincere friend upon the earth than I am. The Dean confesses that he had some little dislikings to you (I fancy he hears some whispers against you) but I believe his share of this letter will set all matters right. I know he has too much honour to read your part of it; and therefore I may venture to speak my mind freely concerning him. Pray, between ourselves, is he not grown very positive of late? He used formerly to listen to his friends' advice, but now we may as well talk to a sea storm. I could say more, only I fear this letter may miscarry.

Sir,

I beg that impertinent woman, who has unaccountably got your ear, may not interrupt you, while you read the encomium, and while you give it a touch of your brush; for I fear the colours are not strong enough. Cannot you draw another picture of him? I wish you would; for he is a subject fit for the finest hand. What a glorious thing it would be to make him hang himself!

As to business, I have nothing to say about money yet a while; but by the next post you shall have two scholars notes, which will amount to about fourteen or fifteen pounds; and if Mr —— can force himself to do me justice, it will put about twenty-five pounds in your pocket. But then you must remark, that you will put twenty of it out again, and send it to Mrs ——. I have nobody after that to gather for but you; and if money comes in as I expect, you may borrow from, Sir, yours. My tenants are as poor as Job, and as wicked as his wife, or the dogs would have given me some money before this. Mr Jones swears he will not pay you the bond which I gave you, except you come down to receive it; for he thinks it but reasonable that you should honour Belturbet as well as Cavan. Mr Coote would give three of his eyes to see you at Cootehill. All the country long for you. My green geese, &c. are grown too fat. I have twenty lambs,

upon honour, as plump as puffins, and as delicate
as ortolans.   I ate one of them yesterday.   A bull,
a bull: hoh, I cry mercy.   As I return from the
county of Galway next vacation, I intend to make
Dublin my way, in order to conduct you hither.
Our country is now in high beauty, and every inch
of it walkable.   I wish you all happiness till I see
you; and remain, with all respect,

    Your most obedient and very humble servant,

                      THOMAS SHERIDAN.

TO DR SHERIDAN.

Dublin, May 15, 1736.

MRS WHITEWAY and I were fretting, raging,
storming, and fuming, that you had not sent a letter since you got to your Caban (for the V conso-
nant was anciently a B) I mean Cavan: but however, we mingled pity; for we feared you had run
away from school, and left the key under the door.
We were much disappointed, that the spring and
beginning of summer had not introduced the muses,
and that your now walkable roads had not roused
your spirits.   We are here the happiest people in
the universe; we have a year and a half before the
club will meet to be revenged farther on the clergy,* who never offended them; and in England
their parliament are following our steps, only with
two or three steps for our one.   It is well you have

---

* The parliament of Ireland, whose bills for establishing a
modus of the tithe upon hemp, excited Swift's indignation, which
he vented both in prose and verse.

done with the church; but pray take care to get money, else in a year of two more they will forbid all Greek and Latin schools, as popish and jacobite. I took leave of the duke and duchess to-day. He has prevailed on us to make a promise to bestow upon England 25,000l. a year for ever, by lowering the gold coin, against the petition of all the merchants, shopkeepers, &c. to a man. May his own estate be lowered the other forty parts, for we now lose by all gold two and a half *per cent.* He will be a better (that is to say a worse) man by 60,000l. than he was when he came over; and the nation better (that is to say worse) by above half a million; beside the worthy method he hath taken in disposal of employments in church and state. Here is a cursed long libel running about in manuscript on the Legion Club; it is in verse, and the foolish town imputes it to me. There were not above thirteen abused (as it is said) in the original; but others have added more, which I never saw; though I have once read the true one. What has Fowlbrother done to provoke you? I either never heard, or have forgot your provocations; but he was a fellow I have never been able to endure. If it can be done, I will have it printed; and the title shall be, " Upon a certain bookseller (or printer) in Utopia." Mrs Whiteway will be here to-morrow, and she will answer your sincere, open-hearted letter very particularly: for which I will now leave room. So adieu for one night.

* " Sir, I am most sincerely obliged to you for all the civil things you have said to me, and of me

---

* Mrs Whiteway here begins.—H.

to the Dean. I found the good effects of them this day; when I waited on him, he received me with great good humour, said something had happened since he saw me last, that had convinced him of my merit; that he was sorry he had treated me with so little distinction, and that hereafter I should not be put upon the foot of an humble companion, but treated like a lady of wit and learning, and fortune; that if he could prevail on Dr Sheridan to part with his wife, he would make her his friend, his nurse, and the manager of his family. I approved entirely of his choice, and at the same time expressed my fears, that it would be impossible for you to think of living without her; this is all that sticks with me. But considering the friendship you express to me for the Dean, I hope you will be persuaded to consider his good rather than your own; and send her up immediately; or else it will put him to the expence of giving three shillings and four pence for a wife; and he declares that the badness of pay of his tithes, since the resolutions of the parliament of Ireland, puts this out of his power."

I could not guess why you were so angry at Fowl-brother; till Mrs Whiteway, who you find is now with me, said it was for publishing some works of yours and mine like a rogue: which is so usual to their trade, that I now am weary of being angry with it. I go on, to desire that Mrs Donaldson * will let me know what I owe her, not in justice but generosity. If you could find wine and victuals, I could be glad to pass some part of the summer with

---

* An innkeeper at Cavan.—D. S.

you, if health would permit me; for I have some club enemies, that would be glad to shoot me, and I do not love to be shot: it is a death I have a particular aversion to. But I shall henceforth walk with servants well ordered, and have ordered them to kill my killers; however I would have them be the beginners. I will do what I can with Mr Richardson, who (money excepted) is a very honest man. How is your breathing? As to myself, my life and health are not worth a groat. How shall we get wine to your cabin? I can spare some; and am preparing diaculum to save my skin as far as Cavan; and even to Belturbet. * Pray God preserve you!

I am, &c.

JON. SWIFT.

TO MR BENJAMIN MOTTE.

Dublin, May 25, 1736.

SIR,

I LATELY received a long letter from Mr Faulkner, grievously complaining upon several articles of the ill treatment he hath met with from you, † and of the many advantageous offers he hath made you, with none of which you thought fit to comply. I am not qualified to judge in the fact, having heard but one side; only one thing I know, that the cruel

---

* Mr Richardson's rectory.—F.
† Motte filed a bill in Chancery in England, against Faulkner, for printing Swift's Works, to stop the sale of them there, which made the author write this letter.—F.

oppressions of this kingdom by England are not to be borne. You send what books you please hither, and the booksellers here can send nothing to you that is written here. As this is absolute oppression, if I were a bookseller in this town, I would use all the safe means to reprint London books, and run them to any town in England, that I could, because whoever offends not the laws of God, or the country he lives in, commits no sin. It was the fault of you and other booksellers who printed any thing supposed to be mine, that you did not agree with each other to print them together, if you thought they would sell to any advantage. I believe I told you long ago, that Mr Faulkner came to me, and told me his intention to print every thing that my friends told him they thought to be mine, and that I was discontented at it, but when he urged, that some other bookseller would do it, and that he would take the advice of my friends, and leave out what I pleased to order him, I said no more, but that I was sorry it should be done here.——But I am so incensed against the oppressions from England, and have so little regard to the laws they make, that I do, as a clergyman, encourage the merchants both to export wool and woollen manufactures to any country in Europe, or anywhere else ; and conceal it from the customhouse officers, as I would hide my purse from a highwayman, if he came to rob me on the road, although England hath made a law to the contrary : and so I would encourage our booksellers here to sell your authors books printed here, and send them to all the towns in England, if I could do it with safety and profit ; because (I repeat it) it is no offence against God, or the laws of the country I live in. Mr Faulkner hath dealt so fairly with me, that I have a great opinion of his honesty, although I never dealt with him as a printer or a bookseller; but since my friends told me, those things, called mine, would certainly be printed by some hedge bookseller, I was forced to be passive in the matter. I have some things which I shall leave my executors to publish after my decease, and have directed that they shall be printed in London. For, except small papers, and some treatises writ for the use of this kingdom, I always had those of any importance published in London, as you well know. For my own part, although I have no power any where, I will do the best offices I can to countenance Mr Faulkner. For, although I was not at all pleased to have that collection printed here, yet none of my friends advised me to be angry with him; although, if they had been printed in London by you and your partners, perhaps I might have pretended to some little profit. Whoever may have the hazard or advantage of what I shall leave to be printed in London after my decease, I will leave no other copies of them here; but, if Mr Faulkner should get the first printed copy, and reprint it here, and send his copies to England, I think he would do as right as you London booksellers, who load us with yours. If I live but a few years, I believe I shall publish some things that I think are important; but they shall be printed in London, although Mr Faulkner were my brother. I have been very tedious in telling you my thoughts on this matter, and so I remain, Sir,

Your most humble servant,

JON. SWIFT.

FROM MR FORD.

London, June 3, 1736.

DEAR SIR,

THOUGH you have left off corresponding with me these two years and a half, I cannot leave you off yet; and I think this is the sixth letter I have sent you, since I have heard one word of you from your own hand. My Lord Oxford told me last winter that he had heard from you, and you were then well. Mr Cæsar very lately told me the same. It is always the most welcome news that can come to me: but it would be a great addition to my pleasure to have it from yourself; and you know my sincere regard for you may in some measure claim it.

I have been engaged these five months in a most troublesome lawsuit with an Irish chairman. Those fellows swarm about St James's, and will hardly allow you to walk half a street, or even in the Park, on the fairest day. This rascal rushed into the entry of a tavern to force me into his chair, ran his poles against me, and would not let me pass till I broke his head. He made a jest of it that night; but the next morning an Irish solicitor came, out of profound respect, to advise me to make the fellow amends: he told a dismal story of the surgeon and the bloody shirt, and spoke against his own interest, merely to hinder me, whom he had never seen before, from being exposed. Neither his kind persuasions, nor the prudent counsels of our friends Mr L————, and a few more, could prevail on me. A few days after, the solicitor brought me a bill found by the grand jury, and a warrant under the hand of three justices against John Ford, without any other addition. To show his good will, he would not affront me by executing the warrant; but desired I would go to any justice of peace, and give bail to appear the next quarter sessions. By my not doing it, he found out the mistake of the name, which he said should be rectified in a new bill, and if I would not comply with their demands, after they had tried me for the assaults, they would bring an action of eighty or a hundred pounds damages. I threatened in my turn; at which he laughed, as I should do, if a little child should threaten to knock me down. As they proceeded against me, I thought it time to begin with them, and spoke to an acquaintance of mine, a justice of peace, who sent a warrant for the fellow, upon the waiter's oath, for assaulting me, and by a small stretch of power, committed him to the Gatehouse, where he remained some days for want of bail. I believe his bail would hardly have been judged sufficient, if his Irish solicitor had not gone to another justice, and taken a false oath, that the gentleman who committed him was out of town. This perjury, it seems, cannot be punished, because it was not upon record. We presented bills against each other to the grand jury, among whom there happened luckily to be some gentlemen : and though I did not know them, by their means my bill was found, and his returned *ignoramus.* Then I indicted him in the crown-office, the terror of the low people, where they often plague one another, and always make use of against those of better rank. Still the fellow blustered, and refused to make it up unless I would pay his expences; for his lawyer had persuaded him, that in the end he should recover damages sufficient.

to make amends for all. While he ruined himself
by law, he lost his business; for no gentleman
would take his chair. This brought down his
proud stomach; he came to me two days ago, made
his submissions, we gave reciprocal releases from all
actions, &c. and I have already received the thanks
of above forty gentlemen, for procuring them liberty
to walk the streets in quiet. Thus this great affair
has ended like the Yorkshire petition, which has
been the chief business of the House of Commons
this session. Toward the end, indeed, they found
a little time to show their good will to the church.
It is the general opinion, that the act for repealing
the Test would have passed, if Sir Robert Walpole
had not seen the necessity of his speaking, which he
did in the most artful manner he had ever done in
his life. Several courtiers voted against him, as
well as most of the patriots, and among others, Lord
Bathurst's two sons. In the House of Lords, next to
the Duke of Argyle, your friend Bathurst and Lord
Carteret have shown most rancour against ————.
It is a melancholy reflection, that all the great
officers of state, and the whole bench of bishops,
joined to the tories, could not prevent any one
question in disfavour of the church.

I am asked every day, if there be no hopes of
ever seeing you here again; and am sorry not to
be able to give any account of your intentions. I
doubt my long letters quite tire your patience; and
therefore conclude with assuring you, that nobody
wishes you all happiness more than I do, who am
most entirely yours, &c.

FROM DR SHERIDAN.

June 3, 1736.

DEAR SIR,

Mr Lucas is now in Dublin, who will pay that small bill on demand. I hope Mr ———— will not disappoint us, and then poor Mrs ———— will be relieved. I must set out soon for Dublin. At my return I will wait upon you to bring you home with me. The weather must and shall be good; and you must and shall be in good health; you must and shall come with me.

> My walk it is finish'd,
> My money diminish'd;
> But when you come down,
> I'll hold you a crown
> You'll soon make me rich,
> Or I'll die in a ditch.

Pray think of things beforehand, and do not be giddy as usual. The walk is a hundred and twelve yards long: I hope that will please you. My rolling-stone cost me dear. If I should ever grow rich, as God forbid I should, I would buy two hogsheads of wine at once. You must know I have bought turf for you, which burns like so many tapers. My son writes me word that Mr Vesey's family are angry with me for inserting some lines in the Legion Club touching him. Upon my soul, I never inserted one line in it; and upon the whole I care not whether they believe me or not. All my garden things are in top order. Are not you sick of Dublin this hot weather? How can you stew in such an oven? My sheep begin now to fatten; I hope they will please you very well. You saw the king's speech, I suppose. I am glad to find by it, that he resolves to stand by us. Our breams here are exceedingly good and fat; we dress them with carp sauce. Doctor Walmsley writes me word by last post, that they are making way to bring me to Armagh. Martin is quite outrageous mad, and his relations are now taking out a writ of lunacy; so that if my Lord Orrery would only mention me to the lord-primate, it would do. I know my lord chancellor is so well inclined toward me, that he would willingly join in the request. Consider the lands are worth four hundred a year and the situation much more advantageous. This must be a secret, upon several accounts. So much for business, and no more. My artichokes, I do, not mean my hearty jokes, are in great plenty; so are my strawberries. I hear that the czarina, Kouli Kan, and the emperor will overrun Turkey. You will not know my house when you see it next, it will be so altercated. Pray what says Goody White-way to the world? I hear she gives herself strange airs of late in calling me nothing but Sheridan. This comes of too much familiarity. When I come next to your house, I shall make her keep her distance, especially when company is present; for she wants to be pulled down. My young turnips, carrots, beans, and pease, are in fine order; you must pay half a crown a quart, if you eat any. I shall be very reasonable as to the rest of your diet,

> You shall want nothing fit for mortal man,
> To eat or drink, 'tis all that I do can.
> And all that's expedient,
> From your most obedient,

FROM DR SHERIDAN.

June 5, 1736.

Dear Sir,

I am so tormented, and have been for eight days, that I lie stretched in my bed as I now write : however, I begin to be easier, and I have hopes that I shall be able to attend in my school on Monday. Surely no person can be so stupid as to imagine you wrote the Panegyric on the Legion Club. I have seen and read it in various editions, which indeed makes me imagine every body to be its author; and what they have done to deserve such treatment, is to me a mystery.

I never writ in this posture before ; and therefore wonder not if lines and words be crooked. My pains are likewise great ; and therefore whether I will or not, I must take pains with this letter.

Now as to your coming down here, the weather will be good, the roads pleasant, and my company likewise, to set out with you from Dublin on Thursday fortnight, and to bring you here in three days. I have three deer parks at my command ; Coote's, Fleming's, and Hamilton's. I have at present forty chickens, all fat; twenty sheep of my own, and sixteen lambs (for lamb will be in season a month longer,) geese, turkey, &c.

My hens are hatching,
My house is thatching,
My geese a gagling,
My wife a dragling,
My corn a threshing,
My sheep a washing,
My turf a drawing,
My timber sawing,

My gravel walk raking,
My rollingstone making,
My ale a brewing,
Myself a stewing.
My boys a teaching,
My webs a bleaching,
My daughters reading,
My garden weeding,
My lime a burning,
My milk a churning.
In short, all nature seems to be at work,
Busy as Kouly Kan against the Turk.

I do not wonder that Mr Towers has discarded that graceless whelp; but I wonder more he kept him above a week. He has a genius for mischief would jade even the devil to attend him. If Mrs Whiteway will prove false, I have willows enough to crown me, and ladies enough here to pick and choose, where I like best. The summer has brought them and the flies in great abundance into our country; the latter I think, indeed, less troublesome. All of them long for your coming; but I know not whether you long for them. I am grieved to hear you have lost so much flesh, which indeed is my present case. If my skin were dry, my bones would rattle like a bag of bobbins. However, I make no doubt but to plump us both up by help of some housewife's remedies. My poor dear wife has run mad for joy of your coming: Sure I have a gravel walk finished twelve perches in length, eight gradations of pease, which will last you to October. You cannot imagine what a good housewife I am grown; my garden is well stocked; I have every thing but money: but that is neither here nor there. Mr Jones will order the money by first opportunity. May all happiness attend you.

TO DR SHERIDAN.

Dublin, June 5, 1736.

You must pay your great (as if you had been drunk last night) for this letter, because I am neither acquainted with any frank cur, nor the of frank king. I am glad you have got the piles, because it is a mark of health, and a strong constitution. I believe what you say of the legion-club poem; for it plainly appears a work of a legion-club, for I hear there are fifty different copies; but what is that to me? And you are in the right, that they are not treated according to their merit. You never writ so regular in your life, and therefore when you write to me, always take care to have the piles; I mean any piles except those of lime and stone, and yet piles are not so bad as the stone. I find you intend to be here (by your date) in a dozen days hence. The room shall be ready for you, though I shall never have you in a morning, or at dinner, or in an evening; at all other times I shall be pestered with you. John R——— (for he does not deserve the name of Jack) is gone to his six-miles-off country seat for the summer. I admire at your bill of 10l. odd; for I thought your first was double: or is it an additional one? When you satisfy me, I will send down to him with a vengeance: although except that damned vice of avarice, he is a very agreeable man. As to your venison, vain is one who expects it. I am checking you for your chickens, and could lamb you for your lambs.——*Addenda quædam.*

My wife a rattling,
My children ,tattling.
My money spent is,
And due my rent is.
My school decreasing,
My income ceasing.
All people tease me,
But no man pays me.
My worship is bit,
By that rogue Nisbit,
To take the right way,
Consult friend Whiteway.
Would you get still more ?
Go flatter Kilmore. *
Your geese are old,
Your wife a scold.

Mrs Whiteway is ever your friend, but our old ones have forsaken you as mine have me. My head is very bad ; and I have just as much spirits left as a drowned mouse. Pray do not you give yourself airs of pretending to have flies in summer at Cavan; and such a *no* summer as this : I, who am the best fly-catcher in the kingdom, have not thought it worth my time to show my skill in that art. I believe nothing of your garden improvements, for I know you too well. What you say of your leanness is incredible ; for when I saw you last you were as broad as long. But if you continue to breathe free (which nothing but exercise can give) you may be safe with as little flesh as I, which is none at all.

I had your letter just before this was sealed ; but I cannot answer it now.

JON. SWIFT.

---

* Dr Josiah Hort, then Bishop of Kilmore.—H.

TO LADY BETTY GERMAIN.

June 15, 1736.

MADAM,

I WRITE this letter to your ladyship, in the employment you have chosen of being a go-between the Duke of Dorset and me. I must preface this letter with an honest declaration, That I never proposed any one thing to his grace, wherein I did not chiefly consult his honour and the general opinion of the kingdom. I had the honour to know him from a boy, as I did your ladyship from a child; and yet, excepting great personal civilities, I never was able to obtain the favour of getting one church preferment for any friend, except one too inconsiderable to mention. I writ to, and told my lord duke, that there was a certain family here, called the Grattans, and that they could command ten thousand men: two of them are parsons, as you whigs call them; another is lord mayor of this city, and was knighted by his grace a month or two ago. But there is another cousin of theirs, who is a Grattan, though his name be John Jackson, as worthy a clergyman as any in this kingdom. He lives upon his own small estate, four miles from this town, and in his own parish; but he has four children. He only wants some little addition of a hundred pounds a-year; for he has laid out eight hundred pounds to build upon his own small estate in his own parish, which he cannot leave; and we cannot spare him. He has lain a weight upon my shoulders for many years; and I have often mentioned him to my lord duke as a most deserving person. His grace has now an opportunity to help

him.   One Mr Ward, who died this morning, had
a deanery of small value ; it was a hedge deanery,
my lord duke will tell you what I mean ; we have
many of them in Ireland : but, as it does not require living there, except a month or two in the
year, although it be but of forty or fifty pounds
yearly rent, it will be a great ease to him.   He
is no party man, but a loyal subject.   It is the
deanery of Cloyne : he is well acquainted with the
bishop, who is Dr Berkeley ; I have reasons enough
to complain of my lord duke, who absolutely refused
to provide for a most worthy man, whom he had
made one of his chaplains before he came over : and
therefore, if he will not consent to give this poor
deanery to Mr John Jackson, I will fall out with
him for ever.   I desire your ladyship to let the
duke know all this.

Somebody read a part of a newspaper to me the
other day, wherein your saucy niece is mentioned
as married, with five and forty thousand pounds to
her fortune.   I desire to present her with my most
humble service, and that we may be friends for the
future.   I hope your ladyship still preserves your
health and good humour.   Your virtues I am in no
pain about ; for you are confirmed in them by your
education and birth, as well as by constant practice.
I pray God preserve you long, for the good you do
to the world, and for your happiness hereafter.

I will (notwithstanding your commands to the
contrary) be so bold to tell you, that I am, with the
greatest respect and esteem, Madam,

Your ladyship's most obedient and obliged
humble servant,

JON. SWIFT.

THE ANSWER.

June 23, 1736.

I OUGHT to begin with begging pardon for not answering yours of the 1st of May, before I thank you for that of the 15th of June : but I do not question the newspapers have informed you of the great loss I have had in my brother Henry Berkeley. And what is an addition to the grief for the best-natured, honest, sincere, disinterested, friendly brother, is the having left a wife, three daughters, and two sons, literally without bread to eat : though perhaps that part might soon be made easy, if those of his relations were as willing, as they are able, to help to take care of them, which hitherto they have only the benefit of from my two nieces. She that you call the saucy one, has bestowed her very great fortune (much more than you mention) on Lord Vere Beauclerk, and had my approbation of her own choice, for I think him a very deserving gentleman; and all that know him give him a great character. I am now with them in the country ; but shall go in about a fortnight to Knowle ; and when I am there, will certainly obey your commands to the Duke of Dorset. My brother George and Lady Suffolk are gone to France to make a visit to Lord Berkeley : which I am glad of, as I hope it will induce her to go to Spa and Aix-la-Chapelle, for her health, which I am afraid is very necessary for her, and truly believe is all she wants to make her easy and happy ; or else my brother George is not the honest good-natured man I really take him to be; and she dissembles well, if she is not so happy as she makes me believe, and I heartily wish her.

You order me to write long letters; but you may see by the nothingness of this, I am yet more unfit than ever to observe your orders, though in all things, and at all times,

Your most sincere and truly humble servant,

E. G.

FROM DR SHERIDAN.

June 23, 1736.

DEAR SIR,

IF you can believe me, I can assure you, that we have a great plenty of flies at Cavan; and let me whisper you in this letter, *nec desunt pediculi nec pulices;* but I beseech you not to speak of it. *Si me non fallit observatio*, we shall have more of the Egyptian plagues, *quippe multitudo militum die crastino advnturae est in Cavanniam nostram.* I do not know what the devil they will do for meat. *De nostro cibo, nisi furtim, aut vi abripiant, uxor me capiat, si gustaverint.* The ladies are already bespeaking seats in my field upon the hill, *Spectatum veniunt, veniunt spectentur ut ipsæ.* Ho, brave colonels, captains, lieutenants, and cornets, *adeo hic splendentes congregantur ut ipsis pavonibus pudorem incutiunt*, of which I am an eye-witness, *dejectis capitibus caudas demittunt.* Our bakers are all so busy upon this occasion, that they double the heat of the weather, *atque urunt officinas.* But when the army fires on Friday, *proh Jupiter!* *infernum redolebunt et spirabunt.* The noise of guns, the neighing of the horses, and the women's tongues, *cœlum atque terras miscebunt.*

Grouse pouts are come in
I've some in my bin,
To butter your chin ;
When done with our din-
—ner, through thick and thin
We'll walk out and in,
And care not a pin
Who thinks it a sin.
We make some folks grin,
By lashing their kin, &c.

I could not mention troop-horses, *quin Pegasus noster lusit exultim ut vides; sed jam stabulo inclusus de versibus nihil amplius.* You may be surprised at this motley epistle ; but you must know that I fell upon my head the other day, and the fall shook away half my English and Latin, *cum omnia lingua Gallica, Hispanica, necnon Italica.* I would rather indeed my wife had lost her one tongue, *totaliter, quoniam equidem nullus dubito nisi radicitus evelleretur tonitrui superaret.*

I wish your reverence were here to hear the trumpets ;
Mistake me not, for I mean not the strumpets.

Well, when will you come down, or will you come at all ? I think you may, can, could, might, would, or ought to come. My house is enlarging, and you may now venture to bring your own company with you ; namely, the provost, Archdeacon Wall, the Bishop of Clogher, and ——, by way of enlivening the rest. Do not let my Lord Orrery come with them ; for I know they will not be pleased with his company. My love to my sweetheart Mrs Whiteway, if she continues constant ; if not, my hatred and my gall. Excuse my haste. I hope by the next post to make up for this short epistle. I am,

dear Sir, with all affection and respect, your mos
obedient humble servant,

THOMAS SHERIDAN.

I send you a letter from Mr Carte. *

TO MR NICHOLLS. †

SIR,

THERE is a lady, a cousin of mine, Mrs Whiteway, who hath been scolding me several weeks for
my ingratitude to you, who having sent me two or
more vessels of ale of your own brewing, without
any claim of merit of mine, had never the civility
either to get out of your debt, or to thank you, or
invite you to eat with me, and drink some of your
own ale. She says, that she invites you to-morrow
to dine with her at the deanery, and there take the
opportunity of exposing me for my ill treatment of
you. This is a misfortune I cannot help, but must
endure it patiently; and therefore, if you be not
otherwise engaged, I entreat the favour of you,
which she commands, and that you will let me
know to-morrow morning. I writ this at her house
in fear and dread, therefore take pity of me.

I am, Sir, your most obedient humble servant,

JONATH. SWIFT.

Dated at Mrs Whiteway's house,
    June 5, 1736.

---

* The Historian; see p. 73.—N.
 † This letter, and two others, to Mr Nicholls, surgeon-general of Ireland, are now, for the first time, published in the Dean's
correspondence.

FROM MR DONNELLAN.

Corke, July 2, 1736.

Sir,

I had the favour of your commands with relation to Mr Dunkin ;* and, in pursuance of them, have writ to two of my friends among the senior fellows, and recommended his petition, and your request, in the best and strongest manner I was able. I am, upon many accounts, obliged to execute whatever orders you are pleased to give me, with the greatest readiness and cheerfulness possible: which, I assure you, I do on this occasion, and shall think myself very happy if I can any way promote the success of an affair which you wish well to. But, beside the right that you have to command me, I think Mr Dunkin's case, as Mrs Sican has represented it, really very worthy of compassion, and on that account likewise should be very glad I could be of some service to him. To be sure, he acted a very silly and wrong part in marrying, and in the affair of Dr Cope's daughter; and I fear he has hurt himself very considerably in the opinion of the

---

* A female relation of Mr Dunkin had bequeathed an estate in land, for ever, to the college and fellows of Trinity College, Dublin, upon condition that they should take care of his education, and afterward assist to advance him in the world. The college, in consequence of this request, allowed him at this time an annuity, which he was now soliciting to get increased to 100l. He succeeded in his application; and the Earl of Chesterfield, when he had the government of Ireland, in the year 1746, gave him the school of Enniskilling, which is very richly endowed, and was founded by King Charles I.—D. S.

college by his strange behaviour at the board, without occasion. But I hope all this will be got over, by your appearance in his favour, and that your request will have all that weight with the college that it ought. I reminded my friends (though I hope they had not forgot it) of the considerable services you had done their house at different times, and let them know how much their compliance in this point would oblige you. After this, I think they must be very beasts, if they do not show their gratitude, when they have so fair an opportunity, and idiots, if they neglect purchasing the Dean's favour at so cheap a rate.

My sister and I were very sorry we had not the pleasure of seeing you the morning we called at the deanery-house. We were just then going out of town, and had not another opportunity of taking our leave of you. She desires me to make her compliments to you in a very particular manner. We are both exceedingly busy in getting our little house ready, and hope to remove into it next week. I shall not trouble you, Sir, with a description of it, but, in a few words, it is really a very sweet little spot, and, though so near a great town, has all the advantages of a complete retirement.

Though I am come among a people that I think you are not very fond of, yet, this I must say in their favour, that they are not such brutes as to be insensible of the Dean's merit. Ever since we came down, this town and country rung of your praises, for opposing the reduction of the coin; and they look upon the stop that is likely to be put to that affair, as a second deliverance they owe you.

I hope the late fine weather has contributed to the recovery of your health : I am sure it is what we have all reason to desire the continuance of;

and what I beg you will believe, no one more truly and sincerely wishes, with all other happiness, than, Sir, your most obedient and obliged humble servant,

CHR. DONNELLAN.

TO THE PROVOST AND SENIOR FELLOWS OF TRINITY COLLEGE, DUBLIN. *

Deanery House, July 5, 1736.

REV. AND WORTHY SIRS,

As I had the honour of receiving some part of my education in your university, and the good fortune to be of some service to it while I had a share of credit at court, as well as since, when I had very little or none, I may hope to be excused for laying a case before you, and offering my opinion upon it.

Mr Dunkin, whom you all know, sent me some time ago a memorial intended to be laid before you, which perhaps he hath already done. His request is, that you would be pleased to enlarge his annuity at present, and that he may have the same right, in his turn, to the first church preferment, vacant in your gift, as if he had been made a fellow, according to the scheme of his aunt's will; because the absurdity of the condition in it ought to be imputed to the old woman's ignorance, although her inten-

---

* This letter plainly shows the author's friendship to gentlemen of genius and learning, although unacquainted with them; but, soon after this, Mr Dunkin was introduced to the Dean, who did him farther services, by recommending him to Dr Bolton, Archbishop of Cashell, who ordained him.—F.

tion be very manifest: and the intention of the testator in all wills is chiefly regarded by the law. What I would therefore humbly propose is this, that you would increase his pension to one hundred pounds a-year, and make him a firm promise of the first church-living in your disposal, to the value of two hundred pounds a year, or somewhat more. This I take to be a reasonable medium between what he hath proposed in his memorial, and what you allow him at present.

I am almost a perfect stranger to Mr Dunkin having never seen him above twice, and then in mixed company, nor should I know his person if I met him in the streets. But I know he is a man of wit and parts; which, if applied properly to the business of his function, instead of poetry (wherein it must be owned he sometimes excels,*) might be of great use and service to him.

I hope you will please to remember, that, since your body hath received no inconsiderable benefaction from the aunt, it will much increase your reputation, rather to err on the generous side toward the nephew.

These are my thoughts, after frequently reflecting on the case under all its circumstances; and so I leave it to your wiser judgments. I am, with true respect and esteem, reverend and worthy Sirs,

Your most obedient and most humble servant,
JON. SWIFT.

---

* See the translation of ", Carberiæ Rupes," Vol. XIV. p. 179.—N.

FROM DR SHERIDAN.

July 6, 1735.

DEAR SIR,

I SUSPECT that some secret villain has prevented the lord chancellor to sign my commission; and therefore I entreat the favour of you to know the meaning of it from his excellency; for I had his consent by a recommendation from my Lord Chief Baron Marley, and Mr Justice Ward. The summer is going off fast, so are my best fowl; and you are not yet come. Will you not come for your six hundred and sixty pounds? We have no way to carry it except you come for it yourself: and do not forget to bring the deed of sale with you for the Marahills and Drumcor. I wish you could sail with them hither, to save you the trouble of riding, which I would rather see than fifty pounds, which I would set my hand and seal to. Mr Jones, as I told you before, will not pay any body but yourself; so that you must inevitably come *nolens volens,* right or wrong, whether you can or not. Our venison is plenty: our weather too hot for its carriage. We have not had two hundred drops of rain these six weeks past.

> Our river is dry,
> And fiery the sky;
> I fret and I fry,
> Just ready to die:
> Oh, where shall I fly
> From Phœbus's eye?
> In bed when I lie,
> I soak like a pie;
> And I sweat, oh, I sweat, like a hog in a stye.

I know you love Alexandrines ; for which reason I closed the above madrigal with one.   I think it is of a very good proportion, which I hope you will set to music ; and pray let me have a base and second treble, with what other decorations and graces you can better design than I can direct.   To let you see you can want for nothing, if you come to Cavan, I write you the following catalogue :

Good road,	Right bacon,
A clean house,	Cauliflowers,
A hearty welcome,	Young chickens,
Good ale,	Fat venison,
Good beer,	Small mutton,
Good bread,	Green pease,
Good bed,	Good water,
Young turkies,	Good wine,
Young beans,	Young ducks,
Young lambs,	Carrots,
Grouse pouts,	Parsnip's, Item
Fine trouts,	

A LONG GRAVEL WALK——

I must trouble your reverence with a small sample of some things, to let you see that all I have said is truth.

REFERENCES.

1. Artichoke.	12. Common cabage.
2. Carrot.	13. Turnip.
3. Parsnip.	14. Cauliflowers.
4. Raspberries.	15. Cos lettuce.
5. Gooseberries.	16. Silesia lettuce.
6. Currants, red.	17. Thyme.
7. Currants, black.	18. Sweet marjoram.
8. Purslain.	19. A Cavan fly, and a thousand things beside.
9. Kidney beans.	
10. Common beans.	20. Some of my gravel walk.
11. Red cabbage.	21. Nasturtium.

22. Cucumber.   25. Onion.
23. Orange.   26. Pea.
24. Spinage.

I would send you some of my canal, but the paper could not hold it.

I have nothing more to send but my best wishes, which you can only see in my face, when you come down.

Present my love 9678946846734056789897324 times to my dear Mrs Whiteway, and all her chickens. I am, dear Sir, as I ever must be, your most obedient and very humble servant to command, Dumb Spur it us hose rage it art us. *

FROM MR FORD.

London, July 8, 1736.

You cannot imagine how much I was transported to see a superscription in your hand, after two years and a half intermission. The pleasure I had in not being quite forgot, was soon abated by what you say of your ill health. I doubt you live too much by yourself; and retirement makes the strongest impression upon those who are formed for mirth and society. I have not been these thirty years without a set of cheerful companions, by herding with new ones as the old marry and go off. Why have not you a succession of Grattans and Jacksons? Whatever resentment the men in power may have, every body else would seek your company, upon your own terms; and for those in great sta-

---

* " Dum spiritus hos regit artus."

tions, I am sure, at this time, you would be ashamed to be well with them. If they hate you, it is because they fear you, and know your abilities better than you seem to do yourself: even in your melancholy you write with too much fire for broken spirits. Your giddiness and deafness give me the utmost concern; though I believe you would be less subject to them, and as well taken care of here: nor need you spunge for a dinner, since you would be invited to two or three places every day. I will say no more upon this subject, because I know there is no persuading you.

My legs have been swelled many years: it is above twelve since Beaufort gave me a prescription for them, which I never took till last winter. My Lord Litchfield, and other of my acquaintance, persuaded me to it; and they tell me it had its effect, for I am no judge either of my own bad looks, or large legs, having always found myself perfectly well, except when I had my fever four years ago. I walk constantly every day in the Park, and am forced to be both temperate and sober, because my meat is so much overdone that I do not like it, and my dining acquaintance reserve themselves for a second meeting at night, which I obstinately refuse.

If your rents fall, I do not know what must become of us. I have considerable losses every year: and yet I think Crossthwaite a very honest man. Rents for some time have been ill paid here as well as in Ireland; and farms flung up every day, which have not been raised since King Charles the First's time. The graziers are undone in all parts, and it is bad enough with the farmers. One cause is, their living much higher than they did formerly; another is, the great number of enclosures made of late, enough to supply many more people than England contains. It is certain, all last year a man came off well if he could sell a fat ox at the price he bought him lean. The butchers, by not lowering their meat in proportion, have been the only gainers.

I generally hear once a month or oftener from my sister. She writes to me with great affection ; but I find she is still wrongheaded, and will be so as long as she lives. As she expected unreasonable presents, she makes them much more unreasonably ; and, in my opinion, so ill-judged, that I do not wonder more at her than at those who receive them. I see no difference in giving thirty or forty guineas, or in paying thirty or forty guineas for a thing the person you give it to must have paid. I have heard no reason to doubt Lord Masham. I know nothing of his son, not even by sight. Our friend Lewis is in constant duty with his sick wife, who has been some years dying, and will not die. Unless he calls, as he does upon me for a quarter of an hour at most twice in a year, there is no seeing him. I heartily wish you health and prosperity ; and am ever, most sincerely, your, &c.

My Lord Masham was extremely pleased with your remembering him, and desired me to make his compliments to you.

TO DR SHERIDAN.

July 10, 1736.

I RECEIVED your two letters. The first is mingled with Latin and English, one following the other: now I scorn that way, and put both languages in one. However, for the sake of order, I will begin with answering your second letter before the first, because it deserves one on account of your presents. From bogs, rivers, mountains, mosses, quagmires, heaths, lakes, kennels, ditches, weeds, &c. &c. &c. &c.——Mrs Whiteway was pleased, although very unjustly, to criticise upon every curiosity; she swears the paper of gravel was of your own voiding, as she found by the smell. That your whole artichoke leaf shows its mother to be smaller than a nutmeg, and I confess you were somewhat unwary in exposing it to censure. Your raspberry she compared with the head of a corking-pin, and the latter had the victory. Your currants were invisible, and we could not distinguish the red from the black. Your purslane passed very well with me, but she swore it was houseleek. She denies your Cavan fly to be genuine, but will have it, that for the credit of your town you would have it born there, although Mrs Donaldson confesses it was sent her in a box of brown sugar, and died as it entered the gates. Mrs Whiteway proceeds farther in her malice, declaring your nasturtium to be only a p-ss-abed; your beans as brown as herself, and of the same kind with what we fatten hogs in Leicestershire. In one thing she admires your generosity, that for her sake you would spare a drop or two of your canal water, which by the spongy bottom needs it so much. The only defects of them all, were, that they wanted colour, sight, and smell; yet as to the last, we both acknowledge them all to exhale a general fustiness, which however did much resemble that of your Cavan air.

JON. SWIFT.

TO THE SAME.

I RECEIVED your letter, which began with "lings." You have thirteen in all, and I have got but a hundred and sixty; a trifle! find me ten more than mine, and I will give you ten guineas for the eleventh. Mine are all down, and only twelve which are not entered in a letter, which I will send you when health permits, and I have nothing else to do, and that may be a twelvemonth hence, if my disorder will let me hold out so long. You were born to be happy, for you take the least piece of good fortune cheerfully. I suppose your arithmetic is, that three boys a week are a hundred and fifty nine in a year; and seven guineas a week are three hundred and sixty-five per annum. Can you reckon that the county, and the next, and Dublin, will provide you with thirty lads in all, and good pay, of which a dozen shall be lodgers? Does the cheapness of things answer your expectation? Have you sent away your late younger-married daughter? and will you send away the other? Let me desire you will be very regular in your accounts; because a very honest friend of yours and mine tells me, that with all your honesty, it is an uneasy thing to have any dealings with you that relate to accounts by your frequent forgetfulness and confusion: for you have no notion of regularity: and I do not wonder at it, considering the scattered, confused manner in which you have lived. Mrs Whiteway thanks you for the good opinion you have of her, and I know she always loved and defended you. I cannot tell when I shall be able to travel; I have three other engagements on my hands, but the principal is to see the bishop of Ossory. Yet I dread the lying abroad above five miles. I am never well. Some sudden turns are every day threatening me with a giddy fit; and my affairs are terribly embroiled. I have a scheme of living with you, when the college green club is to meet; for in these times I detest the town, and hearing the follies, corruptions, and slavish practices of those misrepresentative brutes; and resolve, if I can stir, to pass that whole time at Bath or Cavan. I say again, keep very regular accounts, in large books, and a fair hand: not like me, who to save paper confuse every thing. Your mind is honest, but your memory a knave, and therefore the Scotch mean the same thing by " minding," that we do by " remembering." Sirrah, said I to a Scotch footman, why did not you go that errand? Because I did not " mind" it, quoth Sawny. A curse on these twenty soldiers drumming through my liberty twice a-day, and going to a barrack * the government hath placed just under my nose. I think of a line in Virgil Travesty. " The d—l cut their yelping weasons." We expect Lord Orrery and Bishop Rundle next week. This letter was intended for

---

* Afterwards called the Piddle-guard, and kept within the liberties of St Patrick's to suppress riots.—F.

last post, but interruptions and horses hindered it. Poor Mrs Acheson is relapsed at Grange, and worse than ever; I was there yesterday and met Dr Helsham, who hopes she was a little better.—16. Here has nobody been hanged, married, or dead that I hear of: Dr Grattan is confined by a boil; if you ask him where, he will sell you a bargain. My chief country companion now is Philosopher Webster: for the Grattans and Jacksons are neither to be found at home or abroad, except Robin, who cannot stir a foot.

Jon. Swift.

FROM LADY BETTY GERMAIN.

July 11, 1736.

SINCE, it seems, my letters are not for your own perusal, but kept for a female cousin, to her this ought to be addressed; only that I am not yet in spirits to joke. I did not do so ill by your request, as you apprehended by my letter, for I spoke to the duke much sooner than I told you I should, and did so as soon as it was possible for me, or as soon as I could have sent it. But my answer was, that he had that moment received a letter from Lord Orrery, with the most pressing instances for a deserving friend of his, that the duke could not refuse; especially as my Lord Orrery had been most extremely obliging, and, for this whole session, neglected no opportunity to endeavour to make his administration easy: though, at the same time he assured me, he would otherwise have been very glad to oblige you; and does agree, that the gentleman you recommended is a very deserving one also. All this you should have known before, had I been able to write: but I have been laid up with the gout in my hand and foot, and thought it not necessary to make use of a secretary, since I had nothing more pleasing to tell you. I shall always be extremely willing to be employed by you to him; nor do I make any question but you will always recommend the worthy, as it is for your own honour as well as his. No more will I agree, that you never did prevail, on any one occasion; because the very first you did employ me about, was instantly complied with, though against a rule he thought right, and I knew before he had set himself.

Lady Suffolk is now at Spa, with my brother George, for her health; and as I shall go, for my own, to the Bath in September, I fear we shall not meet this great while. And now I must finish this long letter, which has not been quite easy to write, being still your gouty, but faithful humble servant.

FROM DR SHERIDAN.

July 20, 1736.

DEAR SIR,

I RECEIVED yours some day or other this week, by the hands of Mrs Donaldson, who has made affidavit before our town magistrate, that I never borrowed a fly of her in my life; and I have likewise deposed upon oath, that I caught the fly perched upon a rose tree in my own garden: and I would have you to know, that I have above four hundred thousand of the same species; for I counted them last Sunday. If you will not believe me, pray come down and see. Mr Jones has your six hundred and sixty pounds ready, but can get no bills to remit it. I beseech you lose no time; for he is uneasy about it. * * * * * * * * * * * * * * * * *

If you put off the time of coming down longer, you will lose the best things our country can afford. The ladies are full of your coming; viz.

My wife, *	Mrs Jones,
Two Ladies Lanesborough,	Beauty Copeland,
Mrs Maxwell,	Miss Brooke, 1, 2, 3, 4, &c.
Mrs Fitzmaurice,	&c. &c.
Mrs Hort,	All your Cavan mistresses.
Mrs Hamilton,	News.
Mrs Sanderson,	Doctor Thompson's servant
Mrs Nuburgh,	almost cudgelled him to
Mrs Cromer,	death going from a chris-
Mrs White,	tening.
Mrs Nesbitt,	Colonel Nuburgh's fine arch-
Her five daughters,	ed market house, quite fi-
Mrs Stephens,	nished with a grand cupola
Mrs and Miss Clement,	on the top, fell flat to the
Mrs Tighe,	earth. It is now begun up-
Mrs Coote,	on again. *Sic transit glo-*
Miss Pratt,	*ria mundi.*
Mrs Fitzherbert,	

Grouse pouts,
Fine trouts,
Right venison,
For my benison.
Leave your stinking town in haste,
For you have no time to waste.

Let me know what day I shall meet you. Price and I will stretch to Virginia. That all happiness

---

* Who, by the by, hated Dr Swift above all the human race. —D. S.

may for ever attend you is the sincere wish of, dear Sir, your most obedient and very humble servant,

THOMAS SHERIDAN.

FROM DR SHERIDAN. *

July 31, 1736.

DEAR SIR,

I WENT to Belturbet immediately upon the receipt of your letter, and found Mr Jones ready for Mr Henry's draught, and glad of it : and so am I—— But you are a very fine lawyer in calling your deed of sale a mortgage——Instead of cancelling there is more to be done : you must not only cancel, but you must reconvey to me, in a formal manner as if you sold to me——Pray ask advice, and *do* not *do* things hand overhead, as you were going to *do* (observe my style *) like me. If I had not sworn never to set my foot in Dublin, except I were to pass through it for England,† I would go thither next vacation ; but I have sworn solemnly I will not——If I had my few friends out of it, I would not care that all the rest were petrified.

Now you must know that I forbid you the town of Cavan as strenuously as I invited you to it ; for the small-pox is the broom of death at present, and

---

* This was exactly Swift's style to Sheridan upon many occasions ; and now Sheridan, in his pleasant manner, returns the compliment.——H.

+ Sheridan never crossed the Channel to England in his whole life.——H.

sweeps us off here by dozens*—I never had it, which gives me some little palpitations, but no great fear. As soon as I can get five hundred pounds in my pocket, to make a figure with, I may perhaps honour your metropolis with my presence ; and that may be sooner than you imagine, for I have a guinea, a moidore, a cobb, and two Manks pence towards it already.—You may think I swagger, but as I hope to be saved it is true.

How grieved I am that I am out of the way while Doctor King is in Dublin. I wish with all my soul he would take a frolic to come hither, because he would cost me no wine, and I have the best water in Ireland.

My collection of witty sayings, &c. is finished, if I had any friends to recommend them. The best wares of that kind will not go off otherwise. Doctor King promised me his friendship at Oxford. If you would speak a kind word to the public in their behalf, I know they would bring me in *L'argent,* which I now want as much as I formerly did the gift of retention, when I had enough. But—That —is—neither—here—nor there—

My son—I can affirm is thoroughly reformed ; and, as an argument of it, I must acquaint you that his mother finds fault with every thing he does.

My son—is so far poisoned by the serpent his mother, that I cannot get him home, although I sent horses for him.   *   *   *   *   *   *

May all happiness attend you, is the sincere wish of, dear Sir,

Your most obedient and very humble servant,
THOMAS SHERIDAN.

---

* Swift had always a deep horror for this disorder, which since his time has been so effectually disarmed.

FROM LADY HOWTH.

August 6, 1736.

SIR,

I DO not know how this letter may be received, since I never had the favour of an answer to my last. I impute it to the neglect of the post, or any thing rather than to think I am forgot by my old friend. I am now in Connaught, where I assure you I spend the least of my time at cards. I am on horseback almost every day to view the beauties of Connaught, where I am told you have been. I live greatly under ground; for I view all the places under ground. I make nothing of going down sixty steps. I really think, could you lend me a little of your brains, I should be able to come nigh Addison in several of his descriptions of Italy ; for upon my word I think there are several very remarkable things. As you took a journey last winter to Cavan, my lord and I hope you will take one to the county of Kilkenny this winter, where we assure you of a hearty welcome. I must now be troublesome to you; but Lord Athunry begged I would write to you in favour of a young gentleman, one Mr Ireland, who was usher to Mr Garnett, schoolmaster of Tipperary. Mr Garnett died lately : he has given Mr Ireland a very good certificate, and most of the gentlemen in and about Tipperary have recommended Mr Ireland to succeed Mr Garnett ; as you are one of the governors of that school, I hope you will do Mr Ireland all the service you can, which will very much oblige me. Since I began this there came in a trout : it was so large that we had it weighed ; it was a yard and four inches long, twenty-three inches round; his jaw-bone eight inches long, and he weighed thirty-five pound and a half. My lord and I stood by to see it measured. I believe I have tired your patience; so beg leave to assure you I am

Your affectionate friend and humble servant,

L. HOWTH.

Direct to me at Turlaghvan, near Tuam. My lord begs you would accept of his compliments.

FROM THOMAS CARTE, ESQ. *

August 11, 1736.

SIR,

HAVING at last, after a long application and in the midst of sharp rheumatic pains, the effects of a sedentary life, finished " my History of the Life of the first Duke of Ormond, and of the Affairs of Ireland in his Time," I here send you a copy of that work, of which I beg your acceptance. I have endeavoured to follow the instructions you gave me, and hope I have done so in some measure. If it have your approbation in any degree, it will be so much to my satisfaction.

It hath been a long subject of complaint in England, that no history has yet been wrote of it upon authentic and proper materials; and even those who have taken notice of the military actions of our ancestors, have yet left the civil history of the kingdom (the most instructive of any) untouched, for

---

* The well-known historian.

want of a proper knowledge of the antiquities, usages, laws and constitutions of this nation. Rapin de Thoiras, the last writer, was a foreigner, utterly ignorant in these respects: and, writing his history abroad, had no means of clearing up any difficulties that he met with therein. He made, indeed, some use of Rymer's Fœdera: but his ignorance of our customs suffered him to fall into gross mistakes, for want of understanding the phraseology of acts, which have reference to our particular customs. Besides, Rymer's collection contains only such treaties as were enrolled in the Tower, or in the rolls of chancery; he knew nothing of such as were enrolled in the exchequer, and of the public treaties with foreign princes enrolled in this latter office. I have now a list of above four hundred by me. Rymer never made use of that vast collection of materials for an English history, which is preserved in the Cotton library: nor ever consulted any journal of our privy council, whenever he refers to any, still quoting Bishop Burnet for his author. He never read the rolls of parliament, nor any journal of either house, where the chief affairs within the nation are transacted; and did not so much as know there was such a place as the paper-office, where all the letters of the English ambassadors abroad, and all the dispatches of our secretaries of state at home, from the time of Edward the Fourth to the revolution (since which the secretaries have generally carried away their papers) are kept in a good method, and with great regularity; so that he wanted likewise the best materials for an account of our foreign affairs. These defects have made several of our nobility and gentry desire a new history to be wrote, in which the abovementioned, and other materials as authentic as they, may be made use of. They have proposed it to me, and my objections regarding the vastness of the expence as well as labour, that, to satisfy myself, I must have all materials by me, not only copies out of our records, journals, &c. in England; but even copies of negotiations of foreign ambassadors at this court (e. g. of the French; all the negotiations and letters of which, for two hundred years past, I know where to have copied) they have proposed a subscription of a thousand a year, for as many years as the work will require, to defray this expence. The subscription is begun, and will (I believe) be completed this winter; and then that work will employ all my time. One advantage I already find from the very talk of this design, having been offered several collections and memoirs of particular persons, considerable in their time, which I did not know were in being, and which would else no part of them ever see the light: and the manner of the history's being carried on, will probably make every body open their stores.

This is one reason, among many others, which makes me very desirous of having your judgment of the work I have now published, and that you would point out to me such faults as I would fain correct in my designed work. It will be a very particular favour to a person who is, with the greatest esteem and respect, Sir, your very obliged and obedient servant,

THOMAS CARTE.

Mr Awnshaw's, in Red Lion Court in Fleet Street, London.

DR SHERIDAN TO MRS WHITEWAY.

Cavan, August 14, 1736.

DEAR MADAM,

YOUR account of the Dean gives me much grief.
I hope in God he will disappoint all his friends' fears,
and his enemies' hopes.   Nothing can be a greater
affliction to me than my distance from him; and,
what is full as bad, my being so near to one who
has been the occasion of it.   Very rich folks in my
debt have made such apologies for non-payment, that
I now feel for Ireland, but much more for myself,
because I was in hopes of being able to make my
appearance in Dublin with a good grace—namely,
to pay some debts, which I cannot.

My poor Lady Mountcashell has a right to a visit from me; and thither I will venture for a day
and a night—and I will venture to the deanery for
another.   I could wish the best friend I had in
the world (you may guess who I mean) and am
sure is so still, would take a little of my advice—
You may depend upon this, it should be all for my
own advantage.

Now I have done raving—I must turn my pen
which is my tongue's representative, against you for
a while, because I am certain it might be in your
power to paint my Siberia so agreeably to the Dean,
as to send him hither while our good weather lasted.
My new kitchen is disappointed; so is my gravel
walk; but what is worse, his only favourite, my rib
—who dreamed with great pleasure that he would
never come.   I am sorry she is disappointed; for I
am certain she would run away if he had come—
God forgive him for not doing it—I will make all

the haste I can out of this Hell; and I hope my friends, (I beg pardon, I mean my friend) will cast about a little for me—if he does not, I will try England, where the predominant phrase is, down with the Irish. I will say no more, but tell you that you are a false mistress; and if you do not behave yourself better, I will choose another. In the mean time God bless you and my dearest friend the Dean. I am, notwithstanding all your upbraidings, dear Madam, your most obedient humble servant,

THOMAS SHERIDAN.

FROM MR POPE.

August 17, 1736.

I FIND, though I have less experience than you, the truth of what you told me some time ago, that increase of years makes men more talkative but less writative; to that degree, that I now write no letters but of plain business, or plain how-d'yes, to those few I am forced to correspond with, either out of necessity, or love, and I grow laconic even beyond laconism; for sometimes I return only yes, or no, to questionary or petitionary epistles of half a yard long. You and Lord Bolingbroke are the only men to whom I write, and always in folio. You are indeed almost the only men I know, who either can write in this age, or whose writings will reach the next; others are mere mortals. Whatever failings such men may have, a respect is due to them, as luminaries whose exaltation renders their motion a little irregular, or rather causes it to seem so to

others.   I am afraid to censure any thing I hear of
Dean Swift, because I hear it only from mortals,
blind and dull; and you should be cautious of censuring any action or motion of Lord B. because you
hear it only from shallow, envious, or malicious
reporters.   What you writ to me about him I find
to my great scandal repeated in one of yours to
———.   Whatever you might hint to me, was this
for the profane? the thing, if true, should be concealed*; but it is I assure you absolutely untrue, in
every circumstance.   He has fixed in a very agreeable retirement near Fontainbleau, and makes it
his whole business *vacare literis*.   But tell me the
truth, were you not angry at his omitting to write
to you so long?   I may, for I hear from him seldomer than from you, that is twice or thrice a year
at most.   Can you possibly think he can neglect
you, or disregard you?   If you catch yourself at
thinking such nonsense, your parts are decayed.
For believe me, great geniuses must and do esteem
one another, and I question if any others can esteem
or comprehend uncommon merit.   Others only
guess at that merit, or see glimmerings of their
minds: a genius has the intuitive faculty: therefore imagine what you will, you cannot be so sure
of any man's esteem as of his.   If I can think that
neither he nor you despise me, it is a greater honour to me by far, and will be thought so by posterity, than if all the house of lords writ commenda-
tory verses upon me, the commons ordered me to

---

* One of Bolingbroke's Letters to Sir Charles Wyndham
seems to explain this circumstance, written in the same year, in
which he says, "it is reported among you, that I play the Ce-
ladon here," &c.—BOWLES.

print my works, the universities gave me public thanks, and the king, queen, and prince crowned me with laurel. You are a very ignorant man : you do not know the figure his name and yours will make hereafter : I do, and will preserve all the memorials I can, that I was of your intimacy ; *longo, sed proximus, intervallo.* I will not quarrel with the present age ; it has done enough for me, in making and keeping you two my friends. Do not you be too angry at it, and let not him be too angry at it ; it has done, and can do, neither of you any manner of harm, as long as it has not, and cannot burn your works : while those subsist, you will both appear the greatest men of the time, in spite of princes and ministers ; and the wisest, in spite of all the little errors you may please to commit.

Adieu. May better health attend you, than I fear you possess ; may but as good health attend you always as mine is at present ; tolerable, when an easy mind is joined with it.

FROM MRS PENDARVES.

Sept. 2, 1736.

SIR,

I NEVER will accept of the writ of ease you threaten me with ; do not flatter yourself with any such hopes : I receive too many advantages from your letters to drop a correspondence of such consequence to me. I am really grieved that you are so much persecuted with a giddiness in your head : the Bath and travelling would certainly be of use to you. Your want of spirits is a new complaint, and what will not only afflict your particular friends, but every one that has the happiness of your acquaintance. I am uneasy to know how you do, and have no other means for that satisfaction, but from your own hand; most of my Dublin correspondents being removed to Cork, to Wicklow mountains, and the Lord knows where. I should have made this inquiry sooner, but that I have this summer undertaken a work that has given me full employment, which is making a grotto in Sir John Stanley's garden at North End; it is chiefly composed of shells I had from Ireland. My life, for two months past, has been very like a hermit's; I have had all the comforts of life but society, and have found living quite alone a pleasanter thing than I imagined. The hours I could spend in reading have been entertained by Rollin's History of the Ancients, in French. I am very well pleased with it; and think your Annibals, Scipios, and Cyruses, prettier fellows than are to be met with now-a-days. Painting and music have had their share in my amusements. I rose between five and six, and went to bed at eleven. I would not tell you so much about myself, if I had any thing to tell you of other people. I came to town the night before last; and if it does not, a few days hence, appear better to me than at present, I shall return to my solitary cell. Sir John Stanley has been all the summer at Tunbridge.

I suppose you may have heard of Mr Pope's accident; which had like to have proved a very fatal one; he was leading a young lady into a boat, from his own stairs, her foot missed the side of the boat, she fell into the water, and pulled Mr Pope after her; the boat slipped away, and they were immediately out of their depth, and it was with some difficulty they were sayed. The young lady's name is Talbot; she is as remarkable for being a handsome woman, as Mr Pope is for wit. I think I cannot give you a higher notion of her beauty, unless I had named you, instead of him. I shall be impatient till I hear from you again; being, with great sincerity, Sir, your most faithful humble servant,

M. Pendarves.

P. S. I forgot to answer, on the other side, that part of your letter that concerns my sister. I do not know whether you would like her person as well as mine, because sickness has faded her complexion; but it is greatly my interest not to bring you acquainted with her mind, for that would prove a potent rival; and nothing but your partiality to me as an older acquaintance could make you give me the preference.
I beg my particular compliments to Dr Delany.* Sir John Stanley says, if you have not forgot him, he desires to be remembered as your humble servant.

TO MR NICHOLLS.

Sir,
You attended a monstrous haunch of venison to the deanery; and if you and Mrs Nicholls do not

---

* Whom Mrs Pendarves afterwards married.

attend it again to-morow, it shall be thrown into the streets; therefore all excuses must be laid aside. Mrs Whiteway and I shall be all your company, and I will give you a pot of ale to relish it.

I am, with true esteem, Sir, your most obedient humble servant,

J. SWIFT.

Deanery-House, Sept. 6, 1736.
    Monday morning.

Name your most convenient hour to dine, and de not say, when you please.

FROM DR SHERIDAN.

September 15, 1736.

DEAR SIR,

I RECEIVED a letter from Mr Henry by the last post, wherein he tells me that the six hundred and sixty pounds were short by eight pounds of your principal, and that you expected I should send you my promissory note for that, and the interest of your money, which I will do most willingly, when you let me know whether you will charge me five or six *per cent.* that I may draw my note accordingly. Indeed if you pleased, or would vouchsafe, or condescend, or think proper, I would rather that you would, I mean should charge only five *per cent.* because I might be sooner able to pay it. Upon second thoughts, mine eyes being very sore with weeping for my wife, you may let Mrs Whiteway know (to whom pray present my love and best respects) that I have made an experiment of the lake-water, which I sent for, upon myself only twice, before my optics became as clear as ever; for which reason I sent for a dozen bottles of it for Miss Harrison, to brighten her stars to the ruin of all beholders. Remember if she turns basilisk, that her mother is the cause. Tully the carrier (not Tully the orator) is to leave this to-morrow (if he does) by whom I shall send you a quarter of my own small mutton, and about six quarts of nuts to my mistress * in Abbey Street, with a fine pair of Cavan nutcrackers to save her white teeth; and yours too, if she will deign to lend them to you. I would advise you to keep in with that same lady, as you value my friendship (which is your best feather) otherwise you must forgive me if my affections shall withdraw with hers. Alas, my long evenings are coming on, bad weather, and confinement.

Somebody told me (but I forget who) that Mrs Whiteway rid your mare at the Curragh, and won the plate; but surely she would not carry the frolick so far. They say the primate's lady † rid against her; and that Mrs Whiteway, by way of weight, carried the Bishop of Down and Connor behind her. Pray let me know the truth of this.

Mr Faulkner writ to me for some poems of yours which I have. I am collecting them as fast as I can from among my papers; and he shall have them in a post or two, so please to tell him.

Three old women were lately buried at the foot of our steeple here; and so strong was the fermentation of their carcases, that our steeple has visibly

---

* Mrs Whiteway.—D. S.
† Mrs Boulter the primate's lady was very lusty.—D. S.

grown forty foot higher; and what is wonderful, above twenty small ones are grown out of its sides. What surprises me most is, that the bell-rope is not one foot higher from the ground. Be so good as to communicate this to the provost of the college, or Archdeacon Whittingham, or Archdeacon Wall. I would be glad to have all or either of their opinions, as they are the chief virtuosi in this kingdom.

I wish you all happiness, and hope you will out-live every enemy, and then we may hope our church and kingdom will flourish, and so will

    Your obedient and very humble servant,

           THOMAS SHERIDAN.

TO MR RICHARDSON *.

Dublin, Oct. 23, 1736.

SIR,

I HAD the favour of a letter from you about two months ago; but I was then, and have been almost ever since, in so ill a state of health, and lowness of spirits, that I was not able to acknowledge it; and it is not a week since I ventured to write to an old friend upon a business of importance. I have long heard of you and your character; which, as I am certain was true, so it was very advantageous, and gave me a just esteem of you, which your friendly letter has much increased. I owe you many thanks for your goodness to Mr Warburton and his widow.

---

* Of Summerseat, near Colrane.

11

I had lately a letter from her, wherein she tells me of the good office you have done her. I would be glad to know whether she has been left in a capacity of living in any comfortable way, and able to provide for her children : for I am told her husband left her some. He served once a cure of mine ; but I came over to settle here upon the queen's death, when consequently all my credit was gone, except with the late primate, who had many obligations to me, and on whom I prevailed to give that living to Mr Warburton, and make him surrogate, which he lost in a little time. Alderman Barber was my old acquaintance. I got him two or three employments when I had credit with the queen's ministers ; but upon her majesty's death he was stripped of them all. However, joining with Mr Gumley, they both entered into the South Sea scheme, and the alderman grew prodigiously rich : but by pursuing too far, he lost two-thirds of his gains. However, he bought a house with some acres near Richmond, and another in London, and kept fifty thousand pounds, which enabled him to make a figure in the city.——This is a short history of the alderman, who, in spite of his tory principles, got through all the honours of London. I cannot tell whether his office of governor of your society* be for his life, or only annual ; I suppose you can inform me.

Your invitation is friendly and generous, and what I would be glad to accept, if it were possible ; but, Sir, I have not an ounce of flesh about me, and cannot ride above a dozen miles in a day, without

---

* The Londonderry Society, of which Mr Richardson was agent.

being sore and bruised and spent. My head is every day more or less disordered by a giddiness; yet I ride the strand here constantly when fair weather invites me. But if I live till spring next, and have any remainder of health, I determine to venture, although I have some objections. I do not doubt your good cheer and welcome; but you brag too much of the prospects and situations. Dare you pretend to vie with the county of Armagh, which, excepting its cursed roads, and want of downs to ride on, is the best part I have seen of Ireland? I own you engage for the roads from hence to your house; but where am I to ride after rainy weather? Here I have always a strand or a turnpike for four or five miles. Your being a bachelor pleases me well; and as to neighbours, considering the race of squires in Ireland, I had rather be without them. If you have books in large print, or an honest parson with common sense, I desire no more. But here is an interval of above six months; and in the mean time God knows what will become of me, and perhaps of the kingdom, for I think we are going to ruin as fast as it is possible. If I have not tired you now, I promise never to try your patience so much again. I am, Sir, with true esteem,

Your most obedient and obliged servant,
JON. SWIFT.

I hear your brother the clergyman is still alive: I knew him in London and Ireland, and desire you will present him with my humble service.

TO THE RIGHT HONOURABLE SIR JOHN STANLEY, BART.

Dublin, Oct. 30, 1736.

SIR,

I HAVE had, for several months, a strong application made me, by a person for whose virtue, honour, and good sense, I have a great esteem, to write to you in behalf of one of your tenants here, whose case I send you enclosed; and if he relates it with truth and candour, I expect you will comply with his request, because I have known you long, and have always highly esteemed and loved you, as you cannot deny: I know you will think it hard for me, or any one, to interfere in a business of property; but I very well understand the practice of Irish tenants to English landlords, and of those landlords to their tenants. Yet, if what Mr Wilding desires is rightly represented, that he has been a great improver, his offers reasonable, his gains by no means exorbitant, and his payments regular, you neither must nor shall act as an Irish racking squire. I have inquired about this tenant, and hear a good account of his honesty; and that worthy friend, who recommends him to me, durst not deceive me: so I fully reckon that you will obey my commands, or show me strong reasons to the contrary; in which case I will break with that friend, and drive your tenant out of doors, whenever he presumes to open his lips again to me on any occasion.

I have one advantage by this letter, that it gives me a fair occasion of inquiring after your health, and where you live, and how you employ your leisure, and what share I keep in your good-will.

As to myself, years and infirmities have sunk my spirits to nothing. My English friends are all either dead or in exile, or by a prudent oblivion, have utterly dropped me ; having loved this present world. And as to this country, I am only a favourite of my old friends the rabble, and I return their love because I know none else who deserve it. May you live long happy and beloved, as you have ever been by the best and wisest of mankind. And if ever you happen to think of me, remember that I have always been, and shall ever continue, with the truest respect and esteem, Sir,

Your most obedient and obliged servant,
JON. SWIFT.

I know not the present state of your family ; but, if there be still near you the ladies I had the honour to know, I desire to present them with my most humble service.

I am now at the age of blundering in letters, syllables, words, and half-sentences, as you see, and must pardon.

FROM LADY BETTY GERMAIN.

Nov. 2, 1736.

I AM sorry to be so unlucky in my late errands between his grace and you ; and he also is troubled at it, as the person you recommend is, indeed, what you say, a very worthy person ; but Mr Molloy, who was Lord George's second tutor, had the promise of the next preferment, so he cannot put him by this. I wish I was more fortunate in my undertakings; but I verily believe it is a common calamity to most men in power, that they are often, by necessity, prevented from obliging their friends; and many worthy people go unrewarded. Whether you call this a court answer, or not, I am very positively sure, he is heartily vexed when it is not in his power to oblige you. I have been very much out of order, or you should have heard from me before: and I am now literally setting out for the Bath. So adieu! dear Dean.

FROM MRS BARBER.

Bath, Nov. 3, 1736.

SIR,

I SHOULD long since have acknowledged the honour of your kind letter, but that I found my head so disordered by writing a little, that I was fearful of having the gout in it; so I humbly beseech you to pardon me; nor think me ungrateful, nor in the least insensible of the infinite obligations I lie under to you, which, Heaven knows, are never out of my mind.

How shall I express the sense I have of your goodness, in inviting me to return to Ireland, and generously offering to contribute to support me there? But would it not be base in me, not to try to do something for myself rather than be burdensome where I am already so much indebted?

As to the friend who you say, Sir, is in so much better circumstances, I should be very unjust, if I did not assure you that friend has never failed of being extremely kind to me.

I find I need not tell you that I am not able to pursue the scheme of letting lodgings, your goodness and compassion for my unhappy state of health, has made you think of it for me; it is impracticable, but am desirous to try if I can do any good by selling Irish linen, which I find is coming much into repute here: in that way, my daughter, who is willing to do every thing in her power, can be of service, but never in the other.

If I should go from Bath, I have reason to think that the remainder of my life would be very miserable, and that I should soon lose the use of my limbs for ever; since I find nothing but the blessing of God on these waters does me any good; beside this, the interest of my children is a great inducement to me, for here I have the best prospect of keeping up an acquaintance for them. My son, * who is learning to paint, goes on well; and, if he be in the least approved of, in all probability he may do very well at Bath; for I never yet saw a painter that came hither, fail of getting more business than he could do, let him be ever so indifferent; and I am in hopes that Con † may settle here. Dr Mead, whose goodness to me is great, may be of vast use to him, if he finds, as I hope he will, that he is worthy of his favour. And if God blesses my sons with success, they are so well inclined, that I do not doubt but they would take a pleasure in supporting me,

---

* Mr Rupert Barber, an eminent painter in crayons and miniature.—F.

† Dr Constantine Barber, a very learned physician, and president of the college of physicians in Dublin. Some of his poems are printed in the collection of his mother.—F.

if I can make a shift to maintain them and myself till then: and I find Mr Barber is very willing to do what he can for them, though his circumstances are far from being what you are told they are; nor, I fear, half so good.

But though I cannot hope to be supported by letting lodgings, I would willingly take a house a little larger than I want for myself, if I could meet with it on reasonable terms; that if any particular friend came, they might lodge in it, which would make it more agreeable: and if I live till my son the painter goes into business, he might be with me. As for Con, if he does not choose to settle here, good Dr Helsham, with his usual friendliness, has promised to honour him with his protection, if he returns to Ireland.

I have now, Sir, told you my schemes, and hope they will be honoured with your approbation; and encouraged by your inexpressible goodness to me, I have at length got resolution enough to beg a favour; which, if you, Sir, condescend to grant, would make me rich, without impoverishing you.

When Dr King of Oxford was last in Ireland, he had the pleasure of seeing your Treatise on Polite Conversation, and gave such an account of it in London, as made numbers of people very desirous to see it. Lady Worsley,* who heard of it from Mrs Cleland, † and many more of my patronesses pressed me to beg it of you, and assured me I might get a great subscription if I had that, and a few of

---

* Wife of Sir Robert Worsley.—B.
† Wife of Major William Cleland, a friend of Mr Pope, and author of the Letter to the Publisher of the Dunciad, prefixed to the first correct edition of that poem.—B.

your original poems; if you would give me leave to publish an advertisement, that you had made me a present of them. This they commanded me to tell you, above a year ago, and I have had many letters since upon that account; but, conscious of the many obligations I already lay under, I have thought it a shame to presume farther upon your goodness: but, when I was last in London, they made me promise I would mention it the next time I wrote to you; and indeed I have attempted it many a time since, but never could till now. I humbly beseech you, Sir, if you do not think it proper, not to be offended with me for asking it; for it was others, that out of kindness to me, put me upon it. They said you made no advantage for yourself, by your writings; and, that since you honoured me with your protection, I had all the reason in the world to think it would be a pleasure to you, to see me in easy circumstances; that every body would gladly subscribe for any thing Dr Swift wrote; and indeed, I believe in my conscience, it would be the making of me. *

There are a great many people of quality here this season; among others, Lady Carteret, and Mrs Spencer, † who commanded me to make their best compliments to you. They came on Mrs Spencer's account, who is better in her health since she drank these waters. I daily see such numbers of people mended by them, that I cannot but wish you would

---

* The Dean complied with this request by presenting Mrs Barber with the copy.
† Daughter of Lord Carteret, married, first to the Honourable John Spencer, brother to the Duke of Marlborough, and afterward to William, second Earl Cowper.—B.

try them: as you are sensible your disorders are chiefly occasioned by a cold stomach, I believe there is not any thing in this world so likely to cure that disorder as the Bath waters; which are daily found to be a sovereign remedy for disorders of that kind: I know, Sir, you have no opinion of drugs, and why will you not try so agreeable a medicine, prepared by Providence alone? If you will not try for your own sake, why will you not, in pity to your country? O may that Being that inspired you to be its defence in the day of distress, influence you to take the best method to preserve a life of so much importance to an oppressed people!

Before I conclude, gratitude obliges me to tell you, that Mr Temple * was here lately, and was exceedingly kind to me and my daughters. He made me a present of a hamper of very fine Madeira, which he said was good for the gout, and distinguished me in the kindest manner. He commanded me to make his best compliments to you, and says he flatters himself you will visit Moor Park once again. Heaven grant you may! and that I may be so blest as to see you, who am, with infinite respect and gratitude, your most obliged, most dutiful, humble servant,

MARY BARBER.

---

* John Temple, Esq. nephew of Sir William Temple, whose grand-daughter he married. He was brother to Lord Viscount Palmerston.—B.

FROM DR KING TO MRS WHITEWAY.

Paris, Nov. 9, O. S. 1736.

MADAM,

As soon as ever you cast your eye on the date of this letter, you will pronounce me a rambler; and that is a charge I will not deny. How I was transported from Edinburgh to this place requires more room to inform you than my paper will allow me. But I will give you a small hint; you know I am a Laplander,* and consequently I have the honour to be well acquainted with some witches of distinction. I speak in the phrase of this country: for the first man I spoke to in Paris, told me, he had the honour to live next door to Mr Knight's hatter. But to our business. I would not have you imagine I forgot my friends, or neglect the great affairs I have undertaken. The next letter you will receive from me shall be dated from London, where I propose to arrive about the twentieth of this month. I will then put the little MS. to the press, and oblige the whole English nation. † As to the history, the Dean may be assured I will take care to supply the dates that are wanting, and which can easily be done in an hour or two. The tracts, if he pleases, may be printed by way of appendix. This will be indeed

---

* This alludes to the Doctor's satire called "The Toast," which he pretends was written originally in Latin by Frederick Scheffer, a Laplander. This poem is now exceedingly scarce. It is reprinted, but without the notes and observations, in the Foundling Hospital for Wit.—N.

† The History of the last Four Years of Queen Anne's Reign. In the following letters, the reader will find the reasons why this was a posthumous publication.

less trouble than the interweaving them in the body
of the history, and will do the author as much honour, and answer the purpose full as well.   This is
all I need say in answer to that part of your letter
which is serious: for I hope you are not in earnest,
when you throw out such horrible reflections against
my friends in Scotland. Will you believe me, when
I tell you upon my word, that I was entertained with
the greatest politeness and delicacy during my short
stay in that country ? I found every thing as neat
and clean in the houses, where I had my quarters,
as even you could desire.   I cannot indeed much
commend Edinburgh ; and yet the s——ks, which
are so much complained of there, are not more offensive than I have found them in every street in
this elegant city, which the French say is the mistress of the world ; *Madame il n'y a qu'un Paris.*
As to my own thoughts of this nation, you shall
know them, when I am out of it : and then I will
write to the Dean, and give him some account of
his old friend my Lord Bolingbroke.   When the
Dean is informed of what that gentleman is doing,
I am apt to be believe it will be a motive to induce
him to hasten the publication of his history.   In the
mean time, I beg of you to assure him, that nothing
shall be wanting on my part to execute his com-
missions very faithfully.   I am truly sensible of
the great obligations I owe him, and of the honour
he hath done me, not in the French sense of that
word.

  I desire my humble service to Miss Harrison,
and tell Mr Swift * I shall be glad of any opportu-

---

* Mr Swift was at this time in Ireland, but returned to Oxford in the spring following.—D. S.

nity to do him a real service. At the same time I assure you, with the greatest truth, that I am, Madam,

Your most humble and most obedient servant,
W. KING.

—————

FROM DR SHERIDAN TO MRS WHITE-WAY.

November 21, 1736.

DEAR MADAM,

I RECEIVED the vexatious account of your disappointment in the nuts and water, which were both in perfection when they left me, and for which I will make the carrier an example as soon as I can lay hold of him. I do believe this same country, wherein I am settled, exceeds the whole world in villany of every kind, and theft. It is not long since a pair of millstones were stolen and carried off from within two miles of Quilca; the thieves traced and pursued as far as Killishandra, and farther they were never more heard of, any more than if they had been dropt into hell. I do believe this dexterity may challenge history to match it. It has made all our country merry, but the poor miller that lost them.

I sincerely congratulate with you upon the recovery of our dear friend the Dean. May he live long to enjoy his friends, and the vexation of his enemies! I have been for a week past composing an Anglolatin letter to him, which is not as yet finished. I hope it will make him a visit upon his birth-day, which I intend to celebrate with some of his own money, and some of his own friends here. Three

tenants have lately run away with thirty pounds of
my rent : I have by good fortune got one rich honest
man in their place, who has commenced from September past, and is to pay me their arrears the next
May ; so that I am well off. I will gather as fast as
I can for the Dean ; but indeed he must have a little
longer indulgence for me. It is very hard that the
Squire ——— should keep my money in his pocket,
when it is nothing out of his. I suppose he intends
it shall keep him in coals for two or three years ; for
the devil a one he burns, except it be sometimes in
his kitchen, and his nursery upon a cold day. I have
this day written a complaint of him to my scholar
—— of ——, who, I hope, will have gratitude
enough to do me justice. There never was known
such a scarcity of money as we have in the North,
owing to the dismal circumstances of some thousands
of families preparing to go off, that have turned their
leases and effects into ready money. Some squires
will have their whole estates left to themselves and
their dogs. O what compassion I have for them!
I have written a little pretty birth-day poem against
St Andrew's-day, which, when corrected, revised,
and amended, I intend for Faulkner to publish. I
do assure you, Madam, it is a very pretty thing (although I say it that should not say it) and as humorous a thing as ever you read in your life ; and
I know the whole world will be in love with it,
as I am with you. But how the devil came you to
tell the Dean you are no longer my mistress? I say,
that you are, and shall be so in spite of the whole
world.

THOMAS SHERIDAN.

DR DUNKIN TO MRS WHITEWAY.

November 30, 1736.

Madam,

I HAD proposed vast pleasure to myself, from the hopes of celebrating the Dean's birth-day with you; but as I have been afflicted with a violent headach all day, which is not yet abated, I could not safely venture abroad. I have, however, as in annual duty bound, attempted to write some lines on the occasion; not indeed with that accuracy the subject deserved, being the crudities of last night's lucubrations, to which I attribute the indisposition of my pate: but if they should in any measure merit your approbation, I shall rejoice in my pain. One comfort, however, I enjoy by absenting myself from your solemnity, that I shall not undergo a second mortification, by hearing my own stuff. Be pleased to render my most dutiful respects agreeable to the Dean: and pardon this trouble from, Madam,

Your most obliged, most obedient servant,
W. DUNKIN.

TO MR POPE.

December 2, 1736.

I THINK you owe me a letter, but whether you do or not, I have not been in a condition to write. Years and infirmities have quite broke me; I mean that odious continual disorder in my head. I neither read, nor write, nor remember, nor converse. All I have left is to walk and ride; the first I can do tolerably; but the latter for want of good weather at this season is seldom in my power; and having not an ounce of flesh about me, my skin comes off in ten miles riding, because my skin and bone cannot agree together. But I am angry, because you will not suppose me as sick as I am, and write to me out of perfect charity, although I should not be able to answer. I have too many vexations by my station and the impertinence of people, to be able to bear the mortification of not hearing from a very few distant friends that are left; and, considering how time and fortune have ordered matters, I have hardly one friend left but yourself. What Horace says, *Singula de nobis anni prædantur*, I feel every month at farthest; and by this computation, if I hold out two years I shall think it a miracle. My comfort is, you began to distinguish so confounded early, that your acquaintance with distinguished men of all kinds was almost as ancient as mine. I mean, Wycherly, Rowe, Prior, Congreve, Addison, Parnell, &c. and in spite of your heart, you have owned me a contemporary. Not to mention Lords Oxford, Bolingbroke, Harcourt, Peterborow: in short, I was the other day recollecting twenty-seven great ministers, or men of wit and learning, who are all dead, and all of my acquaintance, within twenty years past; neither have I the grace to be sorry, that the present times are drawn to the dregs, as well as my own life. May my friends be happy in this and a better life, but I value not what becomes of posterity, when I consider from what monsters they are to spring. My Lord Orrery writes to you to-morrow, and you see I send this under his cover, or at least franked by him. He has 3000l. a year about Cork, and the neighbourhood, and has more than three years rent unpaid; this is our condition in these blessed times. I writ to your neighbour about a month ago, and subscribed my name: I fear he has not received my letter, and wish you would ask him; but perhaps he is still a rambling; for we hear of him at Newmarket, and that Boerhaave has restored his health. How my services are lessened of late with the number of my friends on your side! yet my Lord Bathurst and Lord Marsham and Mr Lewis remain; and being your acquaintance I desire when you see them to deliver my compliments; but chiefly to Mrs Patty Blount, and let me know whether she be as young and agreeable as when I saw her last? Have you got a supply of new friends to make up for those who are gone? and are they equal to the first? I am afraid it is with friends as with times; and that the *laudator temporis acti se puero*, * is equally applicable to both. I am less grieved for living here, because it is a perfect retirement, and consequently fittest for those who are grown good for nothing; for this town and kingdom are as much out of the world as North Wales. My head is so ill that I cannot write a paper full as I used to do; and yet I will not forgive a blank of half an inch from you. I had reason to expect from some of your letters, that we were to hope for more epistles of morality; and I assure you, my acquaintance resent that they have not seen my name at the head of one. The subject of such epistles are more useful to the public, by your manner of handling them, than any of all your writings; and although in so profligate a world as ours they may possibly not much mend our manners, yet

---

* " Ill-natur'd censor of the present age,
    And fond of all the follies of the past.'

posterity will enjoy the benefit, whenever a court happens to have the least relish for virtue and religion.

FROM LORD CASTLE-DURROW.*

Castle-Durrow, Dec. 4, 1736.

Sir,

It is now a month since you favoured me with your letter ; I fear the trouble of another from me may persuade you to excuse my acknowledgments of it ; but I am too sensible of the honour you do me, to suffer a correspondence to drop, which I know some of the greatest men in this age have gloried in. How then must my heart be elated! The fly on the chariot wheel is too trite a quotation : I shall rather compare myself to a worm enlivened by the sun, and crawling before it. I imagine there is a tinge of vanity in the meanest insect ; and who knows but even this reptile may pride itself in its curls and twists before its benefactor? This is more than the greatest philosopher can determine. Guesses are the privilege of the ignorant, our undoubted right, and what you can never lay claim to.

I am quite angry with your servant, for not acquainting you I was at your door. I greatly commend both your economy and the company you admit at your table. I am told your wine is excellent. The additional groat is, I hope, for suet to your pudding. I fancy I am as old an acquaintance as

---

* Only son of Thomas Flower, Esq. of Durrow ; created Baron of Castle-Durrow in 1733.

most you have in this kingdom ; though it is not my happiness to be so qualified as to merit that intimacy you profess for a few. It is now to little purpose to repine ; though it grieves me to think I was a favourite of Dean Alrich, the greatest man that ever presided in that high post ; that over Virgil and Horace, Rag * and Philips smoked many a pipe, and drank many a quart with me, beside the expence of a bushel of nuts, and that now I am scarce able to relish their beauties. I know it is death to you to see either of them mangled ; but a scrap of paper I design to enclose, will convince you of the truth, It was in joke to an old woman of seventy, who takes the last line so heinously, that, thanks to my stars, she hates me in earnest. So I devote myself to ladies of fewer years, and more discretion.

This, and such other innocent amusements, I devote myself to in my retirement. Once in two years I appear in the *anus* of the world, our metropolis. His grace, my old acquaintance, told me, I began to contract strange old fashioned rust, and advised me to burst out of my solitude, and refit myself for the public : but my own notion of the world, for some time past, is so confirmed by the sanction of your opinion of it, that I resolve this same rust shall be as dear to me, as that which enhanced the value of poor Dr Woodward's shield ; † though it gave

---

* Edmund Smith, usually called Rag Smith.
+ The character of Dr Cornelius Scriblerus, in the Memoirs of his son Martinus Scriblerus, is intended for Dr Woodward, who wrote a dissertation on an ancient shield ; and Dr Cornelius is represented as having intended to place his son in what he conceived to be an antique shield, to be christened ; but which being given to the maid, with its venerable rust upon it, she scoured it bright, and then it appeared to be nothing more than an old sconce without a nozzle.—H.

such offence to his cleanly maid, that she polished it to none at all.

I shall appear very inconsistent with myself in now telling you, that I still design the latter end of next month for England. You allow I have some pretence to go there. My progress with my son will be farther; for which, perhaps, you too will condemn me, as well as other friends do. I shall be proud of the honour of your commands, and, with your leave, will wait upon you for them. I design to send you a pot of woodcocks for a Christmas-box: small as the present is, pray believe I am, with sincere respect, Sir, your most obedient humble servant,

CASTLEDURROW.

I hope you are as well as the news says. *A propos,* can you agree with me, that the little operator of mine, whom you saw lately at his Grace of Dublin's, has a resemblance of your friend Mr Pope?

Verses by Lord CASTLEDURROW, enclosed in the above letter.

Lætitia's Character of her Lover rendered in metre.

Old women sometimes can raise his desire;
The young, in their turn, set his heart all on fire.
And sometimes again he abhors womankind.
Was ever poor wretch of so fickle a mind!

The Lover's Answer.

Parciùs junctas quatiunt fenestras
Ictibus crebris juvenes protervi;
Nec tibi somnos adimunt: amatque
    Janua limen.   Hor. 1. Od. xxv.

No more shall frolic youth advance
In serenade, and am'rous dance;

Redoubling stroke no more shall beat
Against thy window and thy gate ;
In idle sleep now lie secure,
And never be unbarr'd thy door.

FROM DR KING.

London, Dec. 7, 1736.

Sir,

I ARRIVED here yesterday, and I am now ready to obey your commands.   I hope you are come to a positive resolution concerning the History.   You need not hesitate about the dates, or the references which are to be made to any public papers ; for I can supply them without the least trouble.   As well as I remember, there is but one of those public pieces which you determined should be inserted at length ; I mean Sir Thomas Hanmer's Representation ; this I have now by me.   If you incline to publish the two tracts as an appendix to the History, you will be pleased to see if the character given of the Earl of Oxford in the pamphlet of 1715 agrees with the character given of the same person in the History.   Perhaps on a review you may think proper to leave one of them quite out.   You have (I think) barely mentioned the attempt of Guiscard, and the quarrel between Rechteren and Mesnager.   But as these are facts which are probably now forgot or unknown, it would not be amiss if they were related at large in the notes ; which may be done from the Gazettes, or any other newspapers of those times.   This is all I have to offer to your consideration ; and you see here are no objections which ought to retard the publication of this valuable work one moment. I will only now add, that if you intend this History should be published from the original manuscript, it must be done while you are living: and if you continue in the same mind to intrust me with the execution of your orders, I will perform them faithfully. This I would do, although I did not owe you a thousand obligations, which I shall ever acknowledge. I am, with the greatest truth, Sir,

Your most humble and most obedient servant,
W. KING.

TO MR ALDERMAN BARBER.

Dublin, Dec. 8, 1736.

MY DEAR OLD FRIEND,

I am glad of any occassion to write to you, and therefore business will be my excuse. I had lately a letter from Mrs Warburton, the widow of him for whom I got a living in those parts where your society's estate lies *. The substance of her request is a public affair, wherein you and I shall agree; for neither of us are changed in point of principles. Mr John Williams, your society's overseer, is worried by a set of people in one part of your estate, which is called Salter's Proportion, because he opposed the building of a fanatick meeting-house in that place. This crew of dissenters are so enraged at this refusal, that they have incensed Sir Thomas Webster, the landlord (I suppose under you) of that estate, against him, and are doing all in their power

---

* The Londonderry Society, of which Barber was president.

to get him discharged from your service.   Mr Warburton was his great friend.   By what I understand,
those factious people presume to take your timber at
pleasure, contrary to your society's instructions,
wherein Mr Williams constantly opposes them to
the utmost of his power, and that is one great cause
of their malice.   Long may you live a bridle to the
insolence of dissenters, who, with their pupils the
atheists, are now wholly employed in ruining the
church; and have entered into public associations
subscribed and handed about publickly for that purpose.   I wish you were forced to come over hither,
because I am confident the journey and voyage
would be good for your health: but my ill health
and age have made it impossible for me to go over
to you.   I have often let you know that I have a
good warm apartment for you, and I scorn to add
any professions of your being welcome in summer
or winter, or both : pray God bless you, and grant
that you may live as long as you desire, and be ever
happy hereafter.   Is our friend Bolingbroke well?
He is older than either of us; but I am chiefly concerned about his fortune : for some time ago a friend
of us both writ to me, that he wished his lordship
had listened a little to my thrifty lectures, instead of
only laughing at them.   I am ever, with the truest
affection, dear Mr Alderman,
            Your most hearty friend
                  and obedient humble servant,
                        JON. SWIFT.

This letter, I suppose, will reach you, although I
  have forgot your street and part of the town.

FROM MR PULTENEY.

London, Dec. 21, 1736.

SIR,

I WAS at the Bath when I had the favour of your letter of the 6th of last month. I remember I once wrote to you from thence, therefore I resolved not to hazard another by the cross post, but stay till my return to London, to thank you for your kind remembrance of me. I am now, God be thanked, tolerably well in health again, and have done with all physic and water drinking. My constitution must certainly be a pretty good one; for it has resisted the attacks of five eminent physicians for five months together, and I am not a jot the worse for any of them.

For the future I will preserve myself by your advice, and follow your rules of rising early, eating little, drinking less, and riding daily. I hope this regimen will be long of use to both of us, and that we may live to meet again. I am exceedingly rejoiced at Mr Stopford's good success, and have acknowledged my obligation to the Duke of Dorset, who I dare say will in time do more for him, because he has promised it. My first desire to serve him was solely because I knew you esteemed him. I was confident he must be a deserving man, since John Gay assured me he was a very particular friend of yours. I afterward, upon farther acquaintance, grew to love him for his own sake, and the merit I found in him. Men of his worth and character do an honour to those who recommend them. There is a sentence, I think it is in Tully's Offices, which I admire extremely, and should be tempted to take it for a motto, if ever I took one, *Amicis prodesse,* *nemini nocere.* It is a noble sentiment, and shall be my rule, though perhaps never my motto. I fancy there is no other foundation for naming so many successors to the Duke of Dorset, than because he has served, as they call it, his time out. I am inclined to believe he will go once more among you, and the rather since I am told he gave great satisfaction the last time he was with you. Lord Essex will hardly be the person to succeed him, though I should be glad he was, since I flatter myself he would be willing, on many occasions, to show some regard to my recommendations. I have lately seen a gentleman who is come from France, who assures me, the person you inquire after*, and to whom you gave so many lectures of frugality, is in perfect health, and lives in great plenty and affluence. I own I doubt it; but, if it be true, I am sure it cannot last long, unless an old gentleman would please to die, who seems at present not to have the least inclination toward it, though near ninety years old †. I verily think he is more likely to marry again than die.

Pope showed me a letter he had lately from you. We grieved extremely to find you so full of complaints, and we wished heartily you might be well enough to make a trip here in spring. Shifting the scene was of great service to me; perhaps it may be so to you. I mended from the moment I had crossed the seas, and sensibly felt the benefit of changing air. His majesty is still on the other side. He has escaped being at sea in the tempestuous weather we have had; but when the wind will let

---

* Lord Bolingbroke.
† Lord St John, father of Lord Bolingbroke.

him come, God knows. Lord Chesterfield says, if
he does not come by Twelfth-day, the people will
choose king and queen without him. I must tell
you a ridiculous incident, perhaps you have not
heard it; one Mrs Mapp, a famous she bonesetter
and mountebank, coming to town with a coach and
six horses, on the Kentish road was met by a rabble
of people, who seeing her very oddly and tawdrily
dressed, took her for a foreigner, and concluded she
must be a certain great person's mistress. Upon
this they followed the coach, bawling out, No
Hanover whore! no Hanover whore! the lady
within the coach was much offended, let down
the glass, and screamed louder than any of them,
She was no Hanover whore! she was an English
one! Upon which they cried out, God bless your
ladyship! quitted the pursuit, and wished her a
good journey.

I hope to be able to attend the house next sessions; but not with that assiduity as I have formerly
done. Why should I risk the doing myself any
harm, when I know how vain it is to expect to do
any good? You that have been a long time out
of this country, can have no notion how wicked
and corrupt we are grown. Were I to tell you
of half the rogueries come to my knowledge, you
would be astonished; and yet I dare say I do
not know of half that are practised in one little
spot of ground only; you may easily guess where I
mean.

I will make your compliments to Lord Carteret,
when he comes to town. I am sure he will be
pleased with your kind mention of him; and if you
will now and then let me hear from you, I shall
look on the continuance of your correspondence as
a very particular honour: for I assure you, that I

am, with the greatest truth and esteem, Sir, your most obedient humble servant,

WILLIAM PULTENEY.

FROM MR POPE.

Dec. 30, 1736.

YOUR very kind letter has made me more melancholy, than almost any thing in this world now can do. For I can bear every thing in it, bad as it is, better than the complaints of my friends. Though others tell me you are in pretty good health, and in good spirits, I find the contrary when you open your mind to me: and indeed it is but a prudent part, to seem not so concerned about others, nor so crazy ourselves as we really are: for we shall neither be beloved nor esteemed the more, by our common acquaintance, for any affliction or any infirmity. But to our true friend we may, we must complain, of what (it is a thousand to one) he complains with us; for if we have known him long, he is old, and if he has known the world long, he is out of humour at it. If you have but as much more health than others at your age, 'as you have more wit and good temper, you shall not have much of my pity; but if ever you live to have less, you shall not have less of my affection. A whole people will rejoice at every year that shall be added to you, of which you have had a late instance in the public rejoicings on your birth-day. I can assure you, something better and greater than high birth and quality, must go toward acquiring those demonstrations of public esteem and love. I have seen a royal birth-day uncelebrated, but by one vile ode, and one hired bonfire. Whatever years may take away from you, they will not take away the general esteem, for your sense, virtue, and charity.

The most melancholy effect of years is that you mention, the catalogue of those we loved and have lost, perpetually increasing. How much that reflection struck me, you will see from the motto I have prefixed to my Book of Letters, which, so much against my inclination, has been drawn from me. It is from Catullus,

> Quo desiderio veteres revocamus amores,
> Atque olim amissas flemus amicitias * !

I detain this letter till I can find some safe conveyance ; innocent as it is, and as all letters of mine must be, of any thing to offend my superiors, except the reverence I bear to true merit and virtue. But I have much reason to fear, those which you have too partially kept in your hands, will get out in some very disagreeable shape, in case of our mortality : and the more reason to fear it, since this last month Curll has obtained from Ireland two letters, (one of Lord Bolingbroke, and one of mine, to you, which we wrote in the year 1723) and he has printed them, to the best of my memory, rightly ; except one passage concerning Dawley, which must have been since inserted, since my lord had not that place at that time. Your answer to that letter he has not got ; it has never been out of my

---

* " How pants my heart old friendship to renew!
How pierc'd with grief old loves decay'd I view !"—S.

custody; for whatever is lent is lost (wit as well as money) to these needy poetical readers.

The world will certainly be the better for his change of life. He seems, in the whole turn of his letters, to be a settled and principled philosopher, thanking fortune for the tranquillity he has been led into by her aversion, like a man driven by a violent wind, from the sea into a calm harbour. You ask me if I have got any supply of new friends to make up for those that are gone? I think that impossible; for not our friends only, but so much of ourselves is gone by the mere flux and course of years, that were the same friends to be restored to us, we could not be restored to ourselves, to enjoy them. But, as when the continual washing of a river takes away our flowers and plants, it throws weeds and sedges in their room; so the course of time brings us something, as it deprives us of a great deal; and instead of leaving us what we cultivated, and expected to flourish and adorn us, gives us only what is of some little use by accident. Thus I have acquired, without my seeking, a few chance acquaintance of young men, who look rather to the past age than the present, and therefore the future may have some hopes of them. If I love them, it is because they honour some of those whom I, and the world, have lost, or are losing. Two or three of them have distinguished themselves in parliament; and you will own in a very uncommon manner, when I tell you it is by their asserting of independency, and contempt of corruption. One or two are linked to me by their love of the same studies and the same authors: but I will own to you my moral capacity has got so much the better of my poetical, that I have few acquaintance on the latter score, and none without a casting weight on the former. But I find my heart hardened and blunt to new impressions, it will scarce receive or retain affections of yesterday; and those friends who have been dead these twenty years, are more present to me now, than these I see daily. You, dear Sir, are one of the former sort to me, in all respects, but that we can, yet, correspond together. I do not know whether it is not more vexatious to know we are both in one world, without any farther intercourse. Adieu. I can say no more, I feel so much: let me drop into common things.—Lord Masham has just married his son. Mr Lewis has just buried his wife. Lord Oxford wept over your letter * in pure kindness. Mrs B. sighs more for you than for the loss of youth. She says she will be agreeable many years hence, for she has learned that secret from some receipts of your writing. Adieu.

---

* On this letter Mr Bowles has made the following just and beautifully expressed remark: "These letters, that almost set us among the very persons who wrote them, create, with all their faults, a melancholy interest. We hear of their acquaintance, friends, pursuits, studies, as if we knew them; we see the progress of years and infirmities, and follow them through the gradations from youth to age, from hope to disappointment; and partake of their feelings, their partialities, aversions, hopes, and sorrows, till all is dust and silence."

FROM LORD CASTLE-DURROW.

Castle-Durrow, Jan. 18, 1726-7.

SIR,

I RECEIVED the honour of your letter with that pleasure which they have always given me. If I have deferred acknowledging longer than usual, I should not be at a loss to make an excuse, if I could be so vain as to imagine you required any. Virtue forbids us to continue in debt, and gratitude obliges us at least to own favours too large for us to pay ; therefore I must write rather than reproach myself, and blush at having neglected it when I wait upon you ; though you may retort, blushes should proceed rather from the pen than from silence; which pleads a modest diffidence, that often obtains pardon.

I am delighted with the sketch of your *Imperium*, and beg I may be presented to your first minister, Sir Robert *. Your puddings I have been acquainted with these forty years ; they are the best sweet thing I ever eat. The economy of your table is delicious ; a little and perfectly good, is the greatest treat ; and that elegance in sorting company puts me in mind of Corelli's *orcastro* †, in forming which he excelled mankind. In this respect no man ever judged worse than Lord Chancellor Middleton ; his table the neatest served of

---

* Mrs Brent, the Dean's house-keeper or prime-minister.

† His lordship probably uses this word for *orchestre*. Corelli, the famous Italian musician and composer, and director of the Pope's choir at Rome, was eminent for his skill in forming and disposing the several musicians in a concert.—B.

any I have seen in Dublin, which, to be sure, was entirely owing to his lady. You really surprise me, when you say you know not where to get a dinner in the whole town. Dublin is famous for vanity this way; and I think the mistaken luxury of some of our grandees, and feasting those who come to laugh at us from the other side of the water, have done us as much prejudice as most of our follies. Not any lord-lieutenant has done us more honour in magnificence, than our present viceroy *. He is an old intimate of my youth, and has always distinguished me with affection and friendship. I trust mine are no less sincere for him. I have joy in hearing his virtues celebrated. I wish that he had gratified you in your request. Those he has done most for, I dare affirm, love him least. It is pity there is any allay in so beneficent a temper; but if a friend can be viewed with an impartial eye, faults he has none; and if any failings, they are grafted in a pusillanimity which sinks him into complaisance for men who neither love nor esteem him, and has prevented him buoying up against their impotent threats, in raising his friends. He is a most amiable man, has many good qualities, and wants but one more to make him really a great man.

If you have any commands to England for so insignificant a fellow as I am, pray prepare them against the beginning of next month. At my arrival in town, I shall send a message in form for audience; but I beg to see you in your private capacity, not in your princely authority; for, as both your ministry and senate are full, and that I

---

* The Duke of Dorset.—H.

cannot hope to be employed in either, I fear your revenue is too small to grant me a pension. And as I am not fit for business, perhaps you will not allow me a fit object for one, which charity only prompts you to bestow. Thus, without any view of your highness's favour, I am independent, and with sincere esteem,

Your most obedient humble servant,
CASTLE-DURROW.

TO LADY BETTY GERMAIN.

Jan. 29, 1736-7.

MADAM,

I OWE your ladyship the acknowledgment of a letter I have long received, relative to a request I made to my lord duke. I now dismiss you, Madam, for ever from your office of being a go-between upon any affair I might have with his grace. I will never more trouble him, either with my visits or application. His business in this kingdom is to make himself easy; his lessons are all prescribed him from court; and he is sure, at a very cheap rate, to have a majority of most corrupt slaves and idiots at his devotion. The happiness of this kingdom is of no more consequence to him, than it would be to the great Mogul; while the very few honest or moderate men of the whig party, lament the choice he makes of persons for civil employments, or church preferments.

I will now repeat, for the last time, that I never made him a request out of any views of my own; but entirely by consulting his own honour, and the desires of all good men, who were as loyal as his grace could wish, and had no other fault than that of modestly standing up for preserving some poor remainder in the constitution of church and state.

I had long experience, while I was in the world, of the difficulties that great men lay under, in the points of promises and employments ; but a plain honest English farmer, when he invites his neighbours to a christening, if a friend happen to come late will take care to lock up a piece for him in the cupboard.

Henceforth I shall only grieve silently, when I hear of employments disposed of to the discontent of his grace's best friends in this kingdom ; and the rather, because I do not know a more agreeable person in conversation, one more easy, or of a better taste, with a greater variety of knowledge, than the Duke of Dorset.

I am extremely afflicted to hear that your ladyship's want of health has driven you to the Bath ; the same cause has hindered me from sooner acknowledging your letter. But I am at a time of life when I am to expect a great deal worse ; for I have neither flesh nor spirits left ; while you, Madam, I hope, and believe, will enjoy many happy years, in employing those virtues which Heaven bestowed on you, for the delight of your friends, the comfort of the distressed, and the universal esteem of all who are wise and virtuous.

I desire to present my most humble service to my Lady Suffolk, and your happy brother. I am, with the truest respect, Madam, your, &c.

TO MR POPE.

Feb. 9, 1736-7.

I CANNOT properly call you my best friend, because I have not another left who deserves the name, such a havock have time, death, exile, and oblivion made *. Perhaps you would have fewer complaints of my ill health and lowness of spirits, if they were not some excuse for my delay of writing even to you. It is perfectly right what you say of the indifference in common friends, whether we are sick or well, happy or miserable. The very maid-servants in a family have the same notion: I have heard them often say, Oh, I am very sick, if any body cared for it! I am vexed when my visitors come with the compliment usual here, Mr Dean, I hope you are very well. My popularity that you mention is wholly confined to the common people, who are more constant than those we miscall their betters. I walk the streets, and so do my lower friends, from whom, and from whom alone, I have a thousand hats and blessings upon old scores, which those we call the gentry have forgot. But I have not the love, or hardly the civility, of any one man in power or station; and I can boast that I neither visit or am acquainted with any lord, temporal or spiritual, in the whole kingdom; nor

---

* All these letters of Swift are curious and interesting, as they give us an account of the gradual decay of his intellects and temper, and strength of mind and body; and fill us with many melancholy but useful reflections. We see the steps by which this great genius sunk into *discontent*, into *peevishness*, into *indignity*, into *torpor*, into *insanity* !—Dr WARTON.

am able to do the least good office to the most deserving man, except what I can dispose of in my own cathedral upon a vacancy. What has sunk my spirits more than even years and sickness, is, reflecting on the most execrable corruptions that run through every branch of public management.

I heartily thank you for those lines translated, *Singula de nobis anni,* * &c. You have put them into a strong and admirable light; but, however, I am so partial, as to be more delighted with those which are to do me the greatest honour I shall ever receive from posterity, and will outweigh the malignity of ten thousand enemies. I never saw them before, by which it is plain that the letter you sent me miscarried.——I do not doubt that you have choice of new acquaintance†, and some of them may be deserving: for youth is the season of virtue; corruptions grow with years, and I believe the oldest rogue in England is the greatest. You have years enough before you to watch whether these new acquaintance will keep their virtue when they leave you and go into the world; how long will their spirit of independency last against the temptations of future ministers, and future kings.——As to the new lord-lieutenant, I never knew any of the family; so that I shall not be able to get any job done by him for any deserving friend.

JON. SWIFT.

---

* " The circling years on human pleasures prey,
  They steal my humour and my mirth away."——S.

† His new acquaintance were, probably, Lyttleton, Murray, Lord Cornbury, &c.——BOWLES.

TO MR NICHOLLS.*

Belcamp, March 14th.

SIR,

RIDING this morning to dine here with Mr Grattan, I saw, at his house, the poor lame boy that gives you this ; he was a servant to a ploughman near Lusk, and while he was following the plough a dog bit him in the leg, about eleven weeks ago. One Mrs Rice endeavoured, six weeks, to cure him, but could not, and his master would maintain him no longer. Mr Grattan and I are of opinion that he may be a proper object to be received into Dr Stephens's Hospital. The boy tells his story naturally, and Mr Grattan and I took pity of him. If you find him curable, and it be not against the rules of the hospital, I hope you will receive him.

I am, Sir,

Your most humble servant,

JONATH. SWIFT.

---

* It appears from the list of the governors of Stephens's Hospital, published in the Dublin Almanack, that Mr Nicholls was of that number. This serves to ascertain the person to whom this letter is addressed, for the direction is torn off. It is now published for the first time.

TO MR JOHN TEMPLE. *

Dublin, Feb. 1736-7.

SIR,

THE letter which I had the favour to receive from you, I read to your cousin Mrs Dingley, who lodges in my neighbourhood. She was very well pleased to hear of your welfare ; but a little morti-fied that you did not mention or inquire after her. She is quite sunk with years and unwieldiness: as well as a very scanty support. I sometimes make her a small present as my abilities can reach ; for I do not find her nearest relations consider her in the least.

Jervas told me that your aunt's picture † is in Sir Peter Lely's best manner, and the drapery all in the same hand. I shall think myself very well paid for it, if you will be so good as to order some mark of your favour to Mrs Dingley. I do not mean a pen-sion, but a small sum to put her for once out of debt: and if I live any time, I shall see that she keeps her-self clear of the world ; for she is a woman of as much piety and discretion as I have known.

I am sorry to have been so much a stranger to the state of your family. I know nothing of your lady, or what children you have, or any other cir-cumstances ; neither do I find that Mr Hatch can

---

* John Temple, Esq. was the nephew, and his lady the grand-daughter of Sir William Temple, by his only son, John Temple, who died before his father in 1689. Mr Temple was Solicitor and Attorney General in Ireland, and esteemed an ex-cellent lawyer. He died at Moor-Park, in February 1752.----N.
† Picture of Lady Giffard, sister of Sir William Temple.

inform me in any one point.   I very much approve
of your keeping up your family-house at Moor Park.
I have heard it is very much changed for the better,
as well as the gardens.   The tree on which I carved
those words, *factura nepotibus umbram*, is one of
those elms that stand in the hollow ground just before the house : but I suppose the letters are widen-
ed and grown shapeless by time.

I know nothing more of your brother, than that
he has an Irish title (I should be sorry to see you
with such a feather), and that some reason or other
drew us into a correspondence, which was very
rough.   But I have forgot what was the quarrel. *

This letter goes by my Lord Castle-durrow, who
is a gentleman of very good sense and wit.   I suspect, by taking his son with him, that he designs
to see us no more.   I desire to present my most
humble service to your lady, with hearty thanks of
her remembrance of me.   I am, Sir,

Your most humble faithful servant,

JON. SWIFT.

TO MR PULTENEY.

March 7, 1736-7.

SIR,
    I MUST begin by assuring you, that I did never
intend to engage you in a settled correspondence
with so useless a man as I here am ; and still more
so, by the daily increase of ill health and old age ;
and yet I confess that the high esteem I preserve
for your public and private virtues, urges me on to

* See the correspondence with Lord Palmerstone.

retain some little place in your memory, for the short time I may expect to live.

That I no sooner acknowledged the honour of your letter is owing to your civility, which might have compelled you to write while you were engaged in defending the liberties of your country with more than an old Roman spirit : which has reached this obscure enslaved kingdom, so far, as to have been the constant subject of discourse and of praise among the whole few of what unprostituted people here remain among us.

I did not receive the letter you mentioned from Bath ; and yet I have imagined, for some months past, that the meddlers of the post-offices here and in London have grown weary of their curiosity, by finding the little satisfaction it gave them. I agree heartily in your opinion of physicians ; I have esteemed many of them as learned ingenious men ; but I never received the least benefit from their advice or prescriptions. And poor Dr Arbuthnot was the only man of the faculty who seemed to understand my case, but could not remedy it. But to conquer five physicians, all eminent in their way, was a victory that Alexander and Cæsar could never pretend to. I desire that my prescription of living may be published (which you design to follow) for the benefit of mankind : which, however, I do not value a rush, nor the animal itself, as it now acts ; neither will I ever value myself as a Philanthropus, because it is now a creature (taking a vast majority) that I hate more than a toad, a viper, a wasp, a stork, a fox, or any other that you will please to add.

Since the date of your letter, we understand there is another duke to govern here. Mr Stopford was with me last night ; he is as well provided for, and to his own satisfaction, as any private clergyman. He engaged me to present his best respects and acknowledgments by you. Your modesty, in refusing to take a motto, goes too far. The sentence is not a boast, because it is every man's duty in morals and religion. *

Indeed we differ here from what you have been told of the Duke of Dorset's having given great satisfaction the last time he was with us; particularly in his disposal of two bishopricks, and other church as well as civil preferments. I wrote to a lady in London, his grace's near relation and intimate, that she would no more continue the office of a go-between (as she called herself) betwixt the duke and me, because I never design to attend him again; † and yet I allow him to be as agreeable a person in conversation as I have almost any where met. I sent my letter to that lady under a cover addressed to the duke; and in it I made many complaints against some proceedings, which 1 suppose he has seen. I never made him one request for myself; and if I spoke for another, he was always upon his guard; which was but twice, and for trifles : but failed in both.

The father of our friend in France ‡ may outlive the son; for I would venture a wager, that if you pick out twenty of the oldest men in England, nineteen of them have been the most worthless fellows in

---

* *Amicis prodesse, nemini nocere.* See Mr Pulteney's letter, dated Dec. 21, 1736, p. 107.——H.

† See his Letter to Lady Betty Germain, June 29, 1736-7.——H.

‡ The friend in France appears to be Lord Viscount Bolingbroke, whose father, Sir Henry St John, Bart. had been created Baron St John of Battersea, and Viscount St John, July 2, 1716.——B.

the kingdom. You tell me with great kindness as well as gravity, that I ought, this spring, to make a trip to England, and your motive is admirable, that shifting the scene was of great service to you, and therefore it may be so to me. I answer as an academic, *Nego consequentiam.* And besides comparisons are odious. You are what the French call *plein de vie.* As you are much younger, so I am a dozen years older than my age makes me, by infirmities of mind and body ; to which I add the perpetual detestation of all public persons and affairs in both kingdoms. I spread the story of Mrs Mapp while it was new to us : there was something humorous in it throughout, that pleased every body here. Will you engage for your friend Carteret that he will oppose any step toward arbitrary power ? He has promised me, under a penalty, that he will continue firm, and yet some reports go here of him, that have a little disconcerted me. Learning and good sense he has, to a great degree, if the love of riches and power do not overbalance.

Pray God long continue the gifts he has bestowed you, to be the chief support of liberty to your country, and let all the people say, Amen.

I am, with the truest respect, and highest esteem, Sir, your, &c.

JON. SWIFT.

FROM THE EARL OF ORRERY.

Cork, March 15, 1735-7.

DEAR SIR,

I RECEIVED your commands, by Faulkner, to write to you. But what can I say? The scene of Cork is ever the same; dull, insipid, and void of all amusement. His sacred majesty was not under greater difficulty to find out diversions at Helvoet-sluys, than I am here. The butchers are as greasy, the quakers as formal, and the presbyterians as holy, and full of the Lord, as usual; all things are in *statu quo*; even the hogs and pigs gruntle in the same cadence as of yore. Unfurnished with variety, and drooping under the natural dulness of the place, materials for a letter are as hard to be found, as money, sense, honesty, or truth. But I will write on; Ogilby, Blackmore, and my Lord Grimston,* have done the same before me.

I have not yet been upon the Change; but am told, that you are the idol of the court of aldermen. They have sent you your freedom. The most learned of them having read a most dreadful account, in Littleton's dictionary, of Pandora's gold box, it was unanimously agreed, not to venture so valuable a present in so dangerous a metal. Had these sage counsellors considered, that Pandora was a woman, (which, perhaps, Mr Littleton forgets to mention) they would have seen, that the ensuing evils arose from the sex, and not from the ore. But

---

* Author of " Love in a Hollow Tree."---H.

I shall speak with more certainty of these affairs, when I have taken my seat among the greybeards.

My letters from England speak of great combustions. Absalom continues a rebel to royal David: the Achitophels of the age are numerous and high-spirited. The influence of the comet seems to have strange effects already. In the mean time, here live we, drones of Cork, wrapped up in our own filth, *procul a Jove et procul a fulmine.* Heaven, and all good stars protect you! For let the thunder burst where it will, so that you are safe, and un-singed, who cares whether Persia submits its government to the renowned Kouli Khan, or that beardless unexperiencd youth, the Sophi. At least the Vicar of Bray and I shall certainly be con-tented.

ORRERY.

FROM THE SAME.

Cork, March 18, 1736-7.

DEAR SIR,

THIS is occasioned by a letter I have received from Mr Pope, of which I send you a copy in my own hand, not caring to trust the original to the accidents of the post. I likewise send you a part of a fifth volume of Curll's Thefts, in which you will find two letters to you (one from Mr Pope, the other from Lord Bolingbroke) just published, with an impudent preface by Curll. You see, Curll, like his friend the Devil, glides through all key-holes, and thrusts himself into the most private ca-binets.

I am much concerned to find that Mr Pope is still uneasy about his letters ; but, I hope, a letter I sent him from Dublin (which he has not yet received) has removed all anxiety of that kind.   In the last discourse I had with you on this topic, you remember you told me he should have his letters ; and I lost no time in letting him know your resolution.   God forbid that any more papers belonging to either of you, especially such papers as your familiar letters, should fall into the hands of knaves and fools, the professed enemies of you both in particular, and of all honest and worthy men in general !

I have said so much on this subject, in the late happy hours you allowed me to pass with you at the deanery, that there is little occasion for adding more upon it at present ; especially as you will find, in Mr Pope's letter to me, a strength of argument that seems irresistible.   As I have thoughts of going to England in June, you may depend upon a safe carriage of any papers you think fit to send him.   I should think myself particularly fortunate, to deliver to him those letters he seems so justly desirous of.   I entreat you, give me that pleasure ! It will be a happy reflection to me in the latest hours of my life ; which, whether long or short, shall be constantly spent in endeavouring to do what may be acceptable to the virtuous and the wise.   I am, dear Sir, your very faithful and obliged humble servant,

ORRERY.

MR. POPE TO THE EARL OF ORRERY. *

My Lord,

AFTER having condoled several times with you on your own illness, and that of your friends, I now claim some share myself; for I have been down with a fever, which yet confines me to my chamber. Just before, I wrote a letter to the Dean, full of my heart; and, among other things, pressed him (which, I must acquaint your lordship, I had done twice before, for near a twelvemonth past) to secure me against that rascal printer, by returning me my letters, which (if he valued so much) I promised to send him copies of, merely that the originals might not fall into such ill hands, and thereby a hundred particulars be at his mercy; which would expose me to the misconstruction of many, the malice of some, and the censure, perhaps, of the whole world. A fresh incident made me press this again, which I enclose to you, that you may show him, The man's declaration, " That he had these two letters of the Dean's from your side the water," with several others yet lying by, (which I cannot doubt the truth of, because I never had a copy of either) is surely a just cause for my request. Yet the Dean, answering every other point of my letter, with the utmost expressions of kindness, is silent upon this : and, the third time silent. I begin to fear he has already lent them out of his hands : and in whatever hands, while they are Irish hands, allow me, my lord, to say, they are in dangerous hands. Weak admirers are

---

* Inclosed in the preceding letter.

as bad as malicious enemies, and operate in these cases alike to an author's disparagement or uneasiness. I think this I made the Dean so just a request, that I beg your lordship to second it, by showing him what I write. I told him as soon as I found myself obliged to publish an edition of letters to my great sorrow, that I wished to make use of some of these : nor did I think any part of my correspondencies would do me a greater honour, and be really a greater pleasure to me, than what might preserve the memory. how well we loved one another. I find the Dean was not quite of the same opinion, or he would not, I think, have denied this. I wish some of those sort of people always about a great man in wit, as well as a great man in power, have not an eye to some little interest in getting the whole of these into their possession : I will venture, however, to say, they would not add more credit to the Dean's memory, by their management of them, than I by mine : and if, as I have a great deal of affection for him, I have with it some judgment at least, I presume my conduct herein might be better confided in.

Indeed, this silence is so remarkable, it surprises me : I hope in God it is not to be attributed to what he complains, a want of memory. I would rather suffer from any other cause than what would be so unhappy to him. My sincere love for this valuable, indeed, incomparable man, will accompany him through life, and pursue his memory, were I to live a hundred lives, as many of his works will live ; which are absolutely original, unequalled, unexampled. His humanity, his charity, his condescension, his candour, are equal to his wit ; and require as good and true a taste to be equally valued. When all this must die, (this last I mean)

I would gladly have been the recorder of so great a part of it as shines in his letters to me, and of which my own are but as so many ackowledgments. But, perhaps, before this reaches your hands, my cares may be over ; and Curll, and every body else, may say and lie of me as they will : the Dean, old as he is, may have the task to defend me.

TO MR GIBSON.

March 23, 1736-7.

Mr Gibson,

I desire you will give my hearty thanks to Mr Richardson for the fine present he has made me ; and I thank you for your care in sending it me in so good a condition. I have invited several friends to dine upon it with me to-morrow, when we will drink his health. He has done every thing in the genteelest manner, and I am much obliged to him. I am your friend and servant,

Jon. Swift.

FROM MR POPE.

March 23, 1736-7.

Though you were never to write to me, yet what you desired in your last, that I would write often to you, would be a very easy task : for every day I talk with you, and of you, in my heart ; and I need only set down what that is thinking of. The nearer I find myself verging to that period of life which is to be labour and sorrow, the more I prop myself upon those few supports that are left me. People in this state are like props indeed; they cannot stand alone, but two or more of them can stand, leaning and bearing upon one another. I wish you and I might pass this part of life together. My only necessary care is at an end. I am now my own master too much; my house is too large; my gardens furnish too much wood and provision for my use. My servants are sensible and tender of me; they have intermarried, and are become rather low friends than servants; and to all those that I see here with pleasure, they take a pleasure in being useful. I conclude this is your case too in your domestic life, and I sometimes think of your old housekeeper as my nurse: though I tremble at the sea, which only divides us. As your fears are not so great as mine, and I firmly hope your strength still much greater, is it utterly impossible it might once more be some pleasure to you to see England? My sole motive in proposing France to meet in, was the narrowness of the passage by sea from hence, the physicians having told me the weakness of my breast, &c. is such, as a sea-sickness might endanger my life. Though one or two of our friends are gone, since you saw your native country, there remain a few more who will last so till death; and who I cannot but hope have an attractive power to draw you back to a country, which cannot quite be sunk or enslaved, while such spirits remain. And let me tell you, there are a few more of the same spirit, who would awaken all your old ideas, and revive your hopes of her future recovery and virtue. These look up to you with reverence, and would be animated by the sight of him, at whose soul they have taken fire, in his writings, and derived from thence as much love of their species as is consistent with a contempt for the knaves in it.

I could never be weary, except at the eyes, of writing to you; but my real reason (and a strong one it is) for doing it so seldom, is fear; fear of a very great and experienced evil, that of my letters being kept by the partiality of friends, and passing into the hands and malice of enemies; who publish them with all their imperfections on their head, so that I write not on the common terms of honest men.

Would to God you would come over with Lord Orrery, whose care of you in the voyage I could so certainly depend on; and bring with you your old housekeeper and two or three servants. I have room for all, a heart for all, and (think what you will) a fortune for all. We could, were we together, contrive to make our last days easy, and leave some sort of monument, what friends two wits could be in spite of all the fools in the world. Adieu.

FROM LORD CARTERET.

Arlington Street, March 24, 1736-7.

Sir,

I this day attended the cause * you recommended to me in your letter of the 3d of January: the de-

---

* An appeal depending between certain persons of the name of Delane.

crée was affirmed most unanimously, the appeal
adjudged frivolous, and 100l. costs given to the
respondent. Lord Bathurst attended likewise. The
other lords you mention, I am very little acquainted
with; so I cannot deliver your messages, though I
pity them in being out of your favour. Since you
mention Greek, I must tell you, that my son, at sixteen, understands it better than I did at twenty, and
I tell him, "Study Greek," καὶ οὐδὲν οὐδέποτε τοιοῦτον
ἐνθυμηθήσῃ ὅτι ἄγαν ἐπιθυμήσεις τινός. He knows how
to construe this, and I have the satisfaction to believe
he will fall into the sentiment; and then, if he makes
no figure, he will yet be a happy man.

Your late lord-lieutenant * told me, some time
ago, he thought he was not in your favour. I told
him I was of that opinion, and showed him the
article of your letter relating to himself; I believe
I did wrong: not that you care a farthing for
princes or ministers; but because it was vanity in
me, to produce your acknowledgments to me for
providing for people of learning, some of which I
had the honour to promote at your desire, for which
I still think myself obliged to you. And I have
not heard that since they have disturbed the peace
of the kingdom, or been jacobites, in disgrace to
you and me.

I desire you will make my sincere respects acceptable to Mr Delany. He sent me potted woodcocks in perfection, which Lady Granville, my wife,
and children, have eat, though I have not yet
answered his letter. My Lady Granville, reading
your postscript, bids me tell you, that she will send

---

* The Duke of Dorset....H.

you a present; and if she knew what you liked,
she would do it forthwith.· Let me know, and it
shall be done, that the first of the family may no
longer be postponed by you to the third place.
My wife and Lady Worseley desire their respects
should be mentioned to you rhetorically; but as
I am a plain peer, I shall say nothing, but that I
am, for ever, Sir, your most humble and obedient
servant,

CARTERET.

When people ask me, how I governed Ireland?   I
say, that I pleased Dr Swift.

Quæsitam meritis sume superbiam.

TO MR ALDERMAN BARBER.

'Dublin, March 30, 1737.

DEAR MR ALDERMAN,
    You will read the character of the bearer, Mr
Lloyd, which he is to deliver to you, signed by the
magistrates and chief inhabitants of Colrane.   It
seems your society has raised the rents of that town,
and your lands adjoining, about three years ago, to
four times the value of what they formerly paid;
which is beyond all I have ever heard even among
the most screwing landlords of this impoverished
kingdom; and the consequence has already been,
that many of your tenants in the said town and lands
are preparing for their removal to the plantations in
America; for the same reasons that are driving some

thousands of families in the adjoining northern parts to the same plantations; I mean the oppression by landlords. My dear friend, you are to consider that no society can, or ought in prudence or justice, let their lands at so high a rate as a squire who lives upon his own estate, and is able to distrain in an hour's warning. All bodies corporate must give easy bargains, that they may depend upon receiving their rents, and thereby be ready to pay all the incident charges to which they are subject. Thus, bishops, deans, and chapters, as well as other corporations, seldom or never let their lands even so high as at half the value; and when they raise those rents which are scandalously low, it is ever by degrees. I have many instances of this conduct in my own practice, as well as in that of my chapter. Although my own lands, as dean, be let for four-fifths under their value, I have not raised them a sixth part in twenty-three years, and took very moderate fines. On the other side, I confess there is no reason why an honourable society should rent their estate for a trifle; and therefore I told Mr Lloyd my opinion, that if you could be prevailed on just to double the old rent, and no more, I hoped the tenants might be able to live in a tolerable manner; for I am as much convinced as I can be of any thing human, that this wretched oppressed country must of necessity decline every year. If, by a miracle, things should mend, you may, in a future renewal, make a moderate increase of rent, but not by such leaps as you are now taking; for you ought to remember the fable of the hen, who laid every second day a golden egg; upon which her mistress killed her, to get the whole lump at once. I am told that one condition in your charter obliges you to plant a colony of

English in those parts : if that be so, you are too wise to make it a colony of Irish beggars. Some ill consequences have already happened by your prodigious increase of the rent. Many of your old tenants have quitted their houses in Colrane ; others are not able to repair their habitations, which are daily going to ruin, and many of those who live on your lands in the country, owe great arrears, which they will never be in a condition to pay. I would not have said thus much in an affair, and about persons to whom I am an utter stranger, if I had not been assured, by some whom I can trust, of the poor condition those people in and about Colrane have lain under, since that enormous increase of their rents.

The bearer, Mr Lloyd, whom I never saw till yesterday, seems to be a gentleman of great truth and good sense ; he has no interest in the case, for, although he lives at Colrane, his preferment is some miles farther ; he is now going to visit his father, who lives near Wrexham, not far from Chester, and from thence, at the desire of your tenants in and near Colrane, he is content to go to London, and wait on you there with his credentials. If he has misrepresented this matter to me in any one particular, I shall never be his advocate again.

And now, my dear friend, I am forced to tell you, that my health is very much decayed, my deafness and giddiness are more frequent ; spirits I have none left ; my memory is almost gone. The public corruptions in both kingdoms allow me no peace or quiet of mind. I sink every day, and am older by twenty years than many others of the same age. I hope, and am told, that it is better with you. May you live as long as you desire, for I have lost so many old friends, without getting any new, that I must keep you as a handsel of the former. I am, my dear friend, with great esteem and love,

Your most obedient humble servant,

JON. SWIFT.

When I would write to you, I cannot remember the street you live in.

FROM THE EARL OF ORRERY.

Cork, April 3, 1737.

DEAR SIR,

I AM very glad there are twelve thousand pounds worth of halfpence arrived; they are twelve thousand arguments for your quitting Ireland. I look upon you in the same state of the unfortunate Achæmenides amidst tyrants and monsters——— Do you not remember the description of Polypheme and his den?

——— Domus sanie dapibusque cruentis
Intus opaca, ingens, ipse arduus, altaque pulsat
Sidera, (Dii talem terris avertite pestem!)
Nec visu facilis, nec dictu affabilis ulli :
Visceribus miserorum et sanguine vescitur atro. *

---

* " The cave, though large, was dark ; the dismal floor
Was pav'd with mangled limbs and putrid gore.
One monstrous host, of more than human size,
Erects his head, and stares within the skies.
Bellowing his voice, and horrid is his hue,
Ye Gods, remove this plague from mortal view!
The joints of slaughtered wretches are his food,
And for his wine, he quaffs the streaming blood."

DRYDEN.

Remember also, that

Centum alii curva hæc habitant ad littora vulgo
Infandi Cyclopes, et altis montibus errant. *

Translate these lines and come away with me to Marston; there you shall enjoy *otium cum dignitate;* there you shall see the famous *Sacsockishkash,* and his two pupils, who shall attend your altars with daily incense; there no archbishops can intrude; there you shall be the sole lord and master; while we your subjects shall learn obedience from our happiness.——If you ever can think seriously, think so now; and let me say with the curate of my parish, Consider what has been said unto you, ponder it well, lay it up in your heart, and God of his infinite mercy direct you!——Mrs Whiteway shall be truly welcome to Marston's homely shade. Hector shall fawn upon the doctor; and I myself will be under the direction and government of Sir Robert Walpole.

You tell me, I am to carry a load for you to England; the most acceptable load will be yourself, and that I would carry with as true piety as Æneas bore the ancient Anchises on his shoulders, when he fled from fire, from blood, from Greeks, and from ruined Troy!

Can you expect that lords move regularly? Is it not below our station to think where or when we are to go? But if my coach and six is in order, per-

---

* " Such and so vast as Polypheme appears,
A hundred more this hated island bears :
Like him in caves they shut their woolly sheep,
Like him, their herds on tops of mountains keep :
Like him, with mighty strides they stalk from steep to steep." }
DRYDEN.

haps I may have the honour to start a hare in Steven's-Green about the first of next month. In the month of June I will hope to set sail with you to England. Mr Pope will come out beyond the shore to meet you : you will exchange Cyclops for men ; and if one must fall, surely the choice is right :

Si pereo, manibus hominum periisse juvabit. *

My next shall be longer. I am now forced to bid you farewell ; but hereafter expect my whole life and conversation ; you shall certainly have the cheeses. If you will come to Somersetshire, I will eat one for joy. † The best in England are made in my manor.

I am so well, that I had almost forgot to answer that kind part of your letter. It is only you that can add health and happiness to your very affectionate obliged and faithful servant,

ORRERY.

FROM THE EARL OF OXFORD.

Dover Street, April 7, 1737.

GOOD MR DEAN,

I AM extremely obliged to you for several letters which I, with great shame and concern, acknowledge that I have not answered, as also several re-

---

* " I die content, to die by human hands."   DRYDEN.

† The Earl of Orrery hated cheese to such a degree, that he could scarcely bear the sight of it.—D. S.

membrances of me and my family in your letters, to
Mr Pope : I stand very strongly obliged to you
upon these accounts ; I dare say you will do me
that justice, that you will not attribute my not
writing to proceed from any neglect of you, or
from any forgetfulness : I am certain of this, that I
do retain the warmest esteem and sincerest regard
for you of any one, be he who he will ; and therefore
I hope you will pardon what is passed, and I promise to amend, if my letters would in the least be
agreeable to you.

One reason of my writing to you now is (next to
my asking your forgiveness) this ; I am told that
you have given leave and liberty to some one or
more of your friends to print a history of the last
four years of Queen Anne's reign, wrote by you.

As I am most truly sensible of your constant regard and sincere friendship for my father, even to
partiality (if I may say so), I am very sensible of the
share and part he must bear in such a history ; and
as I remember, when I read over that history of
yours, I can recollect that there seemed to me a
want of some papers to make it more complete,
which was not in our power to obtain ; besides
there were some severe things said, which might
have been then very currently talked of, but now
will want a proper evidence to support ; for these
reasons it is that I do entreat the favour of you,
and make it my earnest request, that you will give
your positive directions, that this history be not
printed and published, until I have had an opportunity of seeing it ; with a liberty of showing it to
some family friends, whom I would consult upon
this occasion. I beg pardon for this ; I hope you
will be so good as to grant my request : I do it with
great deference to you. If I had the pleasure of

seeing you, I could soon say something to you that would convince you I am not wrong : they are not proper for a letter, as you will easily guess.

My wife desires your acceptance of her most humble service ; my daughter is extremely pleased with the notice you are pleased to take of her, she is very well : she brought me another grand-daughter last month : she desires your acceptance of her most humble service, and would be glad of the pleasure of seeing you here in England.

The Duke of Portland so far answers our expectations, that indeed he exceeds them ; for he makes the best husband, the best father, and the best son ; these qualities are, I assure you, very rare in this age.

I wish you would make my compliments to my Lord Orrery ; do you design to keep him with you ? I do not blame you, if you can. I am, with true esteem and regard, Sir, your most obliged and most faithful humble servant,

OXFORD.

I wish Master Faulkner, when he sends any thing to me, would say how you do. *

---

* Mr Faulkner was with Dr Swift when he received this letter ; which he instantly answered, and made Faulkner read it to him : the purport of which was, " that although he loved his lordship's father more than he ever did any man ; yet, as a human creature, he had his faults, and therefore, as an impartial writer, he could not conceal them." The Dean made Faulkner write on the same sheet of paper to his lordship to answer for himself, and to put it into the post-office, as he would not trust a servant with it, that he might vouch the truth, if ever he should hear his character called in question upon this occasion. —F.

TO DR SHERIDAN.

April 9, 1737.

ABOUT a month ago I received your last letter, wherein you complain of my long silence; what will you do when I am so long in answering? I have one excuse which will serve all my friends, I am quite worn out with disorders of mind and body; a long fit of deafness, which still continues, hath unqualified me for conversing, or thinking, or reading, or hearing: to all this is added an apprehension of giddiness, whereof I have frequently some frightful touches. Besides, I can hardly write ten lines without twenty blunders, as you will see by the number of scratchings and blots before this letter is done: into the bargain, I have not one rag of memory left; and my friends have all forsaken me, except Mrs Whiteway, who preserves some pity for my condition, and a few others who love wine that costs them nothing. As to my taking a journey to Cavan, I am just as capa-

---

Notwithstanding what Mr Faulkner has above stated, and no doubt accurately, as it consisted with his own knowledge, it appears from a subsequent letter from Mr Lewis, 8th April 1738, first printed in this edition of the Dean's works, that Swift actually complied with Lord Oxford's reiterated request, and that the manuscript history was revised by his lordship and some of his friends. It seems more than probable, that the remarks which they offered, and the alterations which they proposed, induced the Dean to suspend, or to lay altogether aside, his intention to publish the work in question. See also the Dean's subsequent letter to Lord Oxford, 14th June 1737, and Lord Oxford's answer, 4th July following, in which he again strongly urges the request here made.

ble as of a voyage to China, or of running races at Newmarket.   But, to speak in the *Latinitas Grattaniana ; Tu clamas meretrix primus ;* for we have all expected you here at Easter, as you were used to do.   Your muster-roll of meat is good, but of drink in sup port able.   Yew wann twine.   My stress Albavia has eaten here all your hung beef, and said it was very good.   The affair of high importance in their family is, that Miss Molly hath issued out orders, with great penalties, to be called Mrs Harrison ; which caused many speck you'll ash owns.——I am now come to the noli me tan jerry, which begg ins wyth mad dam.——So I will go on by the strength of my own wit upon points of the high est imp or taunts.   I have been very curious in considering that fruitful word *ling ;* which explains many fine qualities in ladies, such as *grow ling, ray ling, tip ling,* (seldom) *toy ling, mumb ling, grumb ling, curr ling, puss ling, buss ling, strow ling, ramb ling, quarry ling, tat ling, whiff ling, dabb ling, doub ling.*   These are but as ample o fan hunn dread mower ; they have all got cold this winter, big owing tooth in lick lad ink old wet her, an dare ink you rabble.——Well, I triumph over you, Is corn urine cap a city. Pray, tell me, does the land of Quilca pay any rent? or is any paid by the tenant ? or is there not any part of L.50 to be got ?   But before you make complaints of ill payments from your school, I will declare I was never so ill paid as now, even by my richer debtors.   I have finished my will for the last time, wherein I left some little legacy, which you are not to receive till you shall be entirely out of my debt, and paid all you owe to my executors. And I have made very honourable mention of you in the will, as the consideration of my leaving these legacies to you.

Explain this proverb, *Salt dry fish, and the wedding gold, is the vice of women both young and old.* Yes, you have it i nam o mento time.

The old hunks Shepherd has buried his only son, who was a young hunks come to age.

POSTSCRIPT.

Here is a rhime; it is a satire on an inconstant lover.

You are as faithless as a Carthaginian,
To love at once, Kate, Nell, Doll, Martha, Jenny, Anne.

A Specimen of *Latinitas Grattaniana.*

Ego ludam diabolum super duos baculos cum te.
Voca super me cras.
Profecto ego dabo tibi tuum ventrem plenum legis.
Sine me solum cum illo. Ego capiam tempus.
Quid pestis velles tu esse apud ?
Ego faciam te fumare.
Duc uxorem veni super.
Ego dabo tibi pyxidem in aure.
Ego faciam te secare saltum.
Veni, veni, solve tuum scotum, et fac non plura verba.
Id est plus expensi quam veneratio.
Si tu es pro lege, dabo tibi legem, tuum ventrem plenum.
Ut diabolus voluit habere id.
Quid est materia tecum ?
Tu habes vetus proverbium super tuum latus : Nihil est nunquam
   in periculo.
Cape me apud illud, et suspende me.
Ego capio te apud tuum verbum.
Tu venis in farti tempore.
Est formosus corporatus homo in facie.
Esne tu super pro omni die ?
Morsus : Esne tu ibi cum tuis ursis ?
Ille est ex super suam servationem.

Tu es carcer avis.
Ego amo mendacem in meo corde, et tu aptas me ad crinem.
Ego dicam tibi quid : hic est magnus clamor, et parva lana.
    Quid! tu es super tuum altum equum.
Tu nunquam servasti tuum verbum.
Hic est diabolus et omne agere.
Visne tu esse tam bonus, quam tuum verbum ?
Ego faciam porcum vel canem de id.
Ego servo hoc pro pluvioso die.
Ego possum facere id cum digito madido.
Profecto ego habui nullum manum in id.
Esne tu in aure nido ?
Tu es homo extranei renis.
Precor, ambula super.
Ego feci amorem virgini honoris.
Quomodo venit id circum, quod tu ludis stultum ita ?
Vos ibi, fac viam pro meo domino.
Omnes socii apud pedem pilam.
Fæminæ et linteum aspiciunt optimè per candelæ lucem.

TO MR RICHARDSON *.

April 9, 1737.

SIR,

I HAVE wondered, since I have had the favour
to know you, what could possibly put you upon
your civility to me.   You have invited me to your
house, and proposed every thing according to my
own scheme that would make me easy.   You have
loaded me with presents, although it never lay in

---

* See letter to Mr Richardson, dated Oct. 23, 1736.

my power to do you any sort of favour or advantage. I have had a salmon from you of 26lb. weight, another of 18lb. and the last of 14lb. : upon which my ill-natured friends descant, that I am declining in your good-will by the declining of weight in your salmon. They would have had your salmon double the weight: the second should have been of 52lb. the third of 104, and the last of 208lb. It seems this is the way of Dublin computors, who think you country gentlemen have nothing to do but to oblige us citizens, who are not bound to make you the least return, farther than, when you come hither, to meet you by chance in a coffee-house ; and ask you what tavern you dine in, and there pay your club. I intend to deal with you in the same manner ; and if you come to town for three months, I will invite you once to dinner, for which I shall expect to stay a whole year with you ; and you will be bound to thank me for honouring your house. You saw me ill enough when I had the honour to see you at the deanery. Mrs Whiteway, my cousin, and the only cousin I own, remembers she was here in your company, and desires to present her humble service to you ; and no wonder, for you sent so much salmon, that I was forced to give her a part. Some ten days ago there came to see me one Mr Lloyd a clergyman, who lives, as I remember, near Colrane. He had a commission from the people in and about that town which belongs to the London society. It seems that, three years ago, the society increased their rents from 300l. to 1200l. a-year ; since which time the town is declined, the tenants neglect their houses, and the country tenants are not able to live. I writ a letter by him to Alderman Barber, because their demands seem very extravagant : but I had no other reason for doing so than the ample commission he had from the town of Colrane.* I wish I knew your sentiments in this affair. I never saw the gentleman before ; but the commission he had encouraged me so far, that I could not refuse him the letter. Although I was ill enough when I saw you, I am forty times worse at present, and am no more able to be your guest this summer than to travel to America. I have been this month so ill with a giddy head, and so very deaf, that I am not fit for human conversation : besides, my spirits are so low that I do not think any thing worth minding ; and most of my friends, with very great justice, have forsaken me. I find you deal with Faulkner. I have read his Rollin's history. The translator did not want knowledge enough, but is a coxcomb by running into those cant words and phrases which have spoiled our language, and will spoil it more every day. Your presents are so numerous that I had almost forgot to thank you for the cheese : against which there can be no objection but that of too much rennet, for which I so often wish ill to the housewife. I am, Sir, with true esteem,

Your most obedient humble servant,
JON. SWIFT.

---

* This expostulation is dated the 30th of May preceding.

FROM MR RICHARDSON.

April 17, 1737.

REVEREND SIR,

I RETURNED last night from Derry, where I have been for some time past, and where you will be received with great respect. I pleased myself with the hopes of finding at home an account of the time you design being here. My disappointment occasions you this trouble ; and I hope you will suffer that which can do it best to plead my excuse for being so importunate.

Sir, I take the country to be as pleasant the latter end of this, and all the next month, as any in the year ; the fields are putting on their gayest liveries to receive you ; the birds will warble their sweetest notes to entertain you ; and the waters in the river Bann, when they come in view of your apartment, will tumble in great hurry to wait on you, and leave you with reluctance.

I must brag of my situation, and will pawn my credit with you in those matters, that you will pronounce it the most delightful you have seen in Dublin at least.

Sir, I will not conceal from you any longer a self-interest I have in honouring this place with your presence. All the inclosures I intend in my demesne are now finished, and I am ready to begin what I intend by way of ornament ; but until I am fixed in the scheme of the whole, which I would have adapted in the best manner to the place, I would do nothing. I have delayed coming to a final resolution, till I shall have the opportunity of entreating your opinion and assistance after viewing the whole. It will perhaps afford yourself no disagreeable amusement, and occasion something elegant and correct in miniature, where nature has almost done every thing. When you let me know that you have fitted your stages, I will contrive to meet you as far as Armagh or Stewartstown. I will only add, that it is one that loves you, as well as admires you, that is thus troublesome to you; and that I am, with the greatest truth, as well as esteem, Sir,

Your most humble and most obedient servant,
WILLIAM RICHARDSON.

TO MR RICHARDSON.

Dublin, April 30, 1737.

Sir,

IF it had pleased God to restore me to any degree of health, I should have been setting out on Monday next to your house; but I find such a weekly decay, that has made it impossible for me to ride above five or six miles at farthest, and I always return the same day heartily tired. I have not an ounce of flesh or a dram of spirits left me; yet my greatest load is not my years but my infirmities. In England, before I was twenty, I got a cold which gave me a deafness that I could never clear myself of. Although it came but seldom, and lasted but a few days, yet my left ear has never been well since: but when the deafness comes on, I can hear with neither ear, except it be a woman with a treble, and a man with a counter-tenor. This unqualifies me for any mixed conversation: and the fits of deafness increase; for I have now been troubled with it near seven weeks, and it is not yet lessened, which extremely adds to my mortification. I should not have been so particular in troubling you with my ailments, if they had not been too good an excuse for my inability to venture any where beyond the prospect of this town.

I am the more obliged to your great civilities, because I declare, without affectation, that it never lay in my power to deserve any one of them. I find by the conversation I have had with you, that you understand a court very well for your time, and are well known to the minister on the other side. The consequence of which is, that it lies in my power to undo you, only by letting it be known at St James's that you are perpetually sending me presents, and holding a constant correspondence with me by letters, Another unwary step of yours is inviting me to your house, which will render your election desperate, by making all your neighbour squires represent you as a person disaffected to the government. Thus I have you at my mercy on two accounts, unless you have some new court refinements to turn the guilt upon me. I wrote a long letter some weeks ago ; but I could not find by the messenger of your last salmon that he knew any thing of that letter ; for you take, in every circumstance, a special care that I may know nothing more than of a salmon being left at the deanery. Thus there is a secret commerce between your servant and my butler. The first writes a letter to the other—says the carriage is paid, that the salmon weighs so much, and was sent by his master to me. If some of our patriots should happen to discover the management of this intrigue, they would inform the privy council, from which an order would be brought by a messenger to seize on the salmon, have

it opened, and search all its entrails to find some
letter of dangerous consequence to the state. I believe I told you in my former letter, that Mr Lloyd,
a clergyman, minister of Colrane, but who lives
four miles from it, came to me upon his going to
England, to see his old father in Chester, and from
thence goes to London to wait upon the society.
He showed me very ample credentials from the
magistrates of Colrane to deliver to the society,
upon some hard things that colony lies under. It
seems, about three years ago, their lease was out ;
the rent was 300l. a year ; but upon the renewal it
was raised to 1200l. which was beyond what I have
known in leases from corporations. I had never
seen or heard of Mr Lloyd. He is middle aged,
and walks with a stick as if he were infirm. I
wrote by him to Alderman Barber, putting the case
as Mr Lloyd gave it me, who says that the town-
folks and tenants of the estate round Colrane would
be content to double the rent ; but that the present
prodigious addition had made the townsfolks let
their buildings decay, and the country tenants were
in despair. I then wondered you came to mention
nothing of this to me, since you are concerned for
the society. If Mr Lloyd has not fairly represented the matter, he has not behaved himself suitable
to his function : However, pray let me know the
truth of the matter, and how he came to to be employed : only I find that he is not known to any of
my acquaintance that I have seen since.

Pray God preserve you, Sir, and give you all the
good success that I am convinced you deserve.

I am, with true esteem and gratitude, your most
obedient and obliged servant,

JON. SWIFT.

6

TO DR SHERIDAN.

May 22, 1737.

I WILL on Monday (this is Saturday, May 22, as you will read above in the date) send to talk to Mr Smith : but I distrust your sanguinity so much (by my own desponding temper) that I know not whether that affair of your justiceship be fixed, but I shall know next week, and write or act accordingly. I battled in vain with the duke and his clan against the lowering of gold, * which is just a kind settlement upon England of 25,000l. a-year for ever: yet some of my friends differ from me, though all agree that the absentees will be just so much gainers. I am excessively glad that your difficulty of breathing is over ; for what is life but breath? I mean not that of our nostrils, but our lungs. You must in summer ride every half holiday, and go to church every Sunday some miles off. The people of England are copying from us to plague the clergy, but they intend far to outdo the original. I wish I were to be born next century, when we shall

---

* The proclamation for lowering the English and foreign gold coin to the standard of English silver, was published August 9, 1737. Debates with respect to the propriety of this measure ran very high in Dublin. Lord Primate Boulter was the chief supporter of the scheme, which was designed to remedy the scarcity of silver by bringing that of gold nearer to a par with it. Before this measure was adopted, the comparatively low price of gold in England, occasioned the payments from Ireland to that kingdom being made in silver, and consequently drained Ireland of that metal. But the measure was violently opposed by Dean Swift and the bankers, and the public mind was, for a time, not a little agitated on account of the apprehended consequences.

be utterly rid of parsons, of which, God be thanked, you are none at present ; and until your bishop give you a living, I will leave off (except this letter) giving you the title of reverend.   I did write him lately a letter with a witness, relating to his printer of Quadrille (did you ever see it) with which he half ruined Faulkner.   He promises (against his nature) to consider him, but interposed an exception, which I believe will destroy the whole.   Mrs Whiteway gives herself airs of loving you ; but do not trust her too much, for she grows disobedient, and says she is going for to get another favourite. In short, she calls you names, and has neither Mr nor Dr on her tongue, but calls you plain Sheridan, and pox take you.   She is not with me now, else she would read this in spite of me ; and, between ourselves, she sets up to be my governor.   I wish you had sent me the christian name of Knatchbull,* and I would have writ to him ; but I will see him on Monday, if he will be visible.   The poem on Legion Club is so altered and enlarged, as I hear (for I only saw the original) and so damnably murdered, that they have added many of the club to the true number.   I hear it is charged to me, with great personal threatenings from the puppies offended. Some say they will wait for revenge to their next meeting.   Others say the privy-council will summon the suspected author.   If I could get the true copy I would send it you.   Your bishop† writes me word, that the real author is manifest by the work.   Your loss of flesh is nothing, if it be made up with spirit.   God help him who hath neither,

---

* Secretary to Lord Chancellor Wyndham.
† Dr Hort.—H.

I mean myself. I believe I shall say with Horace, *Non omnis moriar;* for half my body is already spent.

FROM THE HON. MISS DAVYS.

May 27, 1737.

Sir,

I know you are always pleased to do acts of charity, which encourages me to take the liberty of recommending a boy about ten years old, the bearer of this, to your goodness, to beg you would employ it in getting him put into the Bluecoat Hospital. I received the enclosed letter from him this morning. Your compliance with this request, and pardon for this trouble, will oblige, Sir, your most humble and most obedient servant,

M. Davys.

TO MR POPE.

Dublin, May 31, 1737.

It is true, I owe you some letters, but it has pleased God, that I have not been in a condition to pay you. When you shall be at my age, perhaps you may lie under the same disability to your present or future friends. But my age is not my disability, for I can walk six or seven miles, and ride a dozen. But I am deaf for two months together, this deafness unqualifies me for all company, except a few friends with counter-tenor voices, whom I can call names, if they do not speak loud enough for my ears. It is this evil that has hindered me from venturing to the Bath, and to Twitenham; for deafness being not a frequent disorder, has no allowance given it; and the scurvy figure a man affected that way makes in company, is utterly insupportable.

It was I began with the petition to you of *Orna me*, and now you come like an unfair merchant, to charge me with being in your debt; which by your way of reckoning I must always be, for yours are always guineas, and mine farthings; and yet I have a pretence to quarrel with you, because I am not at the head of any one of your epistles. I am often wondering how you come to excel all mortals on the subject of morality, even in the poetical way; and should have wondered more, if nature and education had not made you a professor of it from your infancy.

All the letters I can find of yours, I have fastened in a folio cover, and the rest in bundles endorsed; but, by reading their dates, I find a chasm of six years, of which I can find no copies; and yet I keep them with all possible care: but I have been forced, on three or four occasions, to send all my papers to some friends, yet those papers were all sent sealed in bundles, to some faithful friends; however, what I have, are not much above sixty. I found nothing in any one of them to be left out: none of them have any thing to do with party, of which you are the clearest of all men, by your religion, and the whole tenor of your life; while I am raging every moment against the corruption of both kingdoms, especially of this, such is my weakness.

I have read your Epistle of Horace to Augustus: it was sent me in the English edition, as soon as it

could come. They are printing it in a small octavo.
The curious are looking out, some for flattery, some
for ironies in it; the sour folks think they have found
out some : but your admirers here, I mean every
man of taste, affect to be certain, that the profession of friendship to me in the same poem, will not
suffer you to be thought a flatterer. My happiness
is that you are too far engaged, and in spite of you
the ages to come will celebrate me, and know you
are a friend who loved and esteemed me, although
I died the object of court and party hatred.

Pray who is that Mr Glover,* who writ the epic

---

* Few poems, on their first appearance, have been received
with greater applause than Leonidas. Lord Lyttleton, in the
paper called Common Sense, gave it a very high encomium. Dr
Pemberton wrote a long and critical examination of its merits,
equalling it to Homer and Milton. Nothing else was read or
talked of at Leicester House ; and by all the members that were
in opposition to Sir R. Walpole ; and particularly by Lord Cob_
ham and his friends, to whom the poem was dedicated. If at
first it was too much admired, it certainly of late has been too
much neglected. Many parts of it are commendable ; such as,
the parting of Leonidas with his wife and family ; the story of
Ariana and Teribazus ; the hymn of the Magi ; the dream of
Leonidas ; the description of his shield ; the exact description of
the vast army of Xerxes, taken from Herodotus ; the burning
the camp of Xerxes ; and the last conflict and death of the hero.
Many of the characters are drawn with discrimination and truth.
The style, which sometimes wants elevation, is remarkably pure
and perspicuous ; but the numbers want variety, and he has not
enough availed himself of the great privilege of blank verse, to
run his verses into one another, with different pauses. And I
have often (as I had the pleasure of knowing him well) disputed
with him on his favourite opinion, that only iambic feet should
be used in our heroic verses, without admitting any trochaic.
His Medea is still acted with applause. He was one of the best
and most accurate Greek scholars of his time ; and a man of
great probity, integrity, and sweetness of manners. He died No-

poem called Leonidas, which is reprinting here, and has great vogue? We have frequently good poems of late from London. I have just read one upon Conversation,* and two or three others. But the crowd do not encumber you, who, like the orator or preacher, stand aloft, and are seen above the rest, more than the whole assembly below.

I am able to write no more; and this is my third endeavour, which is too weak to finish the paper: I am, my dearest friend, yours sincerely, as long as I can write, or speak, or think.

JON. SWIFT.

TO THE EARL OF OXFORD.

June 14, 1737.

My Lord,

I HAD the honour of a letter from your lordship, dated April the 7th, which I was not prepared to answer until this time. Your lordship must needs have known, that the history you mention, of the four last years of the queen's reign, was written at Windsor, just upon finishing the peace; at which time, your father and my Lord Bolingbroke had a misunderstanding with each other, that was attended with very bad consequences. When I came to

---

vember 25, 1785, aged 74; and has left behind him some curious memoirs, which, it is hoped, will be one day published.—Dr WARTON.

* By Mr Benjamin Stillingfleet, published aferwards in Dodsley's Miscellanies. He was a learned, modest, and ingenious man; a great and skilful botanist. He died in 1771.—Dr WARTON.

Ireland to take this deanery (after the peace was made) I could not stay here above a fortnight, being recalled by a hundred letters to hasten back, and to use my endeavours in reconciling those ministers. I left them the history you mention, which I had finished at Windsor, to the time of the peace. When I returned to England, I found their quarrels and coldness increased. I laboured to reconcile them as much as I was able : I contrived to bring them· to my Lord Masham's, at St James's. My Lord and Lady Masham left us together. I expostulated with them both, but could not find any good consequences. I was to go to Windsor next day with my lord-treasurer : I pretended business that prevented me ; expecting they would come to some ＊＊＊＊＊. ＊ But I followed them to Windsor ; where my Lord Bolingbroke told me, that my scheme had come to nothing. Things went on at the same rate ; they grew more estranged every day. My lord-treasurer found his credit daily declining. In May before the queen died, I had my last meeting with them at my Lord Masham's. He left us together ; and therefore I spoke very freely to them both ; and told them, " I would retire, for I found all was gone." Lord Bolingbroke whispered me, " I was in the right." Your father said, " All would do well." I told him, " That I would go to Oxford on Monday, since I found it was impossible to be of any use." I took coach to Oxford on Monday ; went to a friend in Berkshire ; there staid until the queen's death ; and then to my station here ; where I staid twelve years,

---

＊ Here is a blank left for some word or other ; such as *agreement*, *reconciliation*, or the like.

and never saw my lord your father afterward. They could not agree about printing the History of the Four last Years: and therefore I have kept it to this time, when I determine to publish it in London, to the confusion of all those rascals who have accused the queen and that ministry of making a bad peace; to which that party entirely owes the protestant succession. I was then in the greatest trust and confidence with your father the lord-treasurer, as well as with my Lord Bolingbroke, and all others who had part in the administration. I had all the letters from the secretary's office, during the treaty of peace: out of those, and what I learned from the ministry, I formed that history, which I am now going to publish for the information of posterity, and to control the most impudent falsehoods which have been published since. I wanted no kind of materials. I knew your father better than you could at that time: and I do impartially think him the most virtuous minister, and the most able, that ever I remember to have read of. If your lordship has any particular circumstances that may fortify what I have said in the History, such as letters or materials, I am content they should be printed at the end, by way of appendix. I loved my lord your father better than any other man in the world, although I had no obligation to him on the score of preferment; having been driven to this wretched kingdom, to which I was almost a stranger, by his want of power to keep me in what I ought to call my own country, although I happened to be dropped here, and was a year old before I left it; and to my sorrow, did not die before I came back to it again. I am extremely glad of the felicity you have in your alliances; and desire to present my most humble respects to my Lady Oxford, and your daughter the duchess. As to the History, it is only of affairs which I know very well; and had all the advantages possible to know, when you were in some sort but a lad. One great design of it is, to do justice to the ministry at that time, and to refute all the objections against them, as if they had a design of bringing in popery and the pretender: and farther to demonstrate, that the present settlement of the crown was chiefly owing to my lord your father. I can never expect to see England: I am now too old and too sickly, added to almost a perpetual deafness and giddiness. I live a most domestic life: I want nothing that is necessary; but I am in a cursed, factious, oppressed, miserable country; not made so by nature, but by the slavish, hellish principles of an execrable prevailing faction in it.

Farewell, my lord. I have tired you and myself. I desire again to present my most humble respects to my Lady Oxford, and the duchess your daughter. Pray God preserve you long and happy! I shall diligently inquire into your conduct from those who will tell me. You have hitherto continued right: let me hear that you persevere so. Your task will not be long; for I am not in a condition of health or time to trouble this world, and I am heartily weary of it already; and so should be in England, which I hear is full as corrupt as this poor enslaved country. I am, with the truest love and respect, my lord, your lordship's most obedient and most obliged, &c.

JON. SWIFT.

FROM DR SHERIDAN.

June 22, 1737.

CERVE DECANE,

Ego longus audire a te, nunc Francisci sunt venti intus.   Dominus M'Carty erat apud Sanctas Catherina,* qui olim minabatur me cum scripto, et sue ego ibam ad Dunboyn.   Non reddebam ad Dublinum apis causa debebam nummum, et ego habebam id non ad cicerem.

Meus filius Thomas sedebat nuper pro scholasticâ nave, et perdidit id per malitiam unius domini Hughs, qui gignebat super apud asserem,† et dixit, quod puer erat nimium juvenis pro juramento. Diabolus cape ingratum Socium ; nam olim dedi illum doctrinam pro nihil ; et sic servit me nunc. Quomodo unquam ego non volo capere ad cor, sed ego faciam optimum de malo mercatu.   O qualis mundus est hic !   Sed ego dicam non plus.   Scio quod scio ; et tenebo mentem ad meipsum, et ego solvam id de cum cogitando.

Ego habeo tres libros sapientum dictorum ‡ transcriptos pro te in pulchrâ et magnâ manu, quos mittam ad te per primam opportunitatem, ante ut meus dominus Orrery vadit pro Angliâ ; nam promisit capere illos cum se, et facere pactum pro me cum prælatore.

Corrigo illos libros valde puteus, et jubebas me,

---

* *St Catherine's*, Lady *Mountcashel's* villa about six miles from *Dublin*....D. S.

† When the provost and fellows of the university of *Dublin* meet in council, they call it a Board.—D. S.

‡ The Doctor's collection of Bons Mots—D. S.

5

sic id ego spero non habebis multum agere; nam est non rationabile dare tibi multam molestiam circum sarciendo stylum. Amica Donelson est cito ire ad Dublinum, mittam illos cum illâ.

Ego habeo non ullos nuncios, sed quod nostra tempestas est valde calida, in sic tantum, ut omne nostrum gramen est ustum super, et pecora habent nihil edere. Caremus pluvia valde multum, si Deus placeret mittere—Mitte me verbum quid genus tempestatis est in Dublino, et si placet te mitte ad me rationem tuæ sanitatis. Da meum humile servitium omnibus, qui rogant pro me, Ad Dominum Orrery, ad Doctorem Helsham et cæteris amicorum. Precare cape curam de teipso, et sic obligabis tuum humillimum famulum,

THOMAS SHERIDAN.

Junii die 22°, unum mille septem
    centum et triginta septem.

Servitium et amor dominæ albæ viæ.

FROM MR ALDERMAN BARBER.

London, June 23, 1737.

MOST HONOURED FRIEND,

I was favoured with a letter some time since by the hands of the bearer, Mr Lloyd, and by him take the opportunity of answering it.

I do assure you, Sir, that as the society have always had the greatest regard for your recommendation, so, in this affair, they have given a fresh instance of their respect; for they have resolved to relieve their tenants in Colrain from their hard bargains; and, to that end, have put it in a way that is to the entire satisfation of the bearer.

I hope this will find you in good health, and that the hot weather will contribute thereto; which will be a great satisfaction to all honest men who wish well to their country.

Our friend Mr Pope is very hearty and well, and has obliged the town lately with several things in his way; among the rest, a translation of Horace's Odes; in one of which you are mentioned "as saving your nation:" which gave great offence; and, I am assured, was under debate in the council, whether he should not be taken up for it: but it happening to be done in the late king's time, they passed it by.

I hope you see the paper called Common Sense, which has wit and humour.

I had thoughts of kissing your hand this summer; but we are all in confusion at Derry about power, which will prevent my coming at present; but I am in hopes of having that happiness before I die. I thank God I hold out to a miracle almost; for I am better in my health now than I was many years ago.

Lord Bolingbroke is in France, writing, I am told, the History of his own Time: he is well. You will please to make my compliments to Lord Orrery and Dr Delany.

I have many things to say, which in prudence I must defer.

I shall conclude with my hearty prayers to Almighty God, to preserve your most valuable life for many years, as you are a public blessing to your country, and a friend to all mankind; and to assure you that I am, with sincerity, dear Sir, your most affectionate and most faithful humble servant,

JOHN BARBER.

FROM DR KING.

St Mary Hall, Oxford, June 24, 1737.

SIR,

I DO not know for what reason the worthy gentlemen of the post-office intercepted a letter, which I did myself the honour to write to you about two months ago. I cannot remember I said any thing that could give them the least offence. I did not mention the new halfpence; I did not praise the royal family; I did not blame the prime-minister; I only returned you my thanks for a very kind letter I had just then received from you. It is true I enclosed in that letter a printed paper called Common Sense, in which the author proposes a new scheme of government to the people of Corsica, advising to make their king of the same stuff of which the Indians make their gods. * I thought to afford you some diversion : but, perhaps, it was this made the whole packet criminal.

I have this day received a letter from Mrs Whiteway, in which she tells me that I am to expect the manuscript by Lord Orrery. I will have the pleasure to wait on him as soon as I can do it without crossing the Irish channel: as soon as I receive the papers, you shall hear from me again. I shall have an op-

* This paper was written by Dr King himself.—D. S.

portunity of writing fully to you by Mr Deane Swift, who proposes to set out for Ireland the next vacation. In making mention of this gentleman, I cannot help recommending him to your favour. I have very narrowly observed his conduct ever since I have been here; and I can, with great truth, give him the character of a modest, sober, ingenious young man. He is a hard student, and will do an honour to the society of which he is now a member.

Mrs Whiteway says, that notwithstanding all your complaints, you are in good health and in good spirits. What think you of making a trip to England this fine season, and visiting our Alma Mater? I can offer you an airy cool room during the summer, and a warm bedchamber in the winter; and I will take care that your mutton commons shall be kept long enough to be tender. If you will accept of this invitation, I promise to meet you at Chester, and to conduct you to King Edward's lodgings; and then St Mary Hall may boast of a triumvirate, that is not to be matched in any part of the learned world, Sir Thomas More, Erasmus, and the Drapier. Believe me to be with the greatest esteem, Sir, your most obedient and most humble servant,

WILLIAM KING.

FROM DR KING TO MRS WHITEWAY.

St Mary Hall, Oxon, June 24, 1737.

MADAM,

I HAVE this day the favour of your letter of the 14th, which hath given me great pleasure: however,

I could not help bestowing some maledictions on those gentlemen at the post-office, who have been so impertinent as to intercept our correspondence; for you ought to have received another letter from me, with one enclosed for our friend in some few days after you had the packet from Hartley. This was in answer to the letter you mention, which I got the very next day (as well as I remember) after Hartley went from London.

As soon as I hear of my Lord Orrery's arrival on this side the water, I will wait on him to receive the papers. The moment they are put into my hands I will write to you again.

I do not know why the Dean's friends should think it derogatory, either to his station or character, to print the history by subscription, considering how the money arising by the sale of it is to be applied. I am not for selling the copy to a bookseller: for, unless a sufficient caution be taken, the bookseller, when he is master of the copy, will certainly print it by subscription, and so have all the benefit which the Dean refuses. But I shall be better able to send you my thoughts of this matter, when I have talked with some of my friends, who have had more dealings in this way than I have.

And have you at last got store of copper half-pence, and are content to give us gold and silver in exchange for this new coin? This serves to verify an observation I have frequently made, that the grossest imposition on the public will go down, if the managers have but patience to try it twice, and art enough to give it a new name. The excise scheme, which made such a noise here a few years ago, passed here last winter with little opposition, under a new shape and title. How would the ghost of Wood triumph over the Drapier, and rattle his copper chains, if the spectre were permitted to meet him in his walks? But I am unawares running into politics, without considering that these reflections may occasion the loss of my letter. I have therefore done with your copper. *

You cannot imagine how greatly I am vexed and disappointed, that I have been so long obliged to keep back my conversation-piece. † I have in this respect, wholly complied with the reasoning, or rather with the humours, of some of my friends. They were willing to try their skill in accommodating my Irish affairs; in which, after all, I believe they will be disappointed as much as I have been: for the adversaries I have to deal with, proceed on

---

* With great respect to Dr King, he is somewhat mistaken in his politics; for the great force of Dr Swift's reasoning, in the character of an Irish Drapier, was not so much levelled against a moderate quantity of halfpence in general (which, it is certain, were much wanted in Ireland in the year 1724,) as against Wood's adulterate copper in particular, which was not worth three-pence in a shilling, and which might have been poured in upon the nation from Wood's mint to eternity; as he had neither given security for his honesty, nor obliged himself, like other patentees, to give either gold or silver in exchange for his copper, when it began to grow troublesome: whereas the halfpence, sent over to Ireland in the year 1737, were coined in the Tower, by the express order of the crown, for the conveniency of the kingdom, and were not calculated to do any mischief; or, in fact, could they have done any, as all people were at that time sufficiently and thoroughly apprised, that halfpence were not sterling money, or could legally be tendered in any payment whatsoever; the only use of them being a sort of change in the small crafts and traffick of the world. However, it is certain that an advertisement of three lines, by order of Dr Swift, had there been occasion for it, as there was not, would instantly have stopped their currency. —D. S.

† Meaning The Toast, a satire, in which Dr King assailed many of the persons with whom he was engaged in an Irish law-suit, particularly the Countess of Newburgh.

a principle that will bear no reason, and do no good, not even to themselves, if others are at the same time to receive any benefit by the bargain. However, since you seem so earnestly to desire a second view of this work, I will send you a book by Mr Swift, who intends to go from hence about ten days or a fortnight hence. You will be so kind as to keep it in your own hands until the publication.

As I think it proper to write a postscript in your letter to a certain person, that must be nameless; and finding I have but room for my address to him, I will say no more to you now than that I am, and always must be, Madam, your most obedient and most humble servant,

WILLIAM KING.

P. S. To the gentleman of the post-office who intercepted my last letter addressed to Mrs Whiteway, at her house in Abbey Street, together with a letter enclosed and addressed to the Dean of St Patrick's.

SIR, when you have sufficiently perused this letter, I beg the favour of you to send it to the lady to whom it is directed. I shall not take it ill though you should not give yourself the trouble to seal it again. If any thing I have said about the copper halfpence and excise should offend you, blot it out. I shall think myself much obliged to you, if, at the same time, you will be pleased to send Mrs Whiteway those letters which are now in your hands, with such alterations and amendments as you think proper. I cannot believe that your orders will justify you in detaining letters of business : for as you are a civil officer, I conceive you have not a license to rob on the highway. If I happen to be mistaken, of which I shall be convinced if this letter should be likewise intercepted, I will hereafter change my address, and enrol you and your superior in my catalogue of heroes.

TO WILLIAM GRAHAM, ESQ.

AT DROGHEDA *.

SIR,

As you hold a lease from me, and the chapter of my cathedral of St Patrick's, which came to you by your mother, who was a person I much esteemed, you are obliged, by your lease, to pay annually L.31, 15s.; and yet, whereas you are obliged to pay half yearly, you have thought fit to be two full years in arrear, and now owe us L.63, 10s. This lease is a part of our economy, as we call it; that is to say, it is all applied to the repairs of the cathedral, to the payment of the organist, and other church servants.

Now, Sir, I remember you were at Doctor Sheridan's school, where you were taught all the principles at least of honour and justice; you were left,

---

* This letter, now for the first time printed, was copied from the original, in the Dean's own hand-writing, in the possession of Leonard M'Nally, Esq. of Dublin. It is without a signature, and fairly written. It would appear that the Dean had preserved it as a copy from the folding of the paper, and the superscription endorsed upon it. It appears from Watson's Almanack, that William Graham was a privy-councillor in Ireland, and member in parliament for the town of Drogheda.----A. W. H.

too, a great estate ; and I hear you are at this time one of the privy-council. However, our procurator assures me, that he never received one line in answer to his frequent letters for payment of your rent. I can impute this way of delaying to many causes ; you have either forgot the lectures of Dr Sheridan your master, or you have heard it was an unfashionable thing in a gentleman to pay his just debts, or you are exalted by your great estate, or by your seat in the council ; or, perhaps, you have been drawn into the association against the clergy ; and therefore, you very reasonably conclude, that their churches, especially cathedrals, should suffer, as well as their own maintenance.

However, I am sorry that, although Christianity be much out of fashion, there might not be some remainder of pagan virtues, such as justice, and honour, and learning, and love of our country left, especially to those who have a vote in making laws, or sitting at a council-board.

I often have, in another kingdom, given advice, with good success, to younger men than you, and of greater titles.

If you resent any thing I have said, it will much lessen the credit of your understanding, as well as of your regard to common justice.

I am, Sir,

Your most obedient servant.

Deanery-House, Dublin,
April the 26th 1737.

FROM MR LEWIS.

London, June 30, 1737.

Our friend Pope tells me, you could wish to revive a correspondence with some of your old acquaintances, that you might not remain entirely ignorant of what passes in this country : on this occasion I would offer myself with pleasure, if I thought
the little trifles that come to my knowledge could in
the least contribute to your amusement ; but as you
yourself judge very rightly, I am too much out of
the world, and see things at too great a distance ;
and beside this, my age, and the use I have formerly made of my eyes in writing by candlelight, have
now reduced me almost to blindness, and I see nothing less than the pips of the cards, from which I
have some relief in a long winter evening.   However, to show my dear Dean how much I love him,
I have taken my pen in my hand to scratch him out
a letter, though it be little more than to tell him most
of those he and I used to converse with are dead ;
but I am still alive, and lead a poor animal life.
Lord Masham is much in the same way : he has
married his son, and boards with him : the lady is
the daughter of Salway Winnington, and they all
live lovingly together ; the old gentleman walks
afoot, which makes me fear that he has made settle-
ments above his strength.   I regret the loss of Dr
Arbuthnot every hour of the day : he was the best-
conditioned creature that ever breathed, and the
most cheerful ; yet his poor son George is under the
utmost dejection of spirits, almost to a degree of de-
lirium ; his two sisters give affectionate attendance,
and I hope he will grow better.   Sir William Wynd-

ham makes the first figure in parliament, and is one of the most amiable men in the world: he is very happy in his wife Lady Blandford: but I fear his eldest son will not come into his measures: this may create him some uneasiness.

Lord Bathurst is in Gloucestershire, where he plants, transplants, and unplants: thus he erects an employment for himself independent of a court.

I have the happiness to live near Lord Oxford, who continues that kindness and protection to me that I had from his father. God Almighty has given him both the power and the will to support the numerous family of his sister, which has been brought to ruin by that unworthy man Lord K———. *

Now I name him, I mean Lord Oxford, let me ask you if it be true, that you are going to print a History of the four last years of the queen? if it is, will not you let me see it before you send it to the press? Is it not possible that I may suggest some things that you may have omitted, and give you reasons for leaving out others? The scene is changed since that period of time: the conditions of the peace of Utrecht have been applauded by most part of mankind, even in the two houses of parliament: Should not matters rest here, at least for some time? I presume your great end is to do justice to truth; the second point may perhaps be to make a compliment to the Oxford family: permit me to say as to the first, that though you know perhaps more than any one man, I may possibly contribute a mite; and, with the alteration of one word, viz. by inserting *parva* instead of *magna*, apply to myself that passage of Virgil, *et quorum*

---

* Kinnoul.

pars parva fui. As to the second point, I do not conceive your compliment to Lord Oxford to be so perfect as it might be, unless you lay the manuscript before him, that it may be considered here.

Our little captain blusters, reviews, and thinks he governs the world, when in reality he does nothing: for the first minister stands possessed of all the regal power: the latter prates well in the house, and, by corruption, is absolute master of it: as to other matters, his foreign treaties are absurd, and his management of the funds betray a want of skill: he has a low way of thinking. My dear Dean, adieu; believe me to be, what I really am,

Most affectionately yours,
ERASMUS LEWIS.

FROM THE EARL OF OXFORD.

Dover Street, July 4, 1737.

GOOD MR DEAN,

Your letter of June 14th, in answer to mine of the 7th of April, is come to my hands; and it is with no small concern that I have read it, and to find that you seem to have formed a resolution to put the History of the four last years of the Queen to the press; a resolution taken without giving your friends, and those that are greatly concerned, some notice, or suffering them to have time and opportunity to read the papers over, and to consider them. I hope it is not too late yet, and that you will be so good as to let some friends see them, before they are put to the press; and, as you propose to have the work printed here, it will be easy to give directions to whom you will please to give the liberty of seeing them; I beg

I may be one : this request I again repeat to you, and I hope you will grant it. I do not doubt but there are many who will persuade you to publish it; but they are not proper judges : their reasons may be of different kinds, and their motives to press on this work may be quite different, and perhaps concealed from you.

I am extremely sensible of the firm love and regard you had for my father, and have for his memory ; and upon that account it is, that I now renew my request, that you would at least defer this printing until you have had the advice of friends. You have forgot that you lent me the history to read when you were in England since my father died ; I do remember it well. I would ask your pardon for giving you this trouble ; but upon this affair I am so nearly concerned, that if I did not my utmost to prevent it, I should never forgive myself. *

I am extremely obliged to you for your good and kind concern for me and my family. My wife desires your acceptance of her most humble service ; my daughter desires the same ; they both are sensible of your good wishes for them. I am, with true esteem and respect, dear Sir,

Your obliged and most affectionate
humble servant,
OXFORD.

---

* This letter, it would seem, had the desired effect ; for the manuscript was sent to England, and submitted to the inspection of Lord Oxford and his friends. See the Dean's letter to Lewis, 23d July.

MR POPE TO THE EARL OF ORRERY.

July 12, 1737.

My Lord,

THE pleasure you gave me, in acquainting me of the Dean's better health, is one so truly great, as might content even your own humanity; and whatever my sincere opinion and respect of your lordship prompts me to wish from your hands for myself, your love for him makes me happy. Would to God my weight added to yours, could turn his inclinations to this side, that I might live to enjoy him here through your means, and flatter myself it was partly through my own! But this, I fear, will never be the case; and I think it more probable his attraction will draw me on the other side, which, I protest, nothing less than a probability of dying at sea, considering the weak frame of my breast, would have hindered me from, two years past. In short, whenever I think of him, it is with the vexation of all impotent passions, that carry us out of ourselves only to spoil our quiet, and make us return to a resignation, which is the most melancholy of all virtues.

FROM THE EARL OF ORRERY.

July 23, 1737.

DEAR SIR,

IF I were to tell you who inquire for you, and what they say of you, it would take up more paper than I have in my lodgings, and more time than I stay in town.　Yet London is empty; not dusty, for we have had rain: not dull, for Mr Pope is in it: not noisy, for we have no cars* : not troublesome, for a man may walk quietly about the streets: in short, it is just as I would have it till Monday, and then I quit St Paul's for my little church at Marston.

Your commands are obeyed long ago; Dr King has his cargo †, Mrs Barber her conversation ‡, and Mr Pope his letters.　To-morrow I pass with him at Twickenham : the *olim meminisse* will be our feast.　Leave Dublin, and come to us. Methinks there are many stronger reasons for it than heretofore ; at least I feel them : and I will say with Macbeth, Would thou could'st !

My health is greatly mended ; so, I hope, is yours ; write to me when you can, in your best health, and utmost leisure ; never break through that rule.　Can friendship increase by absence ? Sure it does : at least mine rises some degrees, or seems to rise : try if it will fall by coming nearer : no, certainly it cannot be higher.

Yours most affectionately,

ORRERY.

---

* Alluding to the Irish cars.—D. S.
† The MS. of "The History of the four last Years."—N.
‡ The treatise on "Polite conversation," which the Dean presented to Mrs Barber, and which was published for her benefit.

TO MR LEWIS.

July 23, 1727.

DEAR FRIEND,

WHILE any of those who used to write to me were alive, I always inquired after you. But since your secretaryship in the queen's time, I believed you were so glutted with the office, that you had not patience to venture on a letter to an absent useless acquaintance: and I find I owe yours to my Lord Oxford. The history you mention was written above a year before the queen's death. I left it with the treasurer and Lord Bolingbroke, when I first came over to take this deanery. I returned in less than a month; but the ministry could not agree about printing it. It was to conclude with the peace. I staid in London above nine months; but not being able to reconcile the quarrels between those two, I went to a friend in Berkshire, and on the queen's death came hither for good and all. I am confident you read that history; as this Lord Oxford did, as he owns in his two letters, the last of which reached me not above ten days ago. You know, on the queen's death, how the peace and all proceedings were universally condemned. This I knew would be done; and the chief cause of my writing was, not to let such a queen and ministry lie under such a load of infamy, or posterity be so ill informed, &c. Lord Oxford is in the wrong, to be in pain about his father's character, or his proceedings in his ministry; which is so drawn, that his greatest admirers will rather censure me for partiality; neither can he tell me any thing material out of his papers, which I was not then informed of: nor do I know any body but yourself who could give me more light than what I then received; for I remember I often consulted with you, and took memorials of many important particulars which you told me, as I did of others, for four years together. I can find no way to have the original delivered to Lord Oxford, or to you; for the person who has it will not trust it out of his hands; but, I believe, would be contented to let it be read to either of you, if it could be done without letting it out of his hands*, although perhaps that may be too late. If my health would have permitted me, for some years past, to have ventured as far as London, I would have satisfied both my lord and you. I believe you know that Lord Bolingbroke is now busy in France, writing the History of his own Time: and how much he grew to hate the treasurer you know too well; and I know how much Lord Bolingbroke hates his very memory. This is what the present Lord Oxford should be in most pain at, not about me. I have had my share of affliction sufficient, in the loss of Dr Arbuthnot, and poor Gay and others; and I heartily pity poor Lord Masham. I would fain know whether his son be a valuable young man; because I much dislike his education. When I was last among you, Sir William Wyndham was in a bad state of health: I always loved him, and I rejoice to hear from you the figure he makes. But I know so little of what

---

* As a little before this period, the great abilities of Dr Swift had begun to fail, he had, in order to gratify some of his acquaintance, called for the History of the four last Years of the Queen's Reign once or twice out of his friend's hands, and lent it abroad; by which means part of the contents were whispered about the town, and several had pretended to have read it, who, perhaps, had not seen one line of it.—D. S.

passes, that I never heard of Lady Blandford his present wife.

Lord Bathurst used to write to me, but has dropped it some years.   Pray, is Charles Ford yet alive! for he has dropped me too : or perhaps my illness has hindered me from provoking his remembrance : for I have been long in a very bad condition.   My deafness, which used to be occasional and for a short time, has stuck by me now several months without remission ; so that I am unfit for any conversation, except one or two Stentors of either sex ; and my old giddiness is likewise become chronical, although not in equal violence with my former short fits.

I was never so much deceived in any Scot, as by that execrable Lord K * * * * ; * whom I loved extremely, and now detest beyond expression.

You say so little of yourself, that I know not whether you are in health or sickness, only that you lead a mere animal life ; which, with nine parts in ten, is a sign of health.   I find you have not, like me, lost your memory ; nor, I hope, your sense of hearing, which is the greatest loss of any, and more comfortless than even being blind ; I mean, in the article of company.   Writing no longer amuses me, for I cannot think.   I dine constantly at home, in my chamber, with a grave housekeeper, whom I call Sir Robert ; and sometimes receive one or two friends, and a female cousin, with strong high tenor voices.   I am, &c.

JON. SWIFT.

---

* Lord Kinnoul, whose pecuniary embarrassments had involved, it would seem, his brother-in-law, Lord Oxford.   He is often mentioned with regard in the Journal.

TO MR POPE.

Dublin, July 23, 1737.

I SENT a letter to you some weeks ago, which my Lord Orrery enclosed in one of his, to which I received as yet no answer; but it will be time enough when his lordship goes over, which will be as he hopes in about ten days, and then he will take with him all the letters I preserved of yours, which are not above twenty-five. I find there is a great chasm of some years, but the dates are more early than my two last journeys to England, which makes me imagine, that in one of those journeys I carried over another cargo. But I cannot trust my memory half an hour; and my disorder of deafness and giddiness increase daily. So that I am declining as fast as it is easily possible for me, if I were a dozen years older.

We have had your volume of letters, which I am told are to be printed here. Some of those who highly esteem you, and a few who know you personally, are grieved to find you make no distinction between the English gentry of this kingdom, and the savage old Irish, (who are only the vulgar, and some gentlemen who live in the Irish parts of the kingdom) but the English colonies, who are three parts in four, are much more civilized than many counties in England, and speak better English, and are much better bred. And they think it very hard, that an American, who is of the fifth generation from England, should be allowed to preserve that title, only because we have been told by some of them that their names are entered in some parish in London. I have three or four cousins here who were born in Portugal, whose parents took the same care, and they are all of them Londoners.   Dr Delany, who, as I take it, is of an Irish family, came to visit me three days ago, on purpose to complain of those passages in your letters ; he will not allow such a difference between the two climates, but will assert that North Wales, Northumberland, Yorkshire, and the other northern shires, have a more cloudy ungenial air than any part of Ireland. In short, I am afraid your friends and admirers here will force you to make a palinody.

As for the other parts of your volume of letters, my opinion is, that there might be collected from them the best system that ever was writ for the conduct of human life, at least to shame all reasonable men out of their follies and vices.   It is some recommendation of this kingdom, and of the taste of the people, that you are at least as highly celebrated here as you are at home.   If you will blame us for slavery, corruption, atheism, and such trifles, do it freely, but include England, only with an addition of every other vice.   I wish you would give orders against the corruption of English by those scribblers who send us over their trash in prose and verse, with abominable curtailings and quaint modernisms.   I now am daily expecting an end of life : I have los' all spirit, and every scrap of health ; I sometimes recover a little of my hearing, but my head is ever out of order.   While I have any ability to hold a commerce with you, I will never be silent, and this chancing to be a day that I can hold a pen, I will drag it as long as I am able. Pray let my Lord Orrery see you often ; next to yourself I love no man so well ; and tell him what I say, if he visits you. I have now done, for it is evening, and my head grows worse. May God always protect you, and preserve you long, for a pattern of piety and virtue.

Farewell, my dearest and almost only constant friend. I am ever, at least in my esteem, honour, and affection to you, what I hope you expect me to be,

Yours, &c.

JON. SWIFT.

TO THE RIGHT WORSHIPFUL THE MAYOR, ALDERMEN, SHERIFFS, AND COMMON-COUNCIL OF THE CITY OF CORK.

Deanery House, Dublin,
August 15, 1737.

GENTLEMEN,

I RECEIVED from you, some weeks ago, the honour of my freedom in a silver box, by the hands of Mr Stannard;* but it was not delivered to me in as many weeks more; because, I suppose, he was too full of more important business. Since that time I have been wholly confined by sickness, so that I was not able to return you my acknowledgment; and, it is with much difficulty I do it now, my head continuing in great disorder. Mr Faulkner will be the bearer of my letter, who sets out this morning for Cork.

I could have wished, as I am a private man, that,

---

* Eaton Stannard, Esq. then Recorder of Dublin, and afterward made his Majesty's Prime Serjeant at Law, in the room of Anthony Malone, Esq. who was promoted to the Chancellorship of the Exchequer.—D. S.

in the instrument of my freedom, you had pleased to assign your reasons for making choice of me. I know it is a usual compliment to bestow the freedom of the city on an archbishop, or lord chancellor, and other persons of great titles, merely upon account of their stations or power : but a private man, and a perfect stranger, without power or grandeur, may justly expect to find the motives assigned in the instrument of his freedom, on what account he is thus distinguished. And yet I cannot discover in the whole parchment scrip any one reason offered. Next, as to the silver box, * there is not so much as my name upon it, nor any one syllable to show it was a present from your city. Therefore I have, by the advice of friends, agreeable with my opinion, sent back the box and instrument of freedom by Mr Faulkner, to be returned to you: leaving to your choice, whether to insert the reasons for which you were pleased to give me my freedom, or bestow the box upon some more worthy person whom you may have an intention to honour, because it will equally fit every body. I am, with true esteem and gratitude, Gentlemen,

Your most obedient and obliged servant,

JON. SWIFT.

---

* In consequence of this letter, there was an inscription, and the city arms of Cork, engraved on the box, and reasons on the parchment instrument for presenting him with the freedom of that city.—D. S.

FROM MR FARREN.

Cork, Sept. 14, 1737.

REVEREND SIR,

I AM favoured with yours by Mr Faulkner, and am sorry the health of a man the whole kingdom has at heart, should be so much in danger.

When the box with your freedom was given the recorder, to be presented to you, I hoped he would, in the name of the city, have expressed their grateful acknowledgments for the many services the public have received from you, which are the motives that induced us to make you one of our citizens; and as they will ever remain monuments to your glory, we imagined it needless to make any inscription on the box, and especially as we have no precedents on our books for any such. But, as so great and deserving a patriot merits all distinction that can be made, I have, by the consent and approbation of the council, directed the box to you, and hope, what is inscribed upon it, although greatly inferior to what your merit is entitled to, will however demonstrate the great regard and respect we have for you, on account of the many singular services your pen and your counsel have done this poor country; and am, reverend Sir, your most obedient humble servant,

THOMAS FARREN, Mayor.

FROM LORD BATHURST.

Cirencester, Oct. 5, 1737.

DEAR MR DEAN,

THAT I often think of you is most certain, but if
I should write to you as often, you would think me
extremely troublesome.   I was alarmed some time
ago with hearing that you were much indisposed;
but if later accounts are to be depended upon, you
are now in perfect health.   I should be heartily glad
to have that news confirmed to me by two lines under your hand : however, I write to you under that
supposition, for which reason I have cut out a little
business for you.

That very pretty epistle which you writ many
years ago to Lord Oxford, is printed very incorrect-
ly.   I have a copy (of which I send you a transcript) which has some very good lines in it, that are
not in the printed copy; and besides, if you will
compare it with the original, you will find that you
left off without going through with the epistle.   The
fable of the country and city mouse is as prettily told
as any thing of that kind ever was : possibly, if you
look over your papers, you may find that you finished the whole; if not, I enjoin you as a task, to
go through with it; and I beg of you, do not suffer
an imperfect copy to stand, while it is in your power
to rectify it.*   Adieu ! do me the justice to believe
me most faithfully and unalterably yours.

---

* On the back of the original letter, Dr Swift has observed,
that upon receiving it, he added twenty lines to the poem.   It
is in imitation of the sixth satire of the second book of Horace,

TO MR COPE.

Deanery House, Nov. 11, 1737.

Sir,

I was just going to write to you, when your clerk
brought me your note for thirty-six pounds, which
was more by a third part than I desired, and for
which I heartily thank you. I have been used since
my illness to hear so many thousand lies told of
myself and others, and so circumstantially, that my
head was almost turned; and if I gave them any
credit, it was because one thing I knew perfectly,
that we differed entirely in our opinions of public
management. I did and do detest the lowering of
the gold, because I saw a resolution seven years old
of your House of Commons of a very different nature, and have since seen tracts against it, which to
me were demonstrations; and am assured, as well as
know by experience, that I have not received a penny except from you. However, although I know you
to be somewhat of what we call a giber, yet I am
convinced by your assertions that I was ill informed;
and yet we differ so much in the present politics,
that I doubt it will much affect the good-will you
formerly seemed to bear me. I grant, that the
bishops, the people in employments of all kinds who
receive salaries, and some others, will not lose a penny, by lowering the money, because they must still
have their pay; and, if your estate be set much under value, you will be no sufferer; though I, and

---

and it is printed with the additional lines, in the Works of Mr
Pope.—H.

thousand of others, will soundly feel the smart, and particularly the lower clergy, who I find are out of every body's good graces; but for what reasons I know not. I hear your house is forming a bill * against all legacies to the church, or any public charity, which puts me under a great difficulty; because, by my will, I have bequeathed my whole fortune to build and endow an hospital for lunatics and idiots.† I wish I had any certainty in that matter. You mistook me in one expression; what I said was, that I wished all who were for lowering the gold, were lowered to the dust; and I might explain it, so that it would bear the sense of causing them to repent in dust and ashes. I am, Sir,

Your most obedient humble servant,

JON. SWIFT.

---

* This bill did not pass.—F.

† The Dean drew up a petition to the House of Lords in Ireland, to be excepted in the heads of the bill for a mortmain act, then in agitation, that he might be at liberty to fulfil his benevolent intention: but the bill did not pass. The hospital (endowed by Dr Swift's legacy of above 10,000 pounds) was incorporated by charter, in August 1746. By a printed state, in 1770, it appears, that, by the addition of other legacies, the trustees were enabled at that time to admit thirty-four patients on the establishment; and had also sixteen boarders under cure, at the rate of thirty guineas a year for each.—F.

FROM LORD MOUNTJOY.*

November 17, 1737.

Sir,

I shall, with great pleasure, bring in your petition to-morrow, the House of Lords not sitting until then ; but I find there is a small mistake in point of form, which will be proper to be set right before the petition shall be presented. †

You mention the bill as if it would certainly pass, and be transmitted into England ; instead of which, I must beg the favour of you to say, that " there are heads of a bill depending now before your lordships' committee, in order to prevent," &c. &c., for until such time as it shall have gone through that, no one can declare the fate of it.

I should not be so impertinent as to pretend to direct you in this, but that I apprehend you did not know the progress the bill has taken ; if you will get it writ over again, my servant shall wait to bring it to me, and I shall take care, as soon as the petition is received, to have a clause ready, in pursuance of it, to except your charity. I am, with great respect, Sir,

Your most obedient and most humble servant,
MOUNTJOY.

---

* William Stewart, Viscount Mountjoy, created Earl of Blessinton, Dec. 7, 1745.

† The Dean's petition to be excepted from the mortmain bill in case it should pass. It stated, that he had long since bequeathed his fortune to pious uses, and was determined to remit it abroad for similar purposes if his petition was refused.

FROM MR FORD.

November 22, 1737.

I CANNOT help putting you in mind of me sometimes, though I am sure of having no return. I often read your name in the newspapers, but hardly
have any other account of you, except when I happen to see Lord Orrery. He told me the last time,
that you had been ill, but were pe. fectly recovered.

I hear they are going to publish two volumes
more of your works. I see no reason why all the
pamphlets published at the end of the queen's reign
might not be inserted. Your objection of their being momentary things, will not hold. Killing no
Murder, and many other old tracts, are still read
with pleasure, not to mention Tully's Letters, which
have not died with the times. My comfort is, they
will some time or other be found among my books
with the author's name, and posterity obliged with
them. I have been driven out of a great house,
where I had lodged between four and five years, by
new lodgers, with an insupportable noise, and have
taken a little one to myself in a little court, merely
for the sake of sleeping in quiet. It is in St James's
Place, and called Little Cleveland Court. I believe
you never observed it; for I never did, though I
lodged very near it, till I was carried there to see the
house I have taken. Though coaches come in, it
consists of but six houses in all. Mine is but two
stories high, contrived exactly as I would wish, as I
seldom eat at home. The ground floor is of small
use to me; for the fore parlour is flung into the
entry, and makes a magnificent London hall. The
back one, by their ridiculous custom of tacking a

closet almost of the same bigness to it, is so dark, that I can hardly see to read there in the middle of the day. Up one pair of stairs I have a very good dining-room, which on the second floor is divided into two, and makes room for my whole family, a man and a maid, both at board-wages. Over my bedchamber is my study, the pleasantest part of the house, from whence you have a full view of Buckingham House, and all that part of the park. My furniture is clean and new, but of the cheapest things I could find out. The most valuable goods I have are two different prints of you. I am still in great hopes I shall one day have the happiness of seeing you in it.

Every body agrees the queen's death was wholly owing to her own fault. She had a rupture, which she would not discover ; * and the surgeon who opened her navel, declared if he had known it two days sooner, she should have been walking about the next day. By her concealing her distemper, they gave her strong cordials for the gout in her stomach, which did her great mischief. The king is said to have given her the first account of her condition : she bore it with great resolution, and immediately sent for the rest of her children, to take formal leave of them, but absolutely refused to see the Prince of Wales ; nor could the Archbishop of

---

* Her complaint was, for a long time, only known by the king and her German nurse, Mrs Mailborne, and Lady Sundon, who, by participating in the secret, preserved a great influence over the queen. The shrewdness of Sir Robert Walpole, however, penetrated the mystery, by remarking, that among the physical questions which she put to him after the death of his wife, the queen most frequently adverted to the case of a rupture, which was not Lady Walpole's disease.

Canterbury, when he gave her the sacrament, prevail on her, though she said she heartily forgave the prince. It is thought her death will be a loss, at least in point of ease, to some of the ministers.

Since Lewis has lost his old wife, he has had an old maiden niece to live with him, continues the same life, takes the air in his coach, dines moderately at home, and sees nobody.

It was reported, and is still believed by many, that Sir Robert Walpole upon the loss of his, made Miss Skirret an honest woman; but if it be so, the marriage is not yet owned.

That you may, in health and happiness, see many 30th of Novembers, is the most sincere and hearty wish of yours, &c.

C. Ford.

If you will be so kind as to let me hear from you once again, you may either direct to me at the Cocoa Tree, or to Little Cleveland Court, in St James's Place.

FROM THE CHEVALIER RAMSAY.

At Paris, Nov. 29, 1737.

Reverend Sir,

I received only some weeks ago the works you were pleased to send me, and have perused them with new pleasure. I still find in them all the marks of that original genius and universal beneficence which compose your character. I cannot send you in return, any such valuable compositions of mine; but you will receive, by the first ships that go for

Ireland, my History of the Mareschal de Turenne, the greatest French hero that ever was. I shall be glad to know your opinion of the performance.

I am, with the greatest respect, veneration, and friendship, dear Sir, your most humble, and most obedient servant,

THE CHEVALIER RAMSAY.

Pray allow me to assure Mr Sican of my most humble respects.

If you have any commands for me in this country, or for any of your friends, pray direct for me, under a cover. *A son Altesse Monseigneur le compte d'Evreux, général de la cavallerie à Paris.*

———

FROM LORD BATHURST.

'Scarcliffe Farm, Dec. 6, 1737.

DEAR SIR,

I RECEIVED a letter from you at Cirencester, full of life and spirits, which gave me singular satisfaction; but those complaints you make of the deplorable state of Ireland, made me reflect upon the condition of England, and I am inclined to think it is not much better; possibly the only difference is, that we shall be the last devoured. * I have attended parliament many years, and never found that I could do any good; I have therefore entered upon a new scheme of life, and am determined to look

---

* The promise of Polypheme to Ulysses.—H.

after my own affairs a little. I am now in a small farm-house in Derbyshire, and my chief business is to take care that my agents do not impose upon my tenants. I am for letting them all good bargains, that my rents may be paid as long as any rents can be paid; and when the time comes that there is no money, they are honest fellows, and will bring me in what corn and cattle I shall want. I want no foreign commodities; my neighbour the Duke of Kingston has imported one; * but I do not think it worth the carriage.

I passed through London in my way here, and every body wondered I could leave them, they were so full of speculations upon the great event which lately happened ; † but I am of opinion some time will be necessary to produce any consequences. Some consequences will certainly follow ; but time must ripen matters for them. I could send you many speculations of my own and others upon this subject ; but it is too nice a subject for me to handle in a post-letter. It is not every body who ought to have liberty to abuse their superiors ; if a man has so much wit as to get the majority of mankind on his side, he is often safe; or if he is known to have talents that can make an abuse stick close, he is still safer. You may say, where is the occasion of abusing any body ? I never did in my life : but you have often told truth of persons, who would rather you had abused them in the grossest manner.

---

* Madame la Touche, a French lady.——B.

† The death of Queen Caroline, on Sunday evening, November 20, 1737.——B. It was expected that this event would have occasioned a change of ministry.

I may say in parliament, that we are impoverished at home, and rendered contemptible abroad, because nobody will care to call upon me to prove it;
but I do not know whether I may venture to put
that in a letter, at least in a letter to a disaffected
person; such you will be reputed as long as you
live; after your death, perhaps, you may stand
rectus in curia.

I met our friend Pope in town; he is as sure to
be there in a bustle, as a porpus in a storm.   He
told me that he would retire to Twickenham for a
fortnight; but I doubt it much.   Since I found by
your last, that your hand and your head are both
in so good a condition, let me hear from you sometimes.   And do not be discouraged that I send you
nothing worth reading now: I have talked with nobody for some time past, but farmers and plough-
men; when I come into good company again, I may
possibly be less insipid; but in whatever condition I
am, I shall always be most ambitious of your friendship, and most desirous of your esteem, being most
faithfully and sincerely, dear Sir,

Your obedient humble servant,

BATHURST.

TO MR FAULKNER.

Deanery House, Dec. 15, 1737.

MR FAULKNER,
THE short treatise that I here send you enclosed
was put into my hands by a very worthy person,
of much ancient learning, as well as knowledge in

the laws of both kingdoms.* He is likewise a most
loyal subject to King George, and wholly attached
to the Hanover family, and is a gentleman of as
many virtues as I have any where met. However,
it seems, he cannot be blind or unconcerned at the
mistaken conduct of his country in a point of the
highest importance to its welfare. He has learn-
edly shown, from the practice of all wise nations in
past and late ages, that tillage was the great principle and foundation of their wealth; and recommends
the practice of it to this kingdom with the most
weighty reasons. He mentions the prodigious sums
sent out yearly for importing all sorts of corn, in the
miserable moneyless condition we are now in. To
which I cannot but add, that in reading the resolutions of the last sessions, I have observed in several papers that the honourable House of Commons
seem to be of the same sentiment, although the increase of tillage may be of advantage to the clergy,
whom I conceive to be as loyal a body of men to
the present king and family as any in the nation:
and, by the great providence of God, it is so ordered, that if the clergy be fairly dealt with, whatever
increases their maintenance will more largely increase the estates of the landed men, and the profits
of their farmers.

I desire you, Mr Faulkner, to print the treatise
in a fair letter and a good paper.

I am, your faithful friend and servant,
JON. SWIFT.

---

* Alexander Macaulay, Esq.

TO DR CLANCY.

Deanery House, Christmas Day, 1737.

SIR,

SOME friend of mine lent me a comedy, * which I am told was written by you : I read it carefully, with much pleasure, on account both of the characters and the moral. I have no interest with the people of the playhouse, else I should gladly recommend it to them. I send you a small present,† in such gold as will not give you trouble to change ; for I much pity your loss of sight, ‡ which if it pleased God to let you enjoy, your other talents might have been your honest support, and have eased you of your present confinement. I am, Sir,

Your well-wishing friend and humble servant,

JON. SWIFT.

I know not who lent me the play ; if it came from you, I will send it back to-morrow.

This letter and the packet were sealed with the head of Socrates.

---

* " The Sharper," the principal character of which performance was designed to represent Colonel Chartres.—D. S.

† This packet contained five pounds in small pieces of gold of different kinds ; of which the largest did not exceed the value of five shillings. A little time after (says Dr Clancy) I sent him a parcel of tickets : he kept but one, which he said he had paid for, and afterwards sent me two four pound pieces for more.—See Clancy's Memoirs, Vol. II. page 56.—D. S.

‡ Dr Clancy had pursued the study of physic, and was patronised by Dr Helsham ; but having lost his sight by a cold in 1737, before he could regularly engage in the business of his profession, he kept a Latin school for his support.—D. S.

FROM LADY HOWTH.

Dec. 26, 1737.

DEAR SIR,

KNOWING you to be very poor, I have sent you a couple of wild-ducks, a couple of partridges, a side of venison, and some plover, which will help to keep your house this Christmas. You may make a miser's feast, and drink your blue-eyed nymph * in a bumper, as we do the drapier : and when these are out, let me know, and you shall have a fresh supply. I have sent them by a black-guard, knowing you to be of a very generous temper, though very poor. My lord and husband joins with me in wishing you a merry Christmas, and many of them ; and am sincerely your affectionate friend and sea-nymph.

If I signed my name, and the letter should be found, you and I might be suspected.

FROM DR CLANCY.

Dec. 27, 1737.

REVEREND SIR,

WHEN I strive to express the thorough sense I have of your humanity and goodness, my attempt

---

* Lady Howth having very sparkling blue-grey eyes, Dr Swift used to distinguish her by the name of " the blue-eyed Nymph."—N.

ceases in admiration of them. You have favoured my performance with some degree of approbation, and you have considered my unfortunate condition by a mark of your known benevolence: from my very soul I sincerely thank you. That approbation, which in some more happy periods of my life would have made me proud even to vanity, has now in my distress comforted and soothed my misery.

If I did not fear being troublesome, I should do myself the honour of waiting upon you, if you will be pleased to permit me to do so. At any time I am ready to obey your command; and am, with the utmost respect and gratitude, Sir, your most obliged humble servant,

MIC. CLANCY.

TO MR FAULKNER.

Deanery House, Dublin, Jan. 6, 1737-8.

SIR,

I HAVE often mentioned to you an earnest desire I had, and still have, to record the merit and services of the lord mayor, Humphrey French;* whom I often desired, after his mayoralty, to give me an account of many passages that happened in his mayoralty, and which he has often put off, on the pretence of his forgetfulness, but in reality of his modesty: I take him to be a hero in his kind,

---

* The Dean addressed to Mr French his version of an Ode of Horace.

and that he ought to be imitated by all his successors, as far as their genius can reach. I desire you therefore to inquire among all his friends whom you are acquainted with, to press them to give you the particulars of what they can remember, not only during the general conduct of his life, wherever he had any power or authority in the city, but particularly from Mr Maple, who was his intimate friend, who knew him best, and could give the most just character of himself and his actions.

When I shall have got a sufficient information of all these particulars, I will, although I am oppressed with age and infirmities, stir up all the little spirit I can raise, to give the publick an account of that great patriot ; and propose him as an example to all future magistrates, in order to recommend his virtues to this miserable kingdom. I am, Sir,

Your very humble servant,
Jon. Swift.

TO MR ALDERMAN BARBER.

Dublin, Jan. 17, 1737-8.

My Dear Old Friend,

I have for almost three years past being only the shadow of my former self, with years and sickness, and rage against all public proceedings, especially in this miserable oppressed country. I have entirely lost my memory, except when it is roused by perpetual subjects of vexation. Mr Richardson, who is your manager in your society of Londonderry, tells me he hears you are in tolerable

health and good spirits.   I lately saw him, and he
said he intended soon to wait on you in London.
He is a gentleman of very good abilities, and a
member of parliament here.   He comes often to
town, and then I never fail of seeing him at the
deanery, where we constantly drink your health.
I have not been out of doors, farther than my garden, for several months, and, unless the summer
will assist me, I believe there will be the end of
my travels.   Our friend Lewis has writ to me once
or twice, and makes the same complaint that I do,
so that you are the heartiest person of the three.
I luckily call to mind an affair that many of my
friends have pressed me to.   There is a church living in your gift, and upon your society lands, which
is now possessed by one Doctor Squire, who is so
decayed that he cannot possibly live a month.   This
living, I am told, is about 120l. or something more,
a-year ; I remember I got it for him by the assistance of Sir William Withers and you ; and since it
is now likely to be so soon vacant, I insist upon it,
that if Doctor Squire dies, you will bestow it to Mr
William Dunkin, a clergyman, upon whose character I have lately taken him into my favour.   He is
a gentleman of much wit, and the best English, as
well as Latin, poet in this kingdom : he has 100l. a
year from our university, to be continued till he is
provided for.   He is a pious, regular man, highly
esteemed ; but our bishops, like yours, have little
regard for such accomplishments, while they have
any dunces of nephews or cousins.   I therefore charge
you to use your influence and authority that Mr
Dunkin may have this church living upon the decease of Doctor Squire ; because you know that my
talent was a little (or rather too much) turned to
poetry ; but he is wiser than I, because he writes

no satires, whereby you know well enough how
many great people I disobliged, and suffered by an-
gering great people in favour.   Farewell, my dear
friend of near thirty years standing.   How many
friends have we lost since our acquaintance began!
I desire you will present my most humble service
and respect to my Lord and Lady Oxford.   I am
ever, with great affection and esteem, dear Sir,
        Your most obedient humble servant,
                            JON. SWIFT.

My kind love and service to Mr Pope when you
    see him, and to my old true friend, and yours, Mr
    Lewis.
To show my memory gone, I wrote this letter a
    week ago, and thought it was sent, till I found it
    this morning, which is Jan. 28, 1737-8.

———————

TO MISS RICHARDSON.

January 28, 1737-8.

MADAM,
    I MUST begin my correspondence by letting you
know that your uncle is the most unreasonable person I was ever acquainted with; and next to him,
you are the second, although I think impartially that
you are worse than he.   I never had the honour and
happiness of seeing you; nor can ever expect it, unless you make the first advance by coming up to
town, where I am confined by want of health; and
my travelling days are over.   I find you follow your
uncle's steps, by maliciously bribing a useless man,
who can never have it in his power to serve or divert

you. I have indeed continued a very long friendship with Alderman Barber, who is governor of the London society about your parts: whereon Mr Richardson * came to the deanery, although it was not in my power to do him the least good office, farther than writing to the alderman. However, your uncle came to me several times: and, I believe after several invitations, dined with me once or twice. This was all the provocation I ever gave him; but he had revenge in his breast, and you shall hear how he gratified it. First, he was told, " That my ill stomach, and a giddiness I was subject to, forced me, in some of those fits, to take a spoonful of usquebaugh:" he discovered where I bought it, and sent me a dozen bottles, which cost him three pounds. He next was told, " That as I never drank malt liquors, so I was not able to drink Dublin claret without mixing it with a little sweet Spanish wine:" he found out the merchant with whom I deal, by the treachery of my butler, and sent me twelve dozen pints of that wine, for which he paid six pounds. But what can I say of a man, who, some years before I ever saw him, was loading me every season with salmons, that surfeited myself and all my visitors; whereby it is plain that his malice reached to all my friends as well as myself? At last, to complete his ill designs, he must needs force his niece into the plot; because it can be proved that you are his prime minister, and so ready to encourage him in his bad proceedings; that you have been his partaker and second in mischief, by sending me half a dozen of shirts, although I never once gave you the least cause of displeasure. And what is worse, the few ladies that come to the dean-

---

* Of Kilmacduac.—F.

ery assure me, they never saw so fine linen, or better worked up, or more exactly fitted. It is a happiness they were not stockings, for then you would have known the length of my foot. Upon the whole, Madam, I must deal so plainly as to repeat, that you are more cruel even than your uncle; to such a degree, that if my health and a good summer can put it in my power to travel to Summer-Seat, I must take that journey on purpose to expostulate with you for all the unprovoked injuries you have done me. I have seen some persons who live in your neighbourhood, from whom I have inquired into your character; but I found you had bribed them all, by never sending them any such dangerous presents; for they swore to me, " That you were a lady adorned with all perfections, such as virtue, prudence, wit, humour, excellent conversation, and even good housewifery;" which last is seldom the talent of ladies in this kingdom. But I take so ill your manner of treating me, that I shall not believe one syllable of what they said, until I have it by letter under your own hand. Our common run of ladies here dare not read before a man, and much less dare to write, for fear (as their expression is) of being exposed. So that when I see any of your sex, if they be worth mending, I beat them all, call them names, until they leave off their follies, and ask pardon. And therefore, because princes are said to have long hands, I wish I were a prince with hands long enough to beat you at this distance, for all your faults, particularly your ill treatment of me. However, I will conclude with charity. May you never give me cause to change, in any single article, the opinion and idea I have of your person and qualities! may you ever long continue the delight of your uncle, and your neighbours round, who deserve your good will, and of all who have merit enough to distinguish you !

I am, with great respect and the highest esteem, Madam,

> Your most obedient and
> most obliged humble servant,
>   JON. SWIFT.

FROM THE EARL OF ORRERY TO MRS WHITEWAY.

Duke Street, Westminster, Feb. 14, 1737-8.

MADAM,

I MUST answer a letter I never received. The Dean tells me you wrote to me ; but the seas, or the postmasters, are in possession of the manuscript. Should it fall into Curll's hands, it may come into print, and then I must answer it in print, which will give me a happy opportunity of letting the world know how much I am your admirer and servant.

I agree entirely with the person who writes three or four paragraphs in the Dean's letter. Humour and wit are, like gold and silver, in great plenty in Ireland ; nor is there any body that wants either but that abominable Dean, the bane of all learning, sense, and virtue. I wish we had him here to punish him for his various offences, particularly for his abhorrence of the dear dear fashions of this polite age. Pray, Madam, send him, and you will hear what a simple figure he will make among the great men of our island, who are every day improving themselves in all valuable qualities and noble principles.

I rejoice to hear your fair daughter is in health. I am, to her and you, a most obedient humble servant,

ORRERY.

FROM CHEVALIER RAMSAY.

At Paris, Feb. 20, 1737-8.

I SEND you here enclosed the bill of loading for the small box of books I wrote of to you some time ago. I shall be glad to hear you received them, much more to know if the perusal pleased you: No man having a higher idea of your talents, genius, and capacity, than he, who is, with great respect, reverend Sir,

Your most humble and
most obedient servant,

A. RAMSAY.

FROM MISS RICHARDSON. *

Summer-Seat, February 23, 1737-8.

SIR,

I WAS favoured some time ago with your most obliging letter, wherein you are pleased to say so many civil things to me, that I have been altogether at a loss how to make proper acknowledgments for the honour you have done me. The commendations you are so good as to bestow upon me, would

---

* Afterward Mrs Pratt.

make my vanity insufferable to my neighbours, if I were not conscious that I do not deserve them; and although I shall always account it a great unhappiness to me that I never have been in your company, yet this advantage I have from it, that my faults are unknown to you. If I have any thing commendable about me, I sincerely own myself indebted to you for it, having endeavoured as much as I could to model myself by the useful instructions that are to be gathered from your works; for which my sex in general (although I believe some of them do not think so) is highly obliged to you. The opinion you are pleased to entertain of me, I fancy is owing to my uncle's partiality, who has frequently been so kind as to take pains to make persons unacquainted with me think better of me than afterward they found I deserved. I have great reason to complain of his treatment in this particular; but in all others I have met with so much kindness from him, that I must think it my duty to lay hold of every opportunity that falls in my way to oblige him. Sir, you have it in your power to give me one, by making him a visit at Summer-Seat, where all the skill I have in housekeeping should be employed to have every thing in that manner that would be most pleasing to you, which I know is the most agreeable service I could do for him. You are pleased to wish in your letter that you had hands long enough to beat me. What an honour and happines would I esteem it, to be thought worthy of your correction? But I fear you would find my faults so numerous, that you would think me one of those ladies that do not deserve to be mended.

Your letter would have given me the greatest pleasure of any thing I have ever met with, had it not been for the complaints you make of your health,

which give me a most sensible concern, as they
ought to do every body that has any regard for this
kingdom. I hope the good weather will set you
right, and that the summer will induce you to visit
this northern part of the world. I fear I have by
this time tired out your patience with female impertinence, and given you too great reason to change
the favourable thoughts you did me the honour to
entertain of me; I will forbear to be longer troublesome to you, only I beg leave to add my best wishes
for your good health, that you may live many years
to be a blessing to mankind in general, and this
country in particular. I am, with the highest esteem,
and greatest respect, Sir, your most obedient and
most humble servant,

KATH. RICHARDSON.

TO MR FAULKNER.

March 8, 1737-8.

SIR,

SOME of my friends wonder very much at your
delaying to publish that treatise of Polite Conversation, &c. when you so often desired that I should
hasten to correct the several copies you sent me ;
which, as ill as I have been, and am still, I dispatched as fast as I got them. I expect you would
finish it immediately, and send it to me ; I hope
you have observed all the corrections. I hear you
have not above four or five pages remaining. I find
people think you are too negligent ; and, if you delay longer, what you fear may come to pass, that

the English edition may come over before you have your own ready.

I am your humble servant,

JON. SWIFT.

TO MR ALDERMAN BARBER.

Dublin, March 9, 1737-8.

MY DEAR AND CONSTANT FRIEND,

I RECEIVED yours of February 11th, and find, with great pleasure, that we preserve the same mutual affection we ever professed, as well as the same principles in church and state.   As to what you hint, as if I were not cautious enough in making recommendations, you know I have conversed too long with ministers to offend upon that article, which I never did but once, and that when I was a beginner.   You may remember that, on Mr Addison's desire, I applied to my Lord Treasurer Oxford in favour of Mr Steele, and his lordship gave me a gentle rebuke, which cured me for ever; although I got many employments for my friends, where no objection could be made, yet I confess, that Doctor Delany, the most eminent preacher we have, is a very unlucky recommender; for he forced me to countenance Pilkington; introduced him to me, and praised the wit, virtue, and humour of him and his wife: whereas he proved the falsest rogue, and she the most profligate whore in either kingdom. *   She was taken in the fact by her own hus-

---

* It must be remembered that Barber, during his mayoralty, had made Pilkington his chaplain upon Swift's recommendation.

band: he is now suing for a divorce, and will not compass it; she is suing for a maintenance, and he has none to give her. As to Mr Richardson, his father was a gentleman, and his eldest brother is a dean. Their father had but a small fortune; your manager was the younger son; he has an excellent understanding in business, with some share of learning; his prudence obliges him to keep fair with all parties, which, in this kingdom, is necessary for one who has to deal with numbers, as the business of your society requires. It is his interest to deal justly with your corporation, because people who envy his employment, would be ready enough to complain; and yet although he has a good estate, I have not heard him taxed with any unjust means in procuring it. He is a bachelor like you and me, and lives with a maiden niece, who is a young woman of very good sense and discretion. He is a member of the House of Commons, and acts as smoothly there as he does in the country. I am so long upon this, because I believe it will give you a true notion of the man; and if you find, by his management, that he gives you, who are the governor, any cause of complaint, let me know the particulars, which I will farther inquire into. I must next say something of Mr Dunkin. I told you he was a man of genius, and the best poet we have, and, you know, that is a trade wherein I have meddled too much for my quiet, as well as my fortune; but I find it generally agreed that he is a thorough churchman in all regards. His aunt, to whom he was legal heir, bequeathed her whole estate to his university, only leaving him an allowance of 70l. per annum, to support him till he was better provided for; but I prevailed on the provost and fellows to make it 100l. a-year. Yesterday I sent for Mr Dunkin, and catechised him strictly on his principles, and was fully satisfied in them by himself, as I was before by many of his friends; therefore I insist that you shall think of nobody else, much less of Mr Lloyd, who is not to be compared in any one view. Doctor Squire may linger out for some time, as consumptive people happen to do, but is past hopes of recovery. My dear friend, I cannot struggle with disorders so well as you; for, as I am older, my deafness is very vexatious, and my memory almost entirely gone, except what I retain of former times and friends; beside frequent returns of that cruel giddiness which you have seen me under, although not as yet with so much violence. You, God be praised, keep your memory and hearing, and your health is much better than mine, beside the assistance of much abler physicians. If you know Doctor Mead, pray present him with my most humble service and grateful acknowledgments of his favours. Dear Mr Alderman, why do you make excuses for writing long letters? I know nobody who writes better, or with more spirit, with your memory as entire as a young man of wit and humour. I repeat that you present my most humble service to my Lord and Lady Oxford, and my old friend Mr Lewis. What is become of Mr Ford? Is he alive? I never hear from him. We thank your good city for the present it sent us of a brace of monsters, called blasters, or blasphemers, or bacchanalians (as they are here called in print), whereof Wotsdail the painter, and one Lints (a painter too, as I hear), are the leaders. Pray God bless you my dear friend, and let us have a correspondence as long as I live. I am ever,

Most dear Sir,

Your constant esteemer, and

most obedient humble servant,

JON. SWIFT.

I have five old small silver medals of Cæsar's, very plain, with the inscription : they were found in an old churchyard. Would my Lord Oxford think them worth taking.

FROM MR ALDERMAN BARBER.

London, March 13, 1737-8.

MOST DEAR AND HONOURED FRIEND,

It was with great pleasure I received yours of the 9th of March, with the state of your health, which was the more agreeable, as it contradicted the various reports we had of you ; for you remember that our newspapers take the privilege of killing all persons they do not like as often as they please. I have had the honour to be decently interred about six times in their weekly memoirs, which I have always read with great satisfaction.

I am very well satisfied with your character of Mr Dunkin, and desire that he would immediately draw up a petition in form, directed to the governor, &c. which petition I desire that you only would underwrite, with your recommendation, and a character of him, which you will please to send to me, to be made use of at my discretion. He need not come over, but inform me, as soon as possible, of Dr Squire's death.

I have made your compliments to Lord and Lady Oxford, who are both well, and rejoiced to hear of your health. They give you their thanks for your remembrance, and are your faithful friends.

His lordship is very well pleased with your present of the medals, and desires you would send them by the first safe hand that comes over. Is it not shocking that that noble lord, who has no vices (except buying manuscripts and curiosities may be called so) has not a guinea in his pocket, and is selling a great part of his estate to pay his debts? and that estate of his produces near 20,000l. a-year. I say is it not shocking! But indeed most of our nobility with great estates are in the same way. My Lord Burlington is now selling in one article, 9000l. a-year in Ireland, for 200,000l. which wont pay his debts.

Dr Mead is proud of your compliments, and returns his thanks and service.

Mr Lewis I have not seen, but hear he is pretty well.

Mr Ford, I am told, is the most regular man living; for from his lodgings to the Mall—to the Cocoa—to the tavern—to bed, is his constant course.

These cold winds of late have affected me; but as the warm weather is coming on, I hope to be better than I am, though, I thank God, I am now in better health than I have been in for many years. Among the other blessings I enjoy, I am of a cheerful disposition, and I laugh, and am laughed at in my turn, which helps off the tedious hours.

I hope the spring will have a good effect upon you, and will help your hearing and other infirmities, and that I shall have the pleasure to hear so from your own hand.

You will please to observe that I am proud of every occasion of showing my gratitude to you, Sir, to whom I must ever own the greatest obligations.

Pray God bless you and preserve you, and believe me always, dear Sir, your most faithful and most obedient humble servant,

JOHN BARBER.

FROM DR KING TO MR DEANE SWIFT. *

St Mary Hall, Oxon, March 15, 1737.

SIR,

I DID not receive your letter of the 4th till yesterday. It was sent after me to London, and from thence returned to Oxford.

I am much concerned that I cannot see you before you go to Ireland, because I intended to have sent by you a packet for the Dean. It has been no fault of mine that he has not heard from me. I have written two letters for him (both enclosed to Mrs Whiteway) since I received the manuscript from Lord Orrery. I wrote again to Mrs Whiteway, when I was last week in London, to acquaint her, that I would write to the Dean by a friend of mine, who is going for Ireland in a few days. I do not wonder my letters by the post have been intercepted, since they wholly related to the publication of ———, † which, I am assured, is a matter by no means agreeable to some of our great men, nor indeed to some of the Dean's particular friends in London. In short, I

---

* Then at Monmouth.——D. S.
† Swift's " History of the four last years of the Queen."—D. S.

8

I have been obliged to defer this publication till I can have the Dean's answer to satisfy the objections which have been made by some of his friends.   I had likewise a particular reason of my own for deferring this work a few months which I have acquainted the Dean with.

I must beg the favour of you to leave behind you the copy of the Toast, at least to show it to nobody in Ireland : for as I am upon the point of accommodating my suit, the publication of the book would greatly prejudice my affairs at this juncture. But this is a caution I believe I needed not have given you.

Your friends in the Hall are all well. We are now very full.

Believe me to be, Sir, your most affectionate and most humble servant,

WILLIAM KING.

Notwithstanding your letter, I am still in some hopes of seeing you before you go for Ireland.

TO MR ALDERMAN BARBER.

Dublin, March 31, 1738.

MY DEAR GOOD OLD FRIEND IN THE
    BEST AND WORST TIMES;

MR RICHARDSON is come to town, and stays only for a wind to take shipping for Chester, from whence he will hasten to attend you as his governor in London.   I have told you that he is a very discreet, prudent gentleman, and I believe your society can

never have a better for the station he is in. I shall
see him some time to-day or to-morrow morning,
and shall desire, with all his modesty, that he press
you to write me a long letter, if your health will
permit; which I believe is better than mine, for I
have a constant giddiness in my head, and what is
more vexatious, as constant a deafness. I forget
every thing but old friendship and old opinions. I
did desire you, that you would at your leisure visit
the few friends I have left, I mean those of them
with whom you have any acquaintance, as my Lord
and Lady Oxford, my Lord Bathurst, the Countess of
Granville, my Lord and Lady Carteret, my Lord
Worsley, my dear friend Mr Pope, and Mr Lewis,
who always loved both you and me. My Lord
Masham, and some others, have quite dropped and
forgot me. Is Lord Masham's son good for any
thing? I did never like his disposition or education. Have you quite forgot your frequent promises of coming over hither, and pass a summer in
attending your government in Derry and Colrane,
as well as your visitation at the deanery? the last
must be for half the months of your stay. Let me
know what is become of my Lord Bolingbroke—
how and where he lives, and whether you ever expect he will come home. Here has run about a report, that the Duke of Ormond has an intention,
and some countenance, to come from his banish-
ment, which I would be extremely glad to find confirmed. That glorious exile has suffered more for
his virtues, than ever the greatest villain did from
the cruellest tyrant. I desire and insist that Mr
Dunkin may have the church living upon Doctor
Squire's decease, who I am still assured cannot long
hold out, and I take it for granted that Mr Richardson will have no objection against him. God

preserve and bless you my dear friend. I am ever, with true esteem and friendship,

Your most obedient humble servant,

JON. SWIFT.

FROM MR^e POPE TO THE EARL OF ORRERY.

April 2, 1738.

I WRITE by the same post that I received your very obliging letter. The consideration you show toward me, in the just apprehension that any news of the Dean's condition might alarm me, is most kind and generous. The very last post I writ to him a long letter, little suspecting him in that dangerous circumstance. I was so far from fearing his health, that I was proposing schemes, and hoping possibilities for our meeting once more in this world. I am weary of it; and shall have one reason more, and one of the strongest that nature can give me (even when she is shaking my weak frame to pieces) to be willing to leave this world, when our dear friend is on the edge of the other. Yet I hope, I would fain hope, he may yet hover a while on the brink of it to preserve to this wretched age a relic and example of the last.

FROM MR LEWIS. *

London, April 8, 1738.

I CAN now acquaint you, my dear Dean, that I have at last had the pleasure of reading your History, in the presence of Lord O———d, and two or three more, who think, in all political matters, just as you do, and are as zealous for your fame and safety as any persons in the world. That part of it which relates to the negociations of peace, whether at London or at Utrecht, they admire exceedingly, and declare they never yet saw that, or any other transaction, drawn up with so much perspicuity, or in a style so entertaining and instructive to the reader in every respect ; but I should be wanting to the sincerity of a friend, if I did not tell you plainly, that it was the unanimous opinion of the company, a great deal of the first part should be retrenched, and many things altered.

1st, They conceive the first establishment of the South Sea Company is not rightly stated, † for no part of the debt then unprovided for was paid ; however, the advantages arising to the public were very considerable ; for, instead of paying for all provisions, cent. per cent. dearer than the common market-price, as we did in Lord Godolphin's times, the credit of the public was imme-

---

* This interesting letter, now first published, points out the reasons why the History of the last four years of Queen Anne did not appear during Swift's life, as he at first intended.

† See the History of the four last years of the Queen, Volume V. p. 265.

diately restored ; and, by means of this scheme, put upon as good a footing as the best private security.

2d, They think the transactions with Mr Buys might have been represented in a more advantageous light, and more to the honour of that administration; and, undoubtedly they would have been so by your pen, had you been master of all the facts. *

3d, The D—— of M———'s † courage not to be called in question.

4th, The projected design of an assassination they believe true, but that a matter of so high a nature ought not to be asserted without exhibiting the proofs. ‡

5th, The present ministers. who are the rump of those whose characters you have painted, shew too plainly, that they have not acted upon republican, or, indeed, any other principles than those of interest and ambition.

6th, Now I have mentioned characters, I must tell you they were clearly of opinion, that if those you have drawn should be published as they now stand, nothing could save the author's printer and publishers from some grievous punishment. As we have no traces of liberty now left, but the freedom of the press, it is the most earnest desire of your friends, that you would strike out all that you have said on that subject.

Thus, my dear Dean, I have laid before you, in a plain manner, the sentiments of those who were

---

* See Vol. V. p. 307.

† Something disparaging to the Duke of Marlborough's personal bravery occurs in the History, p. 173.

‡ See the History, p. 199, where Prince Eugene is said to have meditated, or at least recommended some scheme for assassinating Harley.

present when your history was read; if I have mistaken in any thing, I ask pardon of you and them.

I am not at liberty to name those who were present, excepting only the E— of O———d, who has charged me to return you his thanks for what you have said of his father.

What I have to say from myself is, that there were persons in the company to whose judgment I should pay entire deference. I had no opportunity of paying any on this occasion, for I concurred in the same opinion with them, from the bottom of my heart, and therefore conjure you, as you value your own fame as an author, and the honour of those who were actors in the important affairs that make the subject of your history, and as you would preserve the liberty of your person, and enjoyment of your fortune, you will not suffer this work to go to the press, without making some, or all the amendments proposed. I am, my dear Dean, most sincerely and affectionately yours.

E. L.

I thank you for your kind mention of me in your letter to Lord Oxford.

I had almost forgot to tell you, you have mistaken the case of the D— of S———, which, in truth, was this, that his grace, appearing at court, in the chamber next to the Council-chamber, it was apprehended he would come into the cabinet council, and therefore the intended meeting was put off; whereas one would judge, by your manner of stating it, that the council had met, and adjourned abruptly upon his taking his place there. *

---

* See page 183 of the History, Vol. V. From the various suggestions in this letter producing none of the alterations recom-

I must add, that if you would so far yield to the opinion of your friends, as to publish what you have writ concerning the peace, and leave out every thing that savours of acrimony and resentment, it would, even now, be of great service to this nation in general, and to them in particular, nothing having been yet published on the peace of Utrecht, in such a beautiful and strong manner as you have done it. Once more, my dear Dean, adieu, let me hear from you.

FROM MR MACAULAY.*

April 13, 1738.

REV. SIR,

I HAVE received your letter of this date, and will wait upon you to-morrow morning. I am extremely sorry to find you meet with any thing that affects or perplexes you. I hope I shall never be guilty of such black ingratitude as to admit any

---

mended, it may be concluded that Swift's health was unequal to the task of revising his historical work. The letter is indorsed in the Dean's hand-writing, " Mr Lewis on some mistakes in the History of Four last Years."

* Author of " a Treatise on Tillage," and of a pamphlet in favour of the tithes of the clergy, called, " Property inviolable." To this pamphlet the Dean alludes in the clause of his will, where he leaves Mr Macaulay " the gold box in which the freedom of Dublin was presented to me, as a testimony of the esteem and love I have for him, on account of his great learning, fine natural parts, unaffected piety and benevolence, and his truly honourable zeal in defence of the legal rights of the clergy, in opposition to all their unprovoked oppression."

opportunity of doing you every good office in my power.

I am, with the greatest esteem and gratitude, Rev. Sir, your most obliged and most obedient servant,
ALEXANDER M'AULAY.

DR KING TO MR DEANE SWIFT.

St Mary Hill, Oxon, April 25, 1738.

DEAR SIR,

I HAVE just received your letter by Mr Birt, for which I thank you. It is now more than a month since I wrote to Mrs Whiteway, to acquaint the Dean with the difficulties I met with in regard to the publication of his history, and to desire his advice and directions in what manner I should proceed. I have not yet had any answer; and till I receive one, I can do nothing more. I may probably hear from Ireland before you leave Monmouth; in which case I may trouble you with a packet.

I am pretty much of your opinion about the old poets, and perhaps may confirm you in your whimsies (as you call them) when I have the pleasure of seeing you here again. I heartily wish you a good journey and voyage: but methinks I can hardly excuse you for having been so long absent from us. I wish you had returned to this place, though for one week; because I might have talked over with you all the affair of the history, about which I have been much condemned: and no wonder, since the Dean has continually expressed his dissatisfaction that I have so long delayed the publication of it. However, I have been in no fault: on the contrary, I have consulted the Dean's honour, and the safety of his person. In a word, the publication of this work, as excellent as it is, would involve the printer, publisher, author, and every one concerned, in the greatest difficulties, if not in a certain ruin; and therefore it will be absolutely necessary to omit some of the characters.

I thank you for the promise you make me concerning The Toast.

Your friends here are all well. Believe me, dear Sir, your most obedient humble servant,

WILLIAM KING.

FROM MISS RICHARDSON TO MRS WHITEWAY.

Belturbet, May 6, 1738.

DEAR MADAM,

I RECEIVED the favour of your letter last post. I was deprived of having that pleasure sooner by removing from Summer-seat to this place, the beginning of last month, where I was sent for by my father, to attend him in a fit of the gout, of which he has been very ill these three months past. My sister, who takes care of him and his family, being near the time of her lying-in, I trouble you with this account, that you may know how I am engaged at present, which I fear will prevent me having an opportunity of waiting upon you before my uncle returns.

I most humbly thank you for your kind invitation, and do heartily wish it were any way in my power to let you know the grateful sense I have of my obligations to you. I hope the Dean of St Patrick's is very well: it would have given me infinite plea-

sure to have had the honour of being in his company with you.

When I parted with my uncle, he proposed to
make but a short stay in England at this time ; and
at his return, he intended to leave nothing undone
that he could think of, to prevail with the Dean and
you to spend some time at his house this summer. I
hope you will be so good as to give him all the assistance you can, to persuade the Dean to take that
jaunt: I really believe it would do him great service as to his health: I please myself greatly with
the thoughts of having you there, and your daughter, whom I believe to be a very accomplished
young lady, having had the happiness to be educat-
ed under your direction.   I beg you will make my
compliments to her ; and be assured that I am, with
great respect, Madam, your most obedient and most
humble servant,

KATH. RICHARDSON.

TO MISS HAMILTON * OF CALEDON.

Deanery-House, Dublin, June 8, 1738.

MADAM,

SOME days ago, my Lord Orrery had the assurance
to show me a letter of yours to him, where you did

---

* Miss Hamilton of Caledon in the county of Tyrone, a great
heiress in her own right, with every virtue and accomplishment to
adorn her sex.—F.   So far Mr Faulkner, who, perhaps, thought
that the second part of Miss Hamilton's character was a necessary consequence of the first.   She married Lord Orrery shortly
afterwards.

me the honour to say many things in my favour; I read the letter with great delight; but at the same time I reproached his lordship for his presumption, in pretending to take a lady from me, who had made so many advances, and confessed herself to be nobody's goddess but mine. However, he had the boldness to assure me, that he had your consent to take him for a husband. I therefore command you never to accept him, without my leave, under my own hand and seal. And as I do not know any lady in this kingdom of so good sense, or so many accomplishments, I have at last, with a heavy heart, permitted him to make himself the happiest man in the world; for I know no fault in him, except his treacherous dealing with me.

Pray God make you happy in yourselves, and each other; and believe me to be, with the truest esteem and respect,

Madam,

Your most obedient and obliged servant,

Jon. Swift.

I have neither mourning paper nor gilt at this time; and if I had, I could not tell which I ought to choose.

FROM THE EARL OF ORRERY.

June 13, 1738.

Dear Sir,

I am engaged to-morrow at dinner; but I will try to put it off, and send you word in the morning whether I can meet Mrs Whiteway or not. To

show you what a generous rival I am (now I am sure
of the lady) I should be glad to carry down a letter
from you to my mistress on Friday. She never
drinks any wine: but she told me the other day, to
do you good, she would drink a bottle. I wish you
would insist on it, that I might see whether wine
would alter the sweetness of her temper, for I am
sure nothing else can.

I rejoice to find there is some little amendment in
your health, and I pray God to increase it.

FROM THE SAME.

June 29, 1738.

DEAR SIR,

I HAVE but this paper left, and how can I employ it better than in triumphing over my rival.
Mea est Lavinia conjux. To-morrow Miss Hamilton gives me her heart and hand for ever. Do I
live to see the day when toupets, coxcomical lords,
powdered squires, and awkward beaux, join with
the Dean of St Patrick's in loss of one and the same
object? My happiness is too great, and in pity to
you I will add no more than that I hope to see grief
for this loss strongly wrote in your face even twenty
years hence. Adieu, your generous rival,

ORRERY.

FROM MR ALDERMAN BARBER.

London, July 2, 1738.

MOST HONOURED AND WORTHY SIR,

I HAVE deferred answering the favours of yours of the 9th and 31st of March, in hopes to have something to entertain you with, and I have succeeded in my wishes; for I am sure I give you great pleasure when I tell you the enclosed I received from the hands of my Lord Bolingbroke and Mr Pope, your dearest friends. My lord has been here a few days, and is come to sell Dawley, to pay his debts; and he will return to France, where, I am told, he is writing the History of his own Times; which I heartily rejoice at, (though I am not likely to live to see it published) because so able a hand can do nothing but what must be instructive and entertaining to the next generation. His lordship is fat and fair, in high spirits; but joins with you, and all good men, to lament our present unhappy situation. Mr Pope has a cold, and complains, but he is very well; so well, that he throws out a twelve-penny touch in a week or ten days, with as much ease as a friend of ours formerly used to toast the enemies of their country.

The report of the Duke of Ormond's return is without foundation. His grace is very well in health and lives in a very handsome manner, and has Mr Kelly with him as his chaplain, the gentleman who escaped out of the Tower. A worthy friend of yours and mine passed through Avignon about a month since, and dined with his grace, from whom I have what I tell you.

I hear nothing of Dr Squire's departure: I believe I may say that matter is secured for Mr Dunkin.

I have seen Lord and Lady Oxford, who make you their compliments. He thanks you for your medals. I believe I told you he is selling Wimple, to pay off a debt of 100,000l. That a man without any vice, should run out such a sum, is monstrous. It must be owing to the roguery of his stewards, and his indolency, which is vice enough.

Lord Bathurst is heartily yours; so is Mr Lewis, who wears apace, and the more (would you believe it?) since the loss of his wife.

I do not see Lord —— in an age; his son is married, and proves bad enough; ill-natured and proud, and very little in him. Our friend Ford lives in the same way, as constant as the sun, from the Cocoa tree to the park, to the tavern, to bed, &c.

So far in the historical way, to obey your several commands. You will now give me leave to hope this will find you free from all your complaints, and that I shall have the great pleasure of seeing it very quickly under your own hand. I thank God, I am better than I have been many years, but yet have many complaints; for my asthma sticks close by me, but less gout than formerly, so that though I cannot walk far I ride daily, and eat and drink heartily at noon; and impute my being so much better to my drinking constantly the asses' milk, which is the best specific we have. I wish to God you would try it, I am sure it would do you much good. I take it betimes in the morning, which certainly gives me a little sleep, and often a small breathing or sweat.

If Mr Richardson has not made you his acknowledgments for your great favour and friendship to him, he is much to blame; for to you he owes the continuance of his employment. An alderman of Derry came from thence on purpose to attach him, and he had many articles of impeachment; and I believe he had twenty out of twenty-four of our society against him: and the cry has been against him for two or three years past, and I had no way to save him many times, but only by saying, that while I had the honour to preside in that chair, I would preserve the great privilege every Englishman had, of being heard before he was condemned; and I never put any question against him while he was in Ireland. Well, he came, and after a long and tedious hearing of both sides, the society were of opinion, that he had acted justly and honourably in his office.

I do not deal in politics; I have left them off a long while, only we talk much of war, which I do not believe a word on. A fair lady in Germany * has put the king in a good humour they say.

I shall trouble you no more at present, but to assure you I never think of you but with the utmost pleasure, and drink your health daily, and heartily pray for your long, long life, as you are an honour to your country, and will be the glory of the present and succeeding ages.

I am, dear Sir, your most affectionate humble servant,

J. BARBER.

---

* Amelia Sophia von Walmoden, Countess of Yarmouth.—H.

TO MR FAULKNER.

Thursday, July 13, 1738.

SIR,

I DESIRE you will print the following paper, in what manner you think most proper. You see my design in it: I believe no man had ever more difficulty, or less encouragement, to bestow his whole fortune for a charitable use.

I am your humble servant,

JON. SWIFT.

IT is known enough, that the above-named doctor has, by his last will and testament, bequeathed his whole fortune (except some legacies) to build and endow an hospital, in or near this city, for the support of lunatics, ideots, and those they call incurables: But the difficulty he lies under is, that his whole fortune consists in mortgages on lands, and other the like securities; for, as to purchasing a real estate in lands, for want of active friends, he finds it impossible; so that, much against his will, if he should call in all his money lent, he knows not where to find a convenient estate in a tolerable part of the kingdom, which can be bought; and in the mean time, his whole fortune must lie dead in the hands of bankers. The great misfortune is, that there seems not so much public virtue left among us, as to have any regard for a charitable design; because none but the aforesaid unfortunate objects of charity will be the better for it: However, the said doctor, by calling in the several sums he has lent, can be able, with some difficulty, to purchase three hundred pounds *per annum* in lands for the endowment of the said hospital, if those lands could be now purchased; otherwise he must leave it, as he has done in his will, to the care of his executors, who are very honest, wise, and considerable gentlemen, his friends; and yet he has known some of very fair and deserved credit, prove very negligent trustees. The doctor is now able to lend two thousand pounds, at five *per cent.* upon good security; of which the principal, after his decease, is to be disposed of, by his executors, in buying lands for the farther endowment of the said hospital.

———

[In this place, as referring to the Dean's anxiety to purchase land, and to the difficulties which occurred to prevent him from carrying his intentions into execution, the editor inserts the following four letters; addressed on the subject to Mr Gerrard of Gibstown, near Navan, in the county of Meath. This correspondence, transcribed from the original letters, in the possession of the Gerrard family, by my friend Mr Hartstongue, did not reach me in time to be inserted according to the dates.]

———

TO MR SAMUEL GERRARD,

AT GIBSTOWN, NEAR NAVAN, COUNTY OF MEATH.

Dublin, April 7, 1733.

SIR,

I HEARTILY thank you for you kind remembrance of me in relation to a purchase. But there is one Mr Swift, a relation of mine, whose estate is engaged to me for 2000l. and with whom I am at last

come to a bargain to purchase 150l. per annum, for
which I must, I fear, borrow some money; and,
indeed, as to your proposal, I should never agree to
it, from a maxim that is not much thought of.   I
intend to leave my whole fortune to a public use:
in which case, I take perpetuities to be the most
pernicious, because you are bound for ever to a
certain denomination of money, which is of so uncertain a value in all times; occasioned by the increase of silver and gold, and consequently the decrease of both in value.   By not observing this
caution, most corporations have extremely suffered
by granting perpetuities.   And so the value of
money must decrease in Ireland, let us grow ever
so poor; for we must value money by the standard
of Europe, and not by our own scarcity.   I have
formerly considered this matter, and printed my
thoughts of it; yet I am much obliged to you for
your good intentions.   I am,

> With great truth, Sir,
> Your most obedient servant,
> J. SWIFT.

I go down on Monday to Castle * * * *,* within
four miles of Trim, to see the land surveyed, and
shall return on Thursday following.   The land
belongs to one Deane Swift, Esq. a relation of mine.
I pay 7s. 6d. an acre, which I believe is too dear,
but I am content to pay somewhat too much out
of pity to the difficulties he is under.   I had what
advice I could get from Mr Lightburn of Trim,
and my proctor at Laracor, who said it might be

---

* The ink had here so disappeared from the paper, that the
name of the place could not be ascertained.

worth 7s. per acre round; in that case I pay but 10l. per annum too much. But I wish I may not pay too much by a shilling, which, in 400 acres, will make a difference of 400l. at 20 years purchase.

I wish you had been my adviser.

TO THE SAME,

AT GIBSTOWN, TO BE LEFT AT THE POST-HOUSE IN NAVAN.

Dublin, Feb. 6, 1734-5.

Sir,

I AM very much obliged by your kind endeavours to help me to a purchase of lands, for indeed I am the most helpless man alive in such affairs. My manner of life hath quite estranged me, not knowing how to deal with the cunning of mankind; and my health is so very uncertain, that I dare not venture ten miles from town. I find that Mr Garstin values his land at 10s. an acre, and yet expects to sell it at 24 years purchase. And what friend have I who is able and willing to make the bargain, and inquire into the title, and forty other circumstances. All I am worth, except about 1500l. is out in mortgages; and I cannot command a penny of it, nor get any interest. And the 1500l. I have at the bankers, I am about lending to another person on a mortgage. Yet if I could be tolerably used for the land you mention, I would borrow as much as would make it 2000l. But I look on you as too honest to understand the arts of purchasers or sellers. The neighbouring squires, if they have money, are only proper for such jobs, and if they have none, will all join to cheat a stranger: I have long wished that some skilful man would take me into guardianship.

If I had Mr Garstin's land at 20 years purchase, I would sink the rent to 2s. an acre, and rather have 80l. per annum, well paid, than 100l. upon the rack, and so I should pay 24 years purchase. Your justice and good-will I entirely rely on; and if you had a skilful notable friend, upon whom you could equally rely, something might be done. Mr Swift's land you thought not worth 6s. per acre; this of Mr Garstin's, farther from Dublin, is valued at ten, and 24 years purchase, and the title unknown to me. If the price could be fixed, it would be no difficulty to consult lawyers upon the title. My head is ill, and you may perceive it by my way of writing; and please to excuse it.

I am, with true esteem,
Your most obedient servant,
J. SWIFT.

TO THE SAME,

TO BE LEFT AT THE POST-HOUSE AT NAVAN, COUNTY OF MEATH.

SIR,

As I always conceived a very good opinion of your honour and justice, as well as your good sense, I am more inclined to rely upon them all, than our time of acquaintance usually produceth. What I want is not to be dealt favourably with, but to be safe: I suppose Mr Garstin will enter into all measures to make his title appear good to my lawyers, and then I will readily agree to buy his land at the price you advise me; but if I set to *cant* with Alderman Quail, he is too cunning a man for me to contend with; and if Mr Garstin were my brother, should not advise him to deal with such a *brangling* man, to say no worse of him. However, Mr Garstin's business is to sell as dear as he can; and the money, wheresoever it comes, is the same thing to him. I must borrow 5 or 600l. to make up the sum, which I believe I can do. I am afraid, if the business goes on, I shall desire you to come to town with Mr Garstin, for I neither can, nor will do any thing without you, who are as necessary as my lawyer. Please to answer this letter; and believe me to be,

Your most obedient, &c.

J. SWIFT.

Feb. 11, 1734-5.

I must tell you in confidence, that Mr Garstin's conduct has been much censured. He is said to have been a very ill tenant; he never paid his rents, but till he ran to an ejectment, and hath by extravagance put himself under a necessity of selling this estate. This I have been assured of from some of his neighbours, who have no design to purchase his lands. The characters of men are of great importance to be known on these occasions.

TO THE SAME,

AT GIBSTOWN, IN THE COUNTY OF MEATH, NEAR
NAVAN.

Feb. 20, 1734.

SIR,

I BEG ten thousand pardons for the trouble I have given you. Mr Garstin lies under so ill a character, that I was advised not to deal with him. And, in short, I find such a difficulty in purchasing land, that I resolve not to meddle with it, but leave that trouble to my executors. I find the neighbouring gentlemen, whose land is to be sold, are continually watching like crows over a dead horse ; and we at a distance know not how to deal among them. I have been near 20 years endeavouring to be a purchaser, and have always been baulked, or tried to be cheated. I am much obliged to you for your endeavours, and have not a better opinion of any other man's or gentleman's honesty. I have lately disposed of all my money, no less than 1500l., at interest, at L. 5, 6s. 8d. interest per hundred, which will yield me 80l. per annum. It is to the son-in-law of a friend, who hath a good fortune, and I think it safe. I hope I shall soon see you in town : you slipt out of my hands last time ; but I expect you to be my sojourner whenever you come, when I will tell you the whole scheme of an hospital for lunatics and ideots, a charity I find it the hardest point to settle well. I will never leave any thing to any other use ; I will leave the whole to God's providence how it will be disposed of, who will forgive me if my good intentions miscarry.

I am, Sir, with great esteem and truth, Sir, your most obedient humble servant,

JON. SWIFT.

FROM MR RICHARDSON.

July 25, 1738.

THERE are but very few things would give me a greater concern than the Dean of St Patrick's becoming indifferent toward me ; and yet I fear one of those few things is the cause I have not had a line from you since I came hither.   I beseech you ease me of my present pain, by telling me that you are well ; that summer, which hath but lately reached us here, hath invited you, and tempted you to ride again.

If any thing occurs to you I can do, that is agreeable to you, if you have the least inclination to oblige me, let me know of it.

My hurry here is almost over ; but one affair or other will detain me till the latter end of October, if I get away then.   I cannot say I pass my time disagreeably.   I have had some opportunities of doing good offices ; and, when I am not engaged by business, I live with a few friends that I love, and love me, and, for the most part, go every week with one of them to the country for two or three days.

Your friend Bolingbroke is well, and at present with Mr Pope.   I am told he has sold Dawley. Alderman Barber, who has promised me to write to you by the next post, tells me his lordship inquired much about you and your health.   The alderman plays his cards so as that his credit in the city daily increases.   There is nothing but the vacancy wanted to put Mr Dunkin in possession of the parish of Colrane.

I hear you have seen Pope's " First Dialogue,

1738." Have you seen his "Universal Prayer?" This "Second Dialogue," together with the copy of the inscription intended by the old Duchess of Marlborough for a statue she is to erect of Queen Anne, and a few lines attributed to Lord Chesterfield, on another subject, wait on you enclosed.

Believe that I love as much as I admire you; and that I am, with the most perfect respect, dear Sir, your most obliged and most truly faithful servant,

WILLIAM RICHARDSON.

This packet goes franked by the secretary of the foreign office, who can frank any weight.

I expect the prime serjeant * here this night in his way to France.

LORD GOWER TO A FRIEND OF DEAN SWIFT.

Trentham, Aug. 1, 1738.

SIR,

MR SAMUEL JOHNSON, (author of London, a Satire, and some other poetical pieces) is a native of this country, and much respected by some worthy gentlemen in this neighbourhood, who are trustees of a charity-school † now vacant; the certain salary

---

* Henry Singleton. Esq. whom Dr Swift appointed one of his executors. He was afterwards lord chief-justice of the common pleas, which he resigned upon a pension; and was appointed master of the rolls in Ireland.—D. S.

† Appleby, in Leicestershire. See Boswell's Life of Johnson, 1799, Vol. I. p. 103.

is 60l. a-year, of which they are desirous to make
him master; but, unfortunately, he is not capable
of receiving their bounty, which *would make him
happy for life*, by not being a *Master of Arts;* which,
by the statutes of the school, the master of it must be.

Now these gentlemen do me the honour to think
that I have interest enough in you, to prevail upon
you to write to Dean Swift, to persuade the university of Dublin to send a diploma to me, constitut-
ing this poor man Master of Arts in their University. They highly extol the man's learning and
probity; and will not be persuaded that the university will make any difficulty of conferring such
a favour upon a stranger, if he is recommended by
the Dean. They say he is not afraid of the strictest
examination, though he is of so long a journey;
and will venture it, if the Dean thinks it necessary;
choosing rather to die upon the road, *than be starved
to death in translating for booksellers*, which has
been his only subsistence for some time past.

I fear there is more difficulty in this affair, than
these good-natured gentlemen apprehend; especially as their election cannot be delayed longer than
the 11th of next month. If you see this matter in
the same light as it appears to me, I hope you will
burn this, and pardon me for giving you so much
trouble about an impracticable thing; but, if you
think there is a probability of obtaining the favour
asked, I am sure your humanity, and propensity to
relieve merit in distress, will incline you to serve
the poor man, without my adding more to the
trouble I have already given you, than assuring you
that I am, with great truth, Sir,

Your faithful servant,

GOWER.

TO MR RICHARDSON.

Aug. 5, 1735.

Sir,

It was not my want of friendship and esteem that hindered me from answering your several letters, but merely my disorders in point of health ; for I am constantly giddy, and so deaf, that your friend Mrs Whiteway has almost got into a consumption by bawling in my ears. I heartily congratulate with you on your triumph over your Irish enemies by a *nemine contradicente.*   I leave the rest of this paper to be filled by Mrs Whiteway ; and am, with true esteem and gratitude, your most obedient and obliged servant,

Jon. Swift.

Pray tell my dear friend the alderman, that I love him most sincerely ; but my ill health and worse memory will not suffer me to write a long letter.

TO MR ALDERMAN BARBER.

Aug. 8, 1737.

My Dear and Honoured Friend,

I have received yours of July 27th ; and two days ago had a letter from Mr Pope, with a dozen lines from my Lord Bolingbroke, who tells me he is just going to France, and I suppose, designs to continue there as long as he lives.   I am very sorry he is under the necessity of selling Dawley.   Pray, let me know whether he be tolerably easy in his fortunes; for he has these several years lived very expensively. Is his lady still alive? and has he still a country house and an estate of hers to live on? I should be glad to live so long, as to see his History of his own Times; which would be a work very worthy of his lordship, and will be a defence of that ministry, and a justification of our late glorious queen, against the malice, ignorance, falsehood, and stupidity of our present times and managers. I very much like Mr Pope's last poem, entitled MDCCXXXVIII, called Dialogue II; but I live so obscurely, and know so little of what passes in London, that I cannot know the names of persons and things by initial letters.

I am very glad to hear that the Duke of Ormond lives so well at ease and in so good health, as well as with so valuable a companion. His grace has an excellent constitution at so near to fourscore. Mr Dunkin is not in town, but I will send to him when I hear he is come. I extremely love my Lord and Lady Oxford; but his way of managing his fortune is not to be endured. I remember a rascally butcher, one Morley,* a great land-jobber and knave, who was his lordship's manager, and has been the principal cause of my lord's wrong conduct, in which you agree with me in blaming his weakness and credulity. I desire you will please, upon occasion, to present my humble service to my Lord and Lady Oxford, and to my Lord Bathurst. I just expected the character you give of young

---

* This is the " Mild Morley" of Prior's ballad of Down-Hall. He was originally a butcher, but made a very large fortune as an agent and land-jobber.

*****. I hated him from a boy. I wonder Mr Ford is alive ; perhaps walking preserves him.

I very much lament your asthma. I believe temperance and exercise have preserved me from it.

I seldom walk less than four miles, sometimes six, eight, ten, or more, never beyond my own limits ; or, if it rains, I walk as much through the house, up and down stairs ; and if it it were not for the cruel deafness, I would ride through the kingdom, and half through England ; pox on the modern phrase Great Britain, which is only to distinguish it from Little Britain, where old clothes and old books are to be bought and sold ! However, I will put Dr Sheridan (the best scholar in both kingdoms) upon taking your receipt for a terrible asthma. I wish you were rich enough to buy and keep a horse, and ride every tolerable day twenty miles.

Mr Richardson is, I think, still in London. I assure you, he is very grateful to me, and is too wise and discreet to give any just occasion of complaint, by which he must be a great loser in reputation, and a greater in his fortune.

I have not written as much this many a day. I have tired myself much ; but, in revenge, I will tire you.

I am, dear Mr Alderman,
with very great esteem,
Your most obedient
and most humble servant,
JON. SWIFT.

TO MR POPE AND LORD BOLINGBROKE.

Dublin, Aug. 8, 1738.

My Dear Friend,

I HAVE yours of July 25, and first I desire you will look upon me as a man worn with years, and sunk by public as well as personal vexations. I have entirely lost my memory, uncapable of conversation by a cruel deafness, which has lasted almost a year, and I despair of any cure. I say not this to increase your compassion (of which you have already too great a part) but as an excuse for my not being regular in my letters to you, and some few other friends. I have an ill name in the post-office of both kingdoms, * which makes the letters addressed to me not seldom miscarry, or be opened and read, and then sealed in a bungling manner before they come to my hands. Our friend Mrs B. †. is very often in my thoughts, and high in my esteem; I desire you will be the messenger of my humble thanks and service to her. That superior universal genius you describe, whose handwriting I know toward the end of your letter, has made me both proud and happy; but by what he writes I fear he will be too soon gone to his forest ‡ abroad. He began in the queen's time to be my patron, and then descended to be my friend.

---

* Dr Johnson laughs at Swift and Pope thinking their letters were opened and inspected by the post-master, as an instance of their self-importance.—Dr WARTON.

† Mrs Martha Blount.

‡ Fontainbleau, to which Bolingbroke was again about to retire.

It is a great favour of Heaven, that your health grows better by the addition of years. I have absolutely done with poetry for several years past, and even at my best times I could produce nothing but trifles : I therefore reject your compliments on that score, and it is no compliment in me ; for I take your second dialogue that you lately sent me, to equal almost any thing you ever writ ; although I live so much out of the world, that I am ignorant of the facts and persons, which I presume are very well known from Temple Bar to St James's ; I mean the court exclusive.

I can faithfully assure you, that every letter you have honoured me with, these twenty years and more, are sealed up in bundles, and delivered to Mrs Whiteway, a very worthy, rational, and judicious cousin of mine, and the only relation whose visits I can suffer. All these letters she is directed to send safely to you upon my decease.

My Lord Orrery is gone with his lady to a part of her estate in the north ; she is a person of very good understanding as any I know of her sex. Give me leave to write here a short answer to my Lord B.'s letter in the last page of yours.

MY DEAR LORD,

I am infinitely obliged to your lordship for the honour of your letter, and kind remembrance of me. I do here confess, that I have more obligations to your lordship than to all the world beside. You never deceived me, even when you were a great minister of state : and yet I love you still more, for your condescending to write to me, when you had the honour to be an exile. I can hardly hope to live till you publish your history, and am vain enough to wish that my name should be squeezed in among

the few subalterns, *quorum pars parva fui :* if not,
I will be revenged, and contrive some way to be
known to futurity, that I had the honour to have
your lordship for my best patron; and I will live
and die, with the highest veneration and gratitude,
your most obedient, &c.

P. S. I will here in a postscript correct (if it be
possible) the blunders I have made in my letter. I
have showed my cousin the above letter, and she
assures me, that a great collection of $^{your}_{my}$ letters
to $^{me}_{you}$ * are put up and sealed, and in some very
safe hand.

I am, my most dear and honoured friend, entirely
yours,

JON. SWIFT.

It is now Aug. 24, 1738.

TO MR FAULKNER.

August 31, 1738.

SIR,

I BELIEVE you know that I had a treatise, called
" Advice to Servants," in two volumes. The first
was lost, but this moment Mrs Ridgeway brought it
to me, having found it in some papers in her room ;

---

* It is written just thus in the original. The correspondence
in the present volume seems to be part of the collection here spoken of, as it contains not only the letters of Mr Pope, but of
Dr Swift, both to him and Mr Gay, which were returned to Mr
Pope after Mr Gay's death : though any mention made by Mr
Pope of the return or exchange of letters has been industriously
suppressed in the publication, and only appears by some of the
answers.——WARBURTON.

and truly, when I went to look for the second I could not tell where to find it; if you happen to have it, I shall be glad; if not, the messenger shall go to Mrs Whiteway.   I am,

Your humble servant,

JON. SWIFT.

FROM MRS WHITEWAY TO MR RICHARDSON.

September 16. 1738.

SIR,

I HAVE much pleasure in thinking I have executed your commands and Alderman Barber's, to both your satisfactions; and was greatly pleased yesterday to find the Dean in spirits enough to be able to write you a few lines, because I know it was what you wished for.   I declare it has not been by any omission of mine that it was not done long ago. Beside his usual attendants, giddiness and deafness, I can with great truth say, the miseries of this poor kingdom have shortened his days, and sunk him even below the wishes of his enemies; and as he has lived the patriot of Ireland, like the second Cato, he will resign life when it can be no longer serviceable to his country.

As Sir Robert Walpole has your best wishes, I am so far glad of his recovery.

My daughter is now very well, and most highly obliged to you for what you say about her.   I was so little myself when I wrote to you last, with her illness, that I forgot to entreat the favour of your commands to Miss Richardson, to take the opportunity of the summer season to come to this town; but the week after I wrote to her, and insisted on her company immediately; but by directing my letter to Summerseat instead of Colrane, I had not an answer till yesterday, and then one that did not satisfy me; for it is written with such deference and fear of doing any thing without your positive orders, that I have very little to hope for from her. I shall for ever tax you with want of truth, sincerity, and breach of faith, if you do not command her to come immediately to town.

I showed Mr Dunkin the paragraph in your letter that concerned him; for which, and many other obligations he is under to you, he owns himself most gratefully your obedient, &c. &c. Mr Faulkner will send the books by the first that goes to England.

How could you be so unpolite as to tell a woman you supposed her not to be entertained with scandal? You will not allow us to be learned; books turn our brain; housewifery is below a genteel education; and work spoils our eyes: And will you not permit us to be proficients in gaming, visiting, and scandal? To convince you I am so in the last article, the poem pleased me mightly, and I had a secret pleasure to see the gentleman I showed it to liked it as well as I did; so l find your sex are not without a tincture of that female quality.

You have pressed me so much in every letter to find you employment, that, to be rid of you, I will now do it; for, without mentioning the words, entreat favours, vast obligations, trouble, and a long &c., will you buy for me twenty yards of a pink-coloured English damask? The colour we admire here is called a blue pink. The women will tell you what I mean. If you will be pleased, by the return of the post, to tell what will be the expence, I will pay the money immediately into Henry's bank.

I own I am surprised at what you tell me of Mr Philips; but envy, you know, is the tax on virtue; for no other reason could make him your enemy: and I most heartily wish, whoever is so may meet with the fate they deserve. I have just read so far of this letter, and am so much ashamed of the liberty I have taken to give you so much trouble, that if I have truth in me, were it not for the Dean's letter it should never go to you. If you can pardon me this, I promise for the future never to give you the like occasion of exerting your good nature, to her who is, with the greatest respect, Sir, your most obliged and most obedient humble servant,

M. WHITEWAY.

You forgot to date your letter.

FROM THE BISHOP OF FERNS.*

September 18, 1738.

SIR,

A MESSAGE which I just now received from you by Mr Hughes, gives me some hopes of being restored to my old place. Formerly I was your minister *in musicis:* but when I grew a great man (and by the by you helped to make me so) you turned me off. If you are pleased again to employ me, I shall be as faithful and observant as ever.

---

* Dr Synge.—D. S.

I have heard Mr Hughes sing often at Percival's, * and have a good opinion of his judgment: so has Percival, who, in these affairs, is infallible. His voice is not excellent, but will do: and, if I mistake not, he has one good quality, not very common with the musical gentlemen, *i. e.* he is desirous to improve himself. If Mason and Lamb were of his temper, they would be as fine fellows as they think themselves. I am, Sir,

Your most obedient humble servant,

EDWARD FERNS.

———

TO MRS WHITEWAY.

Mr Swift's gimcracks of cups and balls, † in order to my convenient shaving with ease and dispatch, together with the prescription on half a sheet of paper, was exactly followed, but some inconveniences attended: for I cut my face once or twice, was just twice as long in the performance, and left twice as much hair behind, as I have done this twelvemonth past. I return him therefore all his implements, and my own compliments, with abundance of thanks, because he hath fixed me during life in my old humdrum way. Give me a full and true account of all your healths, and so adieu. I am ever, &c.

JON. SWIFT.

Oct. 3d or 4th, or rather, as the butler says, the second, on Tuesday, 1738.

———

* At Dean Percival's.—D. S.
+ A box of soap and a brush.—D. S.

My service to all your litter; I mean Mrs Harrison, &c. but you will call this high treason. I am still very lame of that left foot. I expect to see as many of you as you please.

FROM THE EARL OF ORRERY TO MR. POPE.

Marston, Oct. 4, 1731.

Sir,

I am more and more convinced that your letters are neither lost nor burnt; but who the Dean means by a safe hand in Ireland is beyond my power of guessing, though I am particularly acquainted with most, if not all, of his friends.. As I know you had the recovery of those letters at heart, I took more than ordinary pains to find out where they were; but my inquiries were to no purpose; and, I fear, whoever has them is too tenacious of them to discover where they lie. "Mrs Whiteway did assure me she had not one of them; and seemed to be under great uneasiness, that you should imagine they were left with her. She likewise told me she had stopped the Dean's letter which gave you that information, but believed he would write such another; and therefore desired me to assure you, from her, that she was totally ignorant where they were."

You may say what you please, either to the Dean or any other person, of what I have told you. I am ready to testify it; and I think it ought to be known, "That the Dean says they are delivered

into a safe hand; and Mrs Whiteway * declares she
has them not. The consequence of their being
hereafter published may give uneasiness to some of
your friends, and of course to you: so I would do
all in my power to make you entirely easy in that
point."

This is the first time that I have put pen to paper
since my late misfortune; and I should say (as an
excuse for this letter) that it has cost me some pain,
did it not allow me an opportunity to assure you,
that I am, dear Sir, with the truest esteem,

Your very faithful and obedient servant,
ORRERY.

FROM MR POPE.

Twitnam, Oct. 12, 1738.

MY DEAR FRIEND,

I COULD gladly tell you every week the many
things that pass in my heart, and revive the memory
of all your friendship to me; but I am not so willing to put you to the trouble of showing it (though
I know you have it as warm as ever) upon little or
trivial occasions. Yet, this once, I am unable to

---

* This lady afterwards gave Mr Pope the strongest assurances
that she had used her utmost endeavours to prevent the publication; nay, went so far as to secrete the book till it was commanded from her, and delivered to the Dublin printer; where-
upon her son-in-law, Deane Swift, Esq. insisted upon writing a
preface, to justify Mr Pope from having any knowledge of it,
and to lay it on the corrupt practices of the printers in London,
but this Mr Pope would not agree to, as not knowing the truth
of the fact.—POPE.

refuse the request of a very particular and very deserving friend: one of those whom his own merit has forced me to contract an intimacy with, after I had sworn never to love a man more, since the sorrow it cost, me to have loved so many, now dead, banished, or unfortunate. I mean Mr Lyttelton, one of the worthiest of the rising generation. His nurse has a son, whom I would beg you to promote to the next vacancy in your choir. I loved my own nurse, and so does Lyttelton: he loves and is loved, through the whole chain of relations, dependants, and acquaintance. He is one who would apply to any person to please me, or to serve mine: I owe it to him to apply to you for this man, whose name is William Lamb; and he is the bearer of this letter. I presume he is qualified for that which he desires; and I doubt not, if it be consistent with justice, you will gratify me in him.

Let this, however, be an opportunity of telling you——What?——what I can tell; the kindness I bear you, the affection I feel for you, the hearty wishes I form for you, my prayers for your health of body and mind, or (the best softenings of the want of either) quiet and resignation. You lose little by not hearing such things as this idle and base generation has to tell you: you lose not much by forgetting most of what now passes in it. Perhaps, to have a memory that retains the past scenes of our country, and forgets the present, is the means to be happier and better contented. But, if the evil of the day be not intolerable (though sufficient, God knows, at any period of life) we may, at least we should, nay we must (whether patiently or impatiently) bear it, and make the best of what we cannot make better, but may make worse. To hear that this is your situation and your temper, and that peace attends you at home, and one or two true friends who are tender about you, would be a great ease to me to know, and know from yourself. Tell me who those are whom you now love or esteem, that I may love and esteem them too; and if ever they come into England, let them be my friends. If, by any thing I can here do, I can serve you, or please you, be certain it will mend my happiness, and that no satisfaction any thing gives me here will be superior, if equal to it.

My dear Dean, whom I never will forget or think of with coolness, many are yet living here who frequently mention you with affection and respect. Lord Orrery, Lord Bathurst, Lord Bolingbroke, Lord Oxford, Lord Masham, Lewis, Mrs P. Blount, allow one woman to the list, for she is as constant to old friendships as any man. And many young men there are, nay all that are any credit to this age, who love you unknown, who kindle at your fire, and learn by your genius. Nothing of you can die, nothing of you can decay, nothing of you can suffer, nothing of you can be obscured, or locked up from esteem and admiration, except what is at the deanery; just as much of you only as God made mortal. May the rest of you (which is all) be as happy hereafter as honest men may expect, and need not doubt; while (knowing nothing more) they know that their Maker is merciful! Adieu,

Yours ever,

A. Pope.

FROM MR POPE TO THE EARL OF ORRERY.

Twitnam, Nov. 7, 1738.

WHEN you get to Dublin (whither I direct this, supposing you will see our dear friend as soon as possible) pray put the Dean in mind of me, and tell him, I hope he received my last. Tell him how dearly I love him, and how greatly I honour him: how greatly I reflect on every testimony of his friendship; how much I resolved to give the best I can of my esteem for him to posterity; and assure him, the world has nothing in it I admire so much; nothing the loss of which I should regret so much, as his genius and his virtues.

TO MRS WHITEWAY.

Nov. 27, 1738.

I NEVER liked a letter from you on your usual days of coming here, for it always brings me bad news. I am heartily sorry for your son's continuing his illness, and that you have now two patients in your house. In the mean time pray take care of your health, chiefly your wicked colic and Mrs Harrison's disposition to a fever. I hope at least things will be better on Thursday,* else I shall be

---

* Dr Swift's birth-day.——D. S.

full of the spleen, because it is a day you seem to regard, although I detest it, and I read the third chapter of Job that morning. * I am deafer than when you saw me last, and indeed am quite cast down. My hearty love and service to Mrs Harrison. I thoroughly pity you in your present circumstances. I am ever yours entirely. God support you.

JON. SWIFT.

FROM MISS RICHARDSON TO MRS WHITEWAY.

Belturbet, Nov. 29, 1738.

DEAR MADAM,

It was a very unequal match that the Dean and you should join in a plot against my uncle and me : you could not fail of carrying your point. Any thing the Dean hath a hand in, is done in the most genteel and surprising manner. I fairly own I am caught : I would be glad to know what my uncle will think of himself when he hears the part he acted in it, I have been so well accustomed to receive presents of value from him, that I thought it had been a piece of edging, or some light thing, which he had committed to your care to be forwarded to me. Never was I so surprised as I was when I read your letter, to think that I had received a present from so great a person as the Dean ; but when I looked upon it, and knew the expense it must be to him, I

---

* This chapter he always read upon his birth-day.——D. S.

was quite confounded : it was too great an honour
for me, who can never deserve the least favour from
him : it is a most beautiful diamond.   I own I am
proud of finery now, which I never was in my life
before.   I am highly obliged to you for your improvement of the ring : the Dean's hair and name
have made it a treasure to me, and I really believe
it will be thought so a thousand years hence, if it
can be kept so long.   I am sure it shall by me, as
long as I live, with as much care as I keep my eyes,
while I have them to look upon it.

My sister, who had the honour of waiting upon
you in town, and brought me the ring very safe, is
full of acknowledgments for your civilities to her,
and returns you her most sincere thanks, with her
humble service.   Pray give mine most affectionately to Miss Harrison.   I am, Dear Madam, your
most obliged and most humble servant,

KATH. RICHARDSON.

FROM MR RICHARDSON.

London, Jan. 2, 1738-9.

SIR,

I AM called upon, by many provocations, to prefer
a bill of indictment against you, and a female accom-
plice of yours; * for that by the use of means very
uncommon, which were in your power only, you
have turned the head of a well-meaning country girl
of plain sense, who had been very useful to me, and

---

* Mrs Whiteway.—D. S.

and esteemed by her acquaintance. I have seen of late many symptoms of her disorder: it is true, that the fascination of your works had before operated strongly upon her; for scarce any opportunity occurred but she poured forth her admiration of the author, and can repeat without book all your poems better than her catechism; however, she could attend to domestic affairs, and give proper directions about matters in the kitchen and larder, &c. and when she did not pore upon your writings, or some other books (I cannot say of the like kind) she was at work, or seeing that things in her province were as they should be: but now truly it appears she apprehends that heretofore she had not discovered her own value and importance. To be taken notice of by a person she has long thought to be the greatest genius any age has produced, and whom she worships with an adoration that to any mortal rises almost to idolatry, has, it is much to be feared, transported her with conceit and vanity, and where it will end, I know not. What you have done proceeded, no doubt, from a malicious intention toward me as well as the poor girl; and I resent it accordingly, as I hope she will do when she returns to her senses.

I was greatly rejoiced, dear Sir, to learn from the prime-serjeant Singleton, that he found you extremely well in every respect, except your hearing; and in that he said you were much better than he expected. That man, who has as true a heart as I ever met with, most entirely loves as well as admires you.

This place affords no news at present. I am detained by affairs of importance that relate to my friends, and cannot yet say when they will allow me to return. I pass my time, now and then, with some of Mr Pope's most intimate friends; and although I would have a great pleasure in being known to him, that of the present age comes next to you in fame, I shall not be introduced to him, unless I shall have the honour not to be thought wholly unworthy to deliver him a letter from the Dean of St Patrick's.

Alderman Barber got a fall in his parlour on his hip, by his foot getting into a hole of the carpet; it brought a fit of the gout upon him, and he is still somewhat lame in his hip; but otherwise in very good health and spirits.

Doctor Squire holds out surprisingly: as soon as the vacancy shall happen, I shall have have notice, and there is no doubt but Mr Dunkin will succeed him.

I am ever, dear Sir, with the highest esteem and respect, your most obliged and most affectionate humble servant,

WILLIAM RICHARDSON.

FROM DR KING.

St Mary-Hall, Oxford, Jan. 5, 1738-9.

SIR,

AT length I have put Rochefoucault to the press, and about ten or twelve days hence it will be published. But I am in great fear lest you should dislike the liberties I have taken. Although I have done nothing without the advice and approbation of those among your friends in this country, who love and esteem you most, and zealously interest themselves in every thing that concerns your character. As they are much better judges of mankind than I am, I very readily submit to their opinion ; however, if after having received the printed copies, which I will send you next week, you shall still resolve to have the poem published as entire as you put it into my hands, I will certainly obey your commands, if I can find a proper person to undertake the work. I shall go to London the latter end of the next week, when I will write to you by a private hand more fully than I can venture to do by the post. *

I was at Twickenham in the Christmas week. Mr Pope had just then received a letter from you, and I had the pleasure of hearing you were well and in good spirits. May those good spirits continue with you to the last hour !

Believe me to be, with the greatest truth, Sir, your most obedient and most faithful servant,

W. K.

Pray do me the honour to present my most humble service to Mrs Whiteway.

FROM MR DEANE SWIFT.

Jan. 12, 1738-9.

Sir,

I HAD so great an honour conferred upon me yesterday, that I know not how to express the obligations I lie under for it ; unless, by endeavouring

---

* The Dean did accordingly much disapprove of the prudential alterations and omissions of Dr King, in the celebrated verses on his own death.

to make myself worthy of your present, I can demonstrate to the world that I daily improve in wisdom and knowledge, by studying in those books, which since the beginning of my life I have ever esteemed to be a complete library of taste, wit, poetry, and politics; yes, and in spite of dulness and prejudice, I will venture to say, of religion also. This I am sure of, that so great a present from so great a person, and in a manner so handsome and extraordinary, it is absolutely impossible I should ever be honoured with again. I always thought I added to my own reputation whenever I pointed out some of those excellencies which shine through every page of them. But to be thought worthy of receiving them from your hands, was infinitely beyond even what my vanity could hope for. I have flattered myself for many years, that to the best of my power I have continually fought under the banners of liberty, and that I have been ready, at a moment's call, either to lay down my life in the defence of it, or, whenever there should appear any probability of success, to vindicate and assert that claim, which every man in every country has by nature a right to insist upon; but, whatever principles have guided my actions hitherto, I shall from this moment enlist myself under the conduct of liberty's general; and whenever I desert her ensigns, to fight under those of tyranny and oppression, then, and not till then will I part with those books which you have so highly honoured me with, and cast them into the flames, that I may never afterwards be reproached either by the sight of them, or the remembrance of the donor. I am, Sir, with the highest esteem, your most obliged and most obedient humble servant,

DEANE SWIFT.

FROM DR KING.

London, Jan. 23, 1738-9.

Sir,

I HOPE you received a letter I wrote to you from Oxford, about the thirtieth of last month, in which I acquainted you with the publication of Rochefoucault; and as I interest myself most heartily in every thing that concerns your character as an author, so I take great pleasure in telling you, that none of your works have been better received by the publick than this poem. I observe this with more than ordinary satisfaction, because I may urge the approbation of the publick as some kind of apology for myself, if I shall find you are dissatisfied with the form in which this poem now appears. But if that should happen, all the rest of your friends on this side of the water must share the blame with me; for I have absolutely conformed myself to their advice and opinion as to the manner of the publication. There are some lines, indeed, which I omitted with a very ill will, and for no other reason but because I durst not insert them, I mean the story of the medals: however, that incident is pretty well known, and care has been taken that almost every reader may be able to supply the blanks. That part of the poem which mentions the death of queen Anne, and so well describes the designs of the ministry, which succeeded upon the accession of the late king, I would likewise willingly have published, if I could have done it with safety; but I do not know whether the present worthy set of ministers would not have construed this passage into high treason, by aid of the new doctrine of innuendos : at least a lawyer, whom I consulted on this occasion, gave me some reason to imagine this might be the case. I am in truth more cautious than I used to be, well knowing that my superiors look on me at present with a very evil eye, as I am the reputed author of the Latin poem I have sent you by the same gentleman, who does me the favour to deliver you this letter : for although that piece has escaped the state inquisition, by being written in a language that is not at present very well understood at court, and might perhaps puzzle the attorney-general to explain, yet the scope of the poem and principal characters being well understood, the author must hereafter expect no mercy, if he gives his enemies any grounds or colour to attack him. But notwithstanding all my caution, if I perceive you dislike this manner and form of the poem, I will, some way or other, contrive that it may be published as you shall direct.

I send you my best wishes, and I hope you will yet live many years in a perfect state for the sake of your friends, for the benefit of your country, and for the honour of mankind ; and I beg you to believe that I am, with the greatest truth, Sir, your most humble and most obedient servant,

W. K.

FROM DR KING. TO MRS WHITEWAY.

Jan. 30, 1738-9.

MADAM,

A VERY kind letter, which I have just received from you, has put me into great confusion. I beg of you to be assured, that I think myself under the highest obligations to you, and that I set a true value on the friendship with which you have honoured me, and shall endeavour to preserve it as long as I live. If our correspondence has been interrupted, it has been wholly owing to the ill treatment I received from the post-office; for some time I did not receive a letter that had not been opened, and very often my letters were delivered to me with the seals torn off. Whether these post-officers really thought me, what I never thought myself, a man of importance, or whether they imagined my letters were a cover for some great name, I do not know; but for my part, I grew peevish, to find my friendships, and all my little chit-chat, must constantly be exposed to the view of every dirty fellow that had leisure or curiosity enough to examine my letters. However, for some little time past, I have not had the same cause of complaint. Your letter was delivered to me in good condition; I begin to think my superiors no longer suspect me of holding any unwarrantable correspondence, especially since I find I may now venture to write to the Dean, even by the Oxford post. Notwithstanding what you say, I am in some pain about Rochefoucault, and doubt much whether he will be satisfied with the manner in which he finds it published; to which I consented in deference to Mr Pope's judgment, and the opinion of others of the Dean's friends in this country, who, I am sure, love and honour him, and kindly concern themselves in every thing that may affect him. The town has received this piece so well, that in all parts, and in all companies, I hear it extremely commended; and not only the Dean's friends, but his greatest enemies, acknowledge that he has not lost any part of his fire, and of that inimitable turn of wit and humour so peculiar to himself. For my part, I never read any of his works either in prose or verse, that I do not call to mind that short character which cardinal Polignac gave him in speaking to me, *Il a l'esprit créateur*, which I mentioned to you in a former letter, if I remember rightly. It may not be amiss to tell you, that one Gally, or Gaillie, since this poem was printed, offered it to sale to a bookseller at Temple-bar; and I am now told that there are two or three copies more in London. Gaillie pretends that he is just come from Ireland, and that he had directions to publish the poem here; so that perhaps the whole may at least appear, whether he will or not.

I am glad to hear that my friend Mr Swift is well. When are we to see him again in Oxford? Since you appeal to him for a voucher, although you need none with me, let him likewise do me the justice to tell you, that he never heard me mention your name but with the greatest esteem and respect; with which I shall ever be, Madam, your most obedient and most faithful servant,

W. K.

I sent the Dean a packet by the gentleman under whose cover I send you this.

TO MR ALDERMAN BARBER.

Dublin, Feb. 16, 1738-9.

MY DEAR GOOD OLD FRIEND,

THE young gentleman * who delivers you this lies under one great disadvantage, that he is one of my relations, and those are of all mortals what I despise and hate, except one Mrs Whiteway and her daughter. You must understand that the mother has the insolence to say, that you have heard of her and know her character. She is a perfect Irish Teague born in Cheshire, and lived, as I remember, at Warrington. The young gentleman who waits upon you, has a very good countenance, has been entered three years at the Temple (as it is the usual custom), but I think was never yet in England, nor does he know any one person there. However, as it is easy to find you, who are so well known and so much esteemed, he will attend you with this letter, and you will please to instruct him in the usual methods of entering himself in the Temple. He is a younger brother, but has an estate of a hundred pounds a-year, which will make shift to support him, in a frugal way. He is also a very good person of a man, and Mrs Whiteway says he has a virtuous disposition. My disorders of deafness, forgetfulness, and other ailments, added to a dead weight of 70 years, make me weary of life. But my comfort is, that in you I find your vigour and health increase. Pray God continue

---

* William Swift, Esq.

both to you. I am, my dear friend, with very great esteem and affection,
Your most obedient, and most humble servant,
JON. SWIFT.

Do you ever see any of our old friends? If you visit Mr Lewis, I must charge you to present him with my kind and hearty service: and how or where is my lord Bolingbroke and Mr Pope?

I am very much obliged to you for the favour you have shown to Mr Richardson. He is a very prudent good gentleman; if you see him, pray make him my compliments. So, my dear friend, once more adieu.

FROM DR KING TO MRS WHITEWAY.

London, March 6, 1738-9.

MADAM,
I DO not remember any thing published in my time, that hath been so universally well received as the Dean's last poem. Two editions have been already sold off, though two thousand were printed at first. In short, all people read it, all agree to commend it; and I have been well assured, the greatest enemies the Dean has in this country, allow it to be a just and beautiful satire. As I am very sincerely and sensibly affected by every thing that may raise the Dean's character as a writer (if any thing can raise it higher) so you may believe I have had the greatest pleasure in observing the suc-

4.

cess and general approbation which this poem has
met with; wherefore I was not a little mortified
yesterday, when the bookseller brought me the
Dublin edition, and at the same time put into my
hands a letter he had received from Faulkner, by
which I perceive the Dean is much dissatisfied with
our manner of publication, and that so many lines
have been omitted, if Faulkner speaks truth, and
knows as much of the Dean's mind as he pretends
to know. Faulkner has sent over several other copies to other booksellers; so that I take it for granted this poem will soon be reprinted here from the
Dublin edition; and then it may be perceived how
much the Dean's friends have been mistaken in
their judgment, however good their intentions have
been. In the mean time I will write to you on this
occasion without any reserve; for I know you love
the Dean, and kindly and zealously interest yourself in every thing that concerns his character; and
if you will believe the same of me, you will do me
great justice.

The Doctor's friends, whom I consulted on this
occasion, were of opinion, that the latter part of
the poem might be thought by the public a little
vain, if so much were said by himself of himself.
They were unwilling that any imputation of this
kind should lie against this poem, considering
there is not the least tincture of vanity appearing
in any of his former writings, and that it is well
known, there is no man living more free from that
fault than he is.

They were of opinion that these lines,

" He lash'd the vice, but spar'd the name,
No individual could resent
Where thousands equally were meant"——

might be liable to some objection, and were not, strictly speaking, a just part of his character; because several persons have been lashed by name, a Bettesworth, and in this poem, Chartres and Whitshed; and for my part, I do not think, or ever shall think, that it is an imputation on a satirist to lash an infamous fellow by name. The lines which begin,

> " Here's Wolston's Tracts, the twelfth edition," &c.

are plainly a mistake; and were omitted for that reason only; for Wolston never had a pension: on the contrary, he was prosecuted for his blasphemous writings; his books were burnt by the hands of the common hangman; he himself was imprisoned, and died in prison. Woolaston, the author of a book called, " The Religion of Nature delineated," was indeed much admired at court, his book universally read, his busto set up by the late queen in her grotto at Richmond with Clarke's and Locke's; but this Woolaston was not a clergyman.

The two last lines,

> " That kingdom he hath left his debtor,
> I wish it soon may have a better"—

I omitted, because I did not well understand them; a *better* what?——There seems to be what the grammarians call an *antecedent* wanting for that word; for neither *kingdom* or *debtor* will do, so as to make it sense, and there is no other antecedent.*

---

* These objections seem entirely hypercritical. The Dean being utterly retired from active life, and even from friendly society, might be well allowed to claim the praise which his worst

The Dean is, I think, without exception, the best and most correct writer of English that has ever yet appeared as an author; I was therefore unwilling any thing should be cavilled at as ungrammatical: he is besides the most patient of criticism of all I ever knew; which perhaps is not the least sign of a great genius——I have therefore ventured to make these objections to you; in which, however, for the most part, I submitted my own opinion to the judgment of others. I had something to add concerning the notes, but I have not room in this paper—but I will give you the trouble of reading another letter. Believe me, Madam, your most obedient and most humble servant,

W. K.

FROM MRS WHITEWAY TO MR RICHARDSON.

March 28, 1739.

Sir,

Two days ago I had the very great pleasure to hear from Mr Swift you were well. The acknow-

---

enemies could hardly deny him. That he had, upon one or two occasions, mentioned notorious characters, did not affect the general proposition, "that he lash'd the vice but spar'd the name," considering the number of his satirical effusions. The grammatical exception to the word *better*, used without a substantive, is also wire-drawn. By a better, in familiar speech or familiar poetry, a better man, or a better member of society, is readily understood.

ledgments he professes in his letters to the Dean and me of your extraordinary civilities to him, make me perfectly ashamed to think how ill I shall acquit myself by only being able to say I most sincerely thank you. What an opportunity have you laid in my way of saying a thousand fine things on this subject; and yet I can only tell you (what you already know to be a great truth), that you have acted in this as you do in every thing, friendly, politely, and genteelly. All the returns I can make, is to give you farther room to exercise a virtue which great minds only feel, that of doing good to an ingenuous worthy honest gentleman. The person I mean is counsellor M'Aulay; one of those who stand candidates for member of parliament to represent the university of Dublin, in the place of Dr Coghill deceased. The Dean of St Patrick's appears openly for him; and I have his leave and command to tell you, if you can do Mr M'Aulay a piece of friendship on this occasion with any person of distinction in England, he will receive the favour as done to himself. After I have mentioned the Dean, how trifling will it be to speak of myself? and yet I most earnestly intreat your interest in this affair; and for this reason, because it will never lie in my way to make you any return; so that only true generosity can inspire you to do any thing at my request. After all, I am not so very unreasonable as to desire a favour of this nature if it be irksome to you. Tell me, sir, can you do any thing in this matter? and will you undertake it? for your word I know can be depended upon. There is one hint that perhaps I am impertinent in offering, that all great bodies of men (or who at least think themselves so) let their inclinations be ever so much in prejudice of one

person (as I take it to be the case of Mr M'Aulay),
yet wait for the interfering of the higher powers ;
so that if, by your good offices, the lord-lieutenant
can be prevailed on to recommend him to the provost and fellows of the university, his interest
would be certainly fixed ; but this, and the manner of doing it, I submit to your superior judgment.

The Dean of St Patrick's presents you his most
affectionate love and service ;—these were his own
words.   He is better both in health and hearing
than I have known him these twelve months ; but
so indolent in writing, that he will scarce put his
name to a receipt for money.   This he has likewise ordered me to tell you as an apology for not
writing to you himself, and not want of the highest esteem for you.

Do you, sir, ever intend to see this kingdom
again ?   What time may we expect it ?   When
may I hope you will perform your promise to let
Miss Richardson spend some months with me ? and
do you ever intend to write again to your friends
in Dublin ?   I am, Sir, with the highest esteem
and respect, your most humble and most obedient
servant,

MAR. WHITEWAY.

FROM MR RICHARDSON TO MRS WHITEWAY.

London, April 5, 1739.

DEAR MADAM,
I AM indeed much ashamed that I have so many
favours from you to acknowledge at one time. You

may believe me when I assure you that my silence has not proceeded from want of respect and esteem for you.   I would not put on the affectation of much business as an excuse to any body, much less to you ; although the truth is, that I am hurried almost out of my life with the attendance and writing about things I have undertaken for some friends.

The Dean's recommendation and yours, without any other consideration whatever, would induce me to do my utmost to serve Mr M'Aulay, as I have told him by this post, when I thought I should not trouble you with a few lines.   He will acquaint you with what I have done, by which you will see that I lost no time ; and I have hopes to obtain the lord-lieutenant's countenance for him.

I will endeavour to introduce Mr Swift * to the acquaintance of some persons before I leave this ; whose countenance and friendship will at least give a young gentleman a good air ——his own merit entitles him to the esteem and regard of such as shall have the happiness to be acquainted with him : I am much obliged to you for introducing me to him. I have only time to add my most hearty thanks for the same, and to assure you that any opportunity of expressing the esteem I have for the Dean, which is the highest, and for you, will ever give me the greatest pleasure.   I am, Madam, your most obliged and most truly faithful servant,

WILLIAM RICHARDSON.

---

* William Swift, Esq. then a student at the Middle Temple. —D. S.

FROM MR RICHARDSON.

London, April 10, 1739.

DEAR SIR,

IT is an age since I had the honour of a line from you. Your friend Mr Alderman Barber, whose veneration for you prompts him to do any thing he can think of that can show his respect and affection, made a present to the university of Oxford of the original picture done for you by Jervas, to do honour to the university by your being placed in the gallery among the most renowned and distinguished personages this island has produced; but first had a copy taken, and then had the original set in a fine rich frame, and sent it to Oxford, after concerting with lord Bolingbroke, the vice-chancellor, and Mr Pope, as I remember, the inscription to be under the picture, a copy whereof is inclosed. The alderman had a very handsome compliment from the vice-chancellor, in the name of all the heads of houses there, and by their direction : wherein there is most honourable mention of the Dean of St Patrick's on that occasion.

Seeing an article in the London Evening Post upon your picture, which was drawn at the request and expence of the chapter of your cathedral, being put up in the deanery, Alderman Barber took the hint, and caused what you see in the London Evening Post of this day to be printed therein. He knows nothing of my writing to you at this time ; but I thought it right that you should be acquainted how intent he is, all manner of ways, to show the effects of the highest friendship, kindled to a flame by the warmest sense of gratitude, and the most exalted esteem and veneration.

Mrs Whiteway, and Mr M'Aulay, can inform you how absolute your commands are with me. Since you recommended him, he is sure of the utmost I can do for him.

Sir, if I have not a few words from you, I shall conclude that you think me troublesome, and are resolved to get rid of my impertinence. It will be two or three months before I can get from hence, although I am impatient to be at home ; but whereever I am, or however engaged, I am always, dear Sir, your most obliged and most truly faithful servant,

WILLIAM RICHARDSON.

My best respects wait upon Mrs Whiteway.

TO THE REVEREND MR KING.

Monday morn.

SIR,

I HAVE often desired to talk with you about the Wednesday dinner, but could never see you. Mrs Sican is to buy the dinner ; for which I advanced a moidore and a double pistole. I hoped you would have wrote to Dr Wilson, and taken some care about the wine, for I have none to spare. Pray let me know whether you are content to take your usual trouble on these occasions.

I am, your obedient humble servant,
J. SWIFT.

FROM DEAN SWIFT AND MRS WHITE-WAY TO MR RICHARDSON.

April 17, 1739.

My very good Friend,

I find that Mrs Whiteway pretends to have been long acquainted with you ; but upon a strict examination I discovered that all the acquaintance was only at the deanery-house, where she had the good fortune to see you once or twice at most. I am extremely obliged to you for your favours to Mr M'Aulay, for whose good sense and virtues of every kind I have highly esteemed him ever since I had the happiness of knowing him. If he succeeds in his election, it will be chiefly by your good offices ; and you have my hearty thanks for what you have already done. I know you often see my honest hearty friend Alderman Barber ; and pray let him know that I command him to continue his friendship to you, although he is your absolute governor. I am very much obliged to the alderman and you for your civilities to young Swift. Mrs Whiteway says he is my cousin ; which will not be to his advantage, for I hate all relations; and I——Sir, I have snatched the pen out of the Dean's hand, who seems, by his countenance, to incline to finish his letter with my faults as he began it. Where there is so large a scope, and such a writer, you may believe I should not like to have my character drawn by him. However, I think for once he is mistaken ; I mean in the article of what he calls vanity, and which I term a laudable ambition, the honour of being known to you, and bragging of it as some merit to myself, to be distinguished by you. Have I not reason to boast, when you tell me my recommendation will have weight with you? and how great must be the obligation that words cannot express? Gratitude, like grief, dwells only in the mind, and can best be guessed at when it was too great to be told, and most certainly lessens when we are capable of declaring it. I never doubted Mr M'Aulay's success if you undertook his cause, nor your indefatigable friendship for those who have the good fortune to gain your esteem. Mr Swift I wish may be in the number. This I am sure of, that his virtue and honour will never give me reason to repent that I introduced him to you, which is the only favour I hoped for him; but you, Sir, never do things by halves.

I know you are hurried on many occasions; therefore I do not expect a letter unless you are perfectly disengaged. Sometimes we are in such a state of indolence, that half an hour is trifled away in doing nothing. When you find yourself in this situation, tell me in two or three lines you are well, and command Miss Richardson to come to me. My daughter most earnestly joins with me in this request, and entreats you to believe that she is, with as great respect as I am, Sir, your most humble and most obedient servant,

M. WHITEWAY,

FROM MR RICHARDSON.

London, April 17, 1739.

DEAR SIR,

I WROTE this morning to Mrs Whiteway a few lines in much hurry, and I write this to you in Guildhall, by Alderman Barber's direction. Beside a letter from you to the Society, whose address is in Mrs Whiteway's letter, he thinks a memorial or petition from Mr Dunkin to the Society will be of use ; and if you write to Mr Pope, the alderman thinks he will get one vote, which he can fix no way of obtaining but through Pope. I am ever, dear Sir, your most obliged and most affectionate humble servant,

WILLIAM RICHARDSON.

I should think it would be right in Mr Dunkin to come over the moment he hears of Squire's death. I wrote by this post to a nephew, to let you know the moment he dies, if the life should be in him when my letter goes to him.

TO THE HONOURABLE THE SOCIETY OF THE GO-
VERNOR AND ASSISTANTS, LONDON, FOR THE
NEW PLANTATION IN ULSTER, WITHIN THE
REALM OF IRELAND, AT THE CHAMBER IN
GUILDHALL, LONDON.

April 19, 1739.

WORTHY GENTLEMEN,
   I HEARTILY recommend to your very worship-
ful society, the reverend Mr William Dunkin, *
for the living of Colrane, vacant by the death of
Dr Squire.   Mr Dunkin is a gentleman of great
learning and wit, true religion, and excellent morals.   It is only for these qualifications that I recommend him to your patronage; and I am confident that you will never repent the choice of such
a man, who will be ready at any time to obey your
commands.   You have my best wishes, and all my
endeavours for your prosperity : and I shall, during my life, continue to be, with the truest respect
and highest esteem,
                   Worthy Sirs,
   Your most obedient and most humble servant,
                                    JON. SWIFT.

---

* See Alderman Barber's letter, March 13, 1738.—N.

FROM MRS WHITEWAY TO MR RICHARDSON:

April 19, 1739.

Sir,

I now give you an opportunity of adding a new petition in your prayers,—From female impertinence, good Lord deliver me. Yet this trouble you brought on yourself; and therefore I will make no apology for it. Mr Dunkin's case comes now under your care. You were the first promoter of it; and to you only are his obligations due. Mr Squire died the 14th of this month; and by this post the Dean has writ to Alderman Barber in Mr Dunkin's favour. He has commanded me to entreat your friendship for him with the alderman and the society: and says, he knows you will pardon him that he does not write to you himself on the occasion; for his head is very much out of order to day. There is one article in the Dean's letter he has left out, and another inserted, much against my inclination. The first is, that he omitted mentioning Mr Dunkin as a worthy good man, which in my opinion is more material than being a poet or a scholar: although, when joined with these, make a most amiable character: the other is, troubling the alderman to know there is such an insignificant person in the world as Mrs Whiteway; but the tyrant Dean will say and do just as he pleases. The enclosed was sent me by Mr Dunkin, not knowing how to direct to you. I now promise you, Sir, to tease you no more with my letters, unless you command me to pay you my most humble respects; and then you shall be obeyed with pleasure, by, Sir, your most obliged and most obedient servant,

MAR. WHITEWAY.

TO MR ALDERMAN BARBER.

Dublin, April 19, 1739.

MY DEAR OLD FRIEND,

AT last Doctor Squire is actually dead; he died
upon the 14th day of this month, and now you have
the opportunity of obliging me in giving Squire's
living in Colrane to Mr William Dunkin, who is an
excellent scholar, and keeps a school in my neighbourhood; besides, he is a very fine poet. My
friend Mr Richardson can give you a better account
of him. It is true, Mr Dunkin is a married man;
however that is of no great moment; and in the
northern country of Ireland, although it be the best
inhabited part of the kingdom, a wife will be convenient. Yet we two old bachelors (I own I am your
senior) could never consent to take so good example,
by endeavouring to multiply the world. I heartily
thank you for your civilities to young Swift. It
seems he is a relation of mine. And there is one
Mrs Whiteway, a widow, the only cousin of my family for whom I have any sort of friendship; it was
she prevailed with me to introduce the young man to
you. He is a younger brother, and his portion is
only 100l. a-year English. You will oblige me if
you can bear seeing him once a quarter at his lodging near the Temple, where he designs to study the
law; and so I have done with ever troubling you,
my dear friend. Where is Mr Lewis? Some months
ago he writ to me with many complaints of his ill
health, and the effect of old age, in both which I can
overmatch you and him, beside my giddy head,
deafness, and forgetfulness into the bargain. I hear
our friend Lord Bolingbroke has sold Dawley; I

wish you could tell me in what condition he is, both as to health and fortune ; and where his lady lives, and how they agree. If you visit my Lord and Lady Oxford and their daughter, who is now as I hear a duchess, or any other friend of ours, let them have the offers of my humble service. May you, my most dear friend, preserve your health, and live as long as you desire! I am ever, with the greatest truth and esteem, your most obedient humble servant, and entire friend,

JON. SWIFT.

I desire you will give my most hearty service to Mr Pope; and let him know that I have provided for Mr Lamb, whom he recommended to me, with a full vicar choralship in my choir. And pray let me know the state of Mr Pope's health.

DR DUNKIN TO MRS WHITEWAY.

April 25, 1737.

MADAM,

As it was through your countenance I had the honour of being first introduced to the most worthy Dean of St Patrick,* I must have thought myself under the highest obligation to you ; but the continuance of your friendship, through so many repeated acts of generosity, and the course of his gracious en-

---

* It was Faulkner who first introduced him to Dr Swift, by taking much pains and trouble to accomplish it.—F.

deavours to raise my reputation and fortune, are such things as I must ever remember and express with a very deep sense of gratitude.

The fatigue of writing so many letters lately in my favour, was indeed what I could not in reason expect even from his humanity, were I worthy of them; and I can only say, the Dean of St Patrick is unwearied in doing good, and that he who could rise to preserve a nation, will descend to relieve an individual.

The sense of my own demerit, and the just awe in which I stand before so great and good a man, will not allow me either that freedom of speech, or writing, which is requisite to let him understand with what love, veneration, and respect of his person I reflect upon the many instances of his tender concern and uncommon zeal for my welfare. This is a duty I most earnestly wish, but am altogether unable to perform, and such as I entreat you, dear Madam, to undertake for me; your compliance in which will be yet another, among the many and weighty obligations laid upon your most dutiful, obedient, devoted servant,

WILLIAM DUNKIN.

TO MR POPE.

Dublin, April 28, 1739.

DEAR SIR,

THE gentleman who will have the honour to deliver you this, although he be one related to me, which is by no means any sort of recommendation; for I am utterly void of what the world calls natural affection, and with good reason, because they are a numerous race degenerating from their ancestors, who were of good esteem for their loyalty and sufferings in the rebellion against King Charles the First. This cousin of mine, who is so desirous to wait on you, is named Deane Swift, because his great grandfather by the grandmother's side was Admiral Deane, who having been one of the regicides, had the good fortune to save his neck by dying a year or two before the Restoration.

I have a great esteem for Mr Deane Swift, who is much the most valuable of any of his family: he was first a student in this university, and finished his studies in Oxford, where Dr King, principal of St Mary Hall, assured me, that Mr Swift behaved himself with good reputation and credit; he hath a very good taste for wit, writes agreeable and entertaining verses, and is a perfect master equally skilled in the best Greek and Roman authors. He has a true spirit for liberty, and with all these advantages is extremely decent and modest. Mr Swift is heir to the little paternal estate of our family at Goodrich in Herefordshire. My grandfather * was so persecuted and plundered two and fifty times by the barbarity of Cromwell's hellish crew, of which I find an account in a book called "Mercurius Rusticus," that the poor old gentleman was forced to sell the better half of his estate to support his family. †
However, three of his sons had better fortune; for, coming over to this kingdom, and taking to the law,

---

* The Rev. Thomas Swift, parson of Godwich, in Herefordshire.
† The account of their sufferings are to be found in Mercurius Rusticus. Edition 1685, p. 82. and are briefly noticed in the Dean's life.

they all purchased good estates, of which Mr Deane Swift has a good share, but with some incumbrance.

I had a mind that this young gentleman should have the honour of being known to you; which is all the favour I ask for him; and that if he stays any time longer in London than he now intends, you will permit him to wait on you sometimes. I am, my dearest friend,

Your most obedient
and most humble servant,
JON. SWIFT.

TO THE SAME.

May 10, 1739.

You are to suppose, for the little time I shall live, that my memory is entirely gone, and especially of any thing that was told me last night, or this morning. I have one favour to entreat from you. I know the high esteem and friendship you bear to your friend Mr Lyttelton, whom you call " the rising genius of this age." His fame, his virtue, honour, and courage, have been early spread, even among us. I find he is secretary to the Prince of Wales; and his royal highness has been for several years chancellor of the university in Dublin. All this is a prelude to a request I am going to make to you. There is in this city one Alexander M'Aulay, a lawyer of great distinction for skill and honesty, zealous for the liberty of the subject, and loyal to the house of Hanover; and particularly to the Prince of Wales, for his highness's love to both kingdoms.

Mr M'Aulay is now soliciting for a seat in parliament here, vacant by the death of Dr Coghill, a civilian, who was one of the persons chosen for this university: and, as his royal highness continues still chancellor of it, there is no person so proper to nominate the representative as himself. If this favour can be procured, by your good-will and Mr Lyttelton's interest, it will be a particular obligation to me, and grateful to the people of Ireland, in giving them one of their own nation to represent this university.

There is a man in my choir, one Mr Lamb; he has at present but half a vicarship; the value of it is not quite fifty pounds *per annum*. You writ to me in his favour some months ago; and, if I outlive any one vicar-choral, Mr Lamb shall certainly have a full place, because he very well deserves it; and I am obliged to you very much for recommending him.

FROM MR SECRETARY LYTTLETON.

London, May 16, 1739.

SIR,

I CANNOT let Mr Swift return to Ireland without my acknowledgments to you for the favour you have done Mr Lamb, * I know that I ought to ascribe it wholly to Mr Pope's recommendation, as I have not the happiness to be known to you

---

* See the last letter.

myself; but give me leave to take this occasion of assuring you how much I wish to be in the number of your friends. I think I can be so even at this distance, and though we should never come to a nearer acquaintance; for the reputation of some men is amiable, and one can love their characters without knowing their persons.

If it could ever be in my power to do you any service in this country, the employing me in it would be a new favour to, Sir, your obliged humble servant,

G. LYTTLETON.

FROM MR POPE.

May 17, 1739.

DEAREST SIR,
EVERY time I see your hand, it is the greatest satisfaction that any writing can give me; and I am in proportion grieved to find, that several of my letters to testify it to you miscarry; and you ask me the same question again which I prolixly have answered before. Your last, which was delivered me by Mr Swift, inquires, where and how is Lord Bolingbroke? who, in a paragraph in my last, under his own hand, gave you an account of himself; and I employed almost a whole letter on his affairs afterward. He has sold Dawley for twenty-six thousand pounds, much to his own satisfaction. His plan of life is now a very agreeable one in the finest country in France, divided between study and exercise; for he still reads or writes five or six hours a-day, and generally hunts twice a-week.

He has the whole forest of Fountainbleau at his command, with the king's stables, dogs, &c., his lady's son-in-law being governor of that place. She resides most part of the year with my lord, at a large house they have hired ; and the rest with her daughter, who is abbess of a royal convent in the neighbourhood.

I never saw him in stronger health or in better humour with his friends, or more indifferent and dispassionate to his enemies. He is seriously set upon writing some parts of the history of his times, which he has begun by a noble introduction, presenting a view of the whole state of Europe, from the Pyrenean treaty. He has hence deduced a summary sketch of the natural and incidental interests of each kingdom ; and how they have varied from, or approached to, the true politics of each, in the several administrations to this time. The history itself will be particular only on such facts and anecdotes as he personally knew, or produces vouchers for, both from home and abroad. This puts into my mind to tell you a fear he expressed lately to me, that some facts in your History of the Queen's Last Years (which he read here with me in 1727) are not exactly stated, and that he may be obliged to vary from them, in relation, I believe, to the conduct of the Earl of Oxford, of which great care surely should be taken. * And he told me, that, when he saw you in 1727, he made you observe them ; and that you promised you would take care.

---

* It may be easily supposed that Swift and Bolingbroke would have differed widely in their account of that statesman's conduct ; whom the former honoured, and the latter detested, beyond all men living.

We very often commemorated you during the five months we lived together at Twickenham: at which place could I see you again, as I may hope to see him, I would envy no country in the world; and think, not Dublin only, but France and Italy, not worth the visiting once more in my life. The mention of travelling introduces your old acquaintance Mr Jervas, who went to Rome and Naples purely in search of health. An asthma has reduced his body, but his spirit retains all its vigour; and he is returned, declaring life itself not worth a day's journey at the expense of parting from one's friends.

Mr Lewis every day remembers you. I lie at his house in town. Dr Arbuthnot's daughter does not degenerate from the humour and goodness of her father. I love her much. She is like Gay, very idle, very ingenious, and inflexibly honest. Mrs Patty Blount is one of the most considerate and mindful women in the world toward others, the least so in regard to herself; she speaks of you constantly. I scarcely know two more women worth naming to you: the rest are ladies, run after music, and play at cards.

I always make your compliments to Lord Oxford and Lord Masham, when I see them. I see John Barber seldom: but always find him proud of some letter from you. I did my best with him, in behalf of one of your friends; and spoke to Mr Lyttelton for the other, who was more prompt to catch then I to give fire, and flew to the prince that instant, who was pleased to please me.

You ask me, how I am at court. I keep my old walk, and deviate from it to no court. The prince shows me a distinction beyond any merit or pretence on my part; and I have received a present from him of some marble heads of poets for my library, and some urns for my garden. The ministerial writers rail at me; yet I have no quarrel with their masters, nor think it of weight enough to complain of them. I am very well with the courtiers I ever was or would be acquainted with: At least, they are civil to me; which is all I ask from courtiers, and all a wise man will expect from them. The Duchess of Marlborough makes great court to me; but I am too old for her mind and body; yet I cultivate some young people's friendship, because they may be honest men: whereas the old ones experience too often proves not to be so, I having dropped ten where I have taken up one, and I hope to play the better with fewer in my hand. There is a Lord Cornbury, a Lord Polworth, a Mr Murray,* and one or two more with whom I would never fear to hold out against all the corruption in the world.

You compliment me in vain upon retaining my poetical spirit: I am sinking fast in prose; and, if I ever write more, it ought (at these years and in these times) to be something, the matter of which will give a value to the work, not merely the manner.

Since my protest (for so I call my dialogue † of 1738) I have written but ten lines, which I will send you. They are an insertion for the next new edition of the Dunciad, which generally is reprinted once in two years. In the second canto, among

---

* The last Lord Marchmont, and the celebrated Lord Mansfield.
† Epilogue to the Satires.—BOWLES.

the authors who live in Fleet-ditch, immediately
after Asnal, verse 300, add these :

> Next plung'd a feeble but a desp'rate pack,
> With each a sickly brother at his back ; *
> Sons of *a day!* just buoyant on the flood,
> Then number'd with the puppies in the mud.
> Ask ye their *names?* I could as soon disclose
> The names of these blind puppies as of those.
> Fast by, like Niobe, her children gone,
> Sits mother Osborne, † stupified to stone ;
> And rueful Paxton ‡ tells the world with tears,
> These are—ah ! no ; these were my Gazetteers."

Having nothing to tell you of my poetry, I come
to what is now my chief care, my health and amusement: the first is better, as to headaches ; worse,
as to weakness and nerves. The changes of weather
affect me much ; otherwise I want not spirits, except when indigestions prevail. The mornings are
my life ; in the evenings I am not dead indeed, but
sleep and am stupid enough. I love reading still,
better than conversation : but my eyes fail ; and, at
the hours when most people indulge in company,
I am tired, and find the labour of the past day sufficient to weigh me down. So I hide myself in

---

* " They print one at the back of the other, to send into the
country."—Pope, *MS. note.* These were daily papers, a number of which, to lessen the expence, were printed at the back of
another.—See the Dunciad.—B.

† Osborne was the assumed name of the publisher of the
Gazetteer.—BOWLES.   The real author was said to be a woman.

‡ " A solicitor, who procured and paid those writers."—Mr
Pope's MS. note.   Afterwards thus altered :

> " And monumental brass this record bears,
>   These are," &c.

bed, as a bird in his nest, much about the same time, and raise and chirp the earlier in the morning. I often vary the scene (indeed at every friend's call) from London to Twickenham; or the contrary, to receive them, or be received by them.

Lord Bathurst is still my constant friend, and yours; but his country-seat is now always in Gloucestershire, not in this neighbourhood. Mr Pulteney has no country-seat; and in town I see him seldom; but he always asks after you. In the summer I generally ramble for a month to Lord Cobham's, the Bath, or elsewhere. In all those rambles my mind is full of you, and poor Gay, with whom I travelled so delightfully two summers. Why cannot I cross the sea? The unhappiest malady I have to complain of, the unhappiest accident of my whole life, is that weakness of the breast, which make the physicians of opinion that a strong vomit would kill me. I have never taken one, nor had a natural motion that way in fifteen years. I went, some years ago, with Lord Peterborow, about ten leagues at sea, purely to try if I could sail without sea-sickness, and with no other view than to make yourself and Lord Bolingbroke a visit before I died.

But the experiment, though almost all the way near the coast, had almost ended all my views at once. Well then, I must submit to live at the distance which fortune has set us at: but my memory, my affections, my esteem, are inseparable from you, and will, my dear friend, be for ever yours.

P. S.—May 19. This I end at Lord Orrery's, in company with Dr King. Wherever I can find two or three that are yours, I adhere to them naturally, and by that title they become mine. I thank you for sending Mr Swift * to me : he can tell you more of me.

A SECOND POSTSCRIPT.

One of my new friends, Mr Lyttelton, was to the last degree glad to have any request from you to make to his master. The moment I showed him your's concerning Mr M'Aulay, he went to him, and it was granted. †—He is extremely obliged for the promotion of Lamb. I will make you no particular speeches from him ; but you and he have a mutual right to each other. *Sint tales animæ concordes.* He loves you, though he sees you not ; as all posterity will love you, who will not see you, but reverence and admire you.

TO MR LYTTELTON.

June 5, 1739.

SIR,

You treat me very hard, by beginning your letter with owing an obligation to me on account of Mr Lamb; which deserves mine and my chapter's thanks, for recommending so useful a person to my choir. It is true I gave Mr Deane Swift a letter to my dear friend Mr Pope, that he might have the happiness to see and know so great a genius in poetry, and so agreeable in all other good

---

* Deane Swift, Esq.—N.
† See the Dean's preceding letter of 10th May 1739.

qualities; but the young man (several years older than you) was much surprised to see his junior in so high a station as secretary to his royal highness the Prince of Wales, and to find himself treated by you in so kind a manner. In one article, you are greatly mistaken : for, however ignorant we may be in the affairs of England, your character is as well known among us, in every particular, as it is in the prince your master's court, and indeed all over this poor kingdom.

You will find that I have not altogether forgotten my old court politics : for, in a letter I writ to Mr Pope, I desired him to recommend Mr M'Aulay to your favour and protection, as a most worthy, honest, and deserving gentleman ; and I perceive you have effectually interceded with the prince, to prevail with the university to choose him for a member to represent that learned body in parliament, in the room of Dr Coghill, deceased.

I have been just now informed, that some of the fellows have sent over an apology, or rather a remonstrance, to the Prince of Wales ; pretending they were under a prior engagement to one Mr Tisdal ; and therefore have desired his royal highness to withdraw his recommendation. A modest request indeed, to demand from their chancellor, what they think is dishonourable in themselves, to give up an engagement! Their whole proceeding, on this occasion, against their chancellor, heir of the crown, is universally condemned here ; and seems to be the last effort of such men, who, without duly considering, make rash promises, not consistent with the prudence expected from them.

I can hardly venture the boldness to desire, that his royal highness may know from you the profound respect, honour, esteem, and veneration, I bear toward his princely virtues. All my friends on your side the water represent him to me in the most amiable light; and the people infallibly reckon upon a golden age in both kingdoms, when it shall please God to make him the restorer of the liberties of his people.

I ought to accuse you highly for your ill-treatment of me, by wishing yourself in the number of my friends: but you shall be pardoned, if you please to be one of my protectors; and your protection cannot be long. You shall therefore make it up, in thinking favourably of me. Years have made me lose my memory in every thing but friendship and gratitude; and you, whom I have never seen, will never be forgotten by me until I am dead. I am, honourable Sir, with the highest respect,

Your most obedient and
obliged humble servant.

FROM MRS WHITEWAY TO MR RICHARDSON.

July 20, 1739.

SIR,

A FORTNIGHT ago I went out of town with the new married couple, my son and daughter; and the day before I had the honour to receive your letter. With great truth I do asssure you, I am much more concerned at the trouble and disappointment you met with in Mr Dunkin's affair than for him, having but a short acquaintance and knowledge, otherwise than knowing him to be a man of sense, virtue, and religion, who would be an ornament to the church, and a credit to those who appeared for him. These were my reasons to wish him well.

One part of your letter, Sir, I can only take notice of with amazement; and do entreat you will indulge me so far as to believe this will be all the answer I can, or ever will, make to it: and yet I am not insensible you have been pleased in some measure to honour me with your esteem. I will not therefore fear the loss of your friendship, because it shall be my study to merit your good opinion: and, unprovoked, I know you to have too much good nature to withdraw it. I never saw a more beautiful silk than was bought for my daughter. If you did not choose it, at least you showed your judgment in the person that was employed. She desires me to say this, that you have forced her to do what she never did in her life, wear any thing that was not paid for; and if hereafter she should run her husband in debt, she will lay all the fault at your door. Mr Swift presents you his most obedient respects, and will oblige you to know him by his assiduity in courting the honour of your acquaintance. I have asked you so many favours, that no one but myself would presume perpetually to dun you thus; and yet I will never leave off until you grant this my request, to command Miss Richardson to town immediately. I now attack you on the foot of charity; an argument you can never resist. Consider my daughter has quitted me; that I am all alone; and her agreeable company will make Molly and her husband spend all their time with me. In short, Sir, If you hesitate one moment longer, I will lay you open to the world, and let them see how much they were mistaken in Mr Richardson, who once in his life broke his word. I have now before me, under your hand, that all my commands should be obeyed. I insist on your promise ; and Miss Richardson is my demand, and that immediately. You see how careful and sparing you gentlemen ought to be in compliments to women, who always keep you to your promise while it makes to their interest ; and as well know how to evade their own when it is contrary to their inclination. I had the favour of a letter from Alderman Barber in answer to one I wrote him. He does not perhaps know the inconveniency he has brought on himself, which is another from me ; and yet you may tell him when I have once more paid my respects to him, I am not so unreasonable as to impose or expect any further notice of Irish impertinence.

I left this paragraph to finish at the deanery, that from his own mouth I might assure you of his love and esteem. He sends his most affectionate service to his dear old friend Alderman Barber. Mr Dunkin likewise presents you his most obedient respects, and hopes you received his letter that he sent some days ago. There is no person a more obedient humble servant to you than my daughter, excepting, dear Sir, your most obedient and most obliged faithful humble servant,

MARTHA WHITEWAY.

The chief circumstance that you would choose to know I had like to have forgot ; which is, that the Dean is in good health, and ever will remember the pains you and the alderman have been at, on his account, for Mr Dunkin.

FROM DR SCOTT.

London, Sept. 7, 1739.

Rev. Sir,

ALTHOUGH I do not imagine that you have any remembrance of a person so little known to you as I am, yet I have taken the liberty to draw a kind of bill of friendship upon you, which I am inclined to believe you will answer, because it is in favour of that kingdom to which you have always stood a sincere and firm friend. We have had here, for some time past, a number of anatomical figures, prepared in wax, which perfectly exhibit all the parts of a human body. They are the work of a French surgeon, * who spent above forty years in preparing them, and who, to bring them to perfection, was at the trouble and expense of dissecting some hundreds of bodies. The present proprietor of them is my friend, and it was by my persuasion that he was prevailed on to send them into Ireland for the instruction of the curious. I presume you have seen them in London, and therefore I am inclined to think you will be of opinion, that a person may gain more perfect knowledge in anatomy, by viewing these preparations only a few times, than he would by attending many dissections. Your encouraging such of your acquaintance as are curious to see these figures, would greatly excite the curiosity of others. This is the favour I have taken the liberty to desire of

---

* Mr Rackstraw, statuary; the anatomical figures were purchased from him by the late Earl of Shelburne, who presented them to the university of Dublin.—D. S.

you, and which I believe you will be the more readily inclined to grant, when I have assured you, that the person who has the care of the figures, has it in his instructions to return the money that may be got by exposing them to view, in Irish linen, so that the kingdom will be no way impoverished by the small expense which gentlemen may be at in procuring useful instruction, or gratifying their curiosity. If the request I have made be such as you cannot favour, my next is, that you will grant me your pardon for having made it.

I intend, God willing, to go into Ireland next spring, after the publication of a work which I have been engaged in for some years past, for the silencing of all infidels, heretics, schismatics of all kinds, and enthusiasts. I thought it necessary, because in the way that the controversy has been hitherto managed against such people, the truth has been rather puzzled and perplexed than cleared, Christianity has been betrayed, and all true religion lost in the world. I have advanced no one new opinion of my own: what I have set forth is what was clearly set forth in the Scriptures from the beginning. I mean in the original Scriptures of the Old Testament, so interpreted as to make them every where consistent with themselves; and to show that the interpretations I have given are not only the true interpretations, but that the Scriptures so interpreted are the revealed word of God. I have demonstrated the truth of them by natural evidence, or by the works of God, and that the works bear evidence to nothing but the truth; that these revealed truths so demonstrated are unquestionable and undeniable; and that they are the only powerful motives by which men are not only moved but enlightened, and enabled to mortify all their lusts, which blind and deceive them here, and will be their everlasting tormentors hereafter, but to work the works of charity, and of that perfect righteousness which is of faith: so that the whole of all true religion, which has been one and the same in all ages, will appear to consist in the mortifications of our bodily and spiritual lusts, which withhold men from the works of righteousness; and in the belief of those demonstrative truths, by which alone we are enlightened, enabled, and moved to subdue them; and in observing those natural memorials, which God has set before us, and in partaking of those reverential ordinances which he has instituted to put us in mind of what we ought to do, in order to eternal life and the motives for so doing. I ask pardon for this digression: and if you have any commands that I am capable of executing here, if you will let me have the honour of receiving them, I shall take great pleasure in obeying you; for I am, with the greatest respect and truth, Sir, your most obedient and and most humble servant,

JOHN SCOTT.

TO THE EARL OF ARRAN.

1739.

My Lord,

I am earnestly desired by some worthy friends of mine, to write to your lordship in favour of the bearer, Mr Moore, minister of Clonmel, who will have the honour to present this letter to your lordship. Those rectorial tithes of Clonmel were granted to the church by letters-patent from King Charles the Second, with the perfect knowledge and full approbation of your great ancestor, the first Duke of Ormond, then lord lieutenant of Ireland. Notwithstanding which, some of the former agents to your lordship's family have greatly distressed the incumbent ministers of Clonmel, which is generally believed to be without the knowledge of his present grace the duke your brother, whom God long preserve. But your lordship's present agent being extremely vigilant of all your lordship's interests, has lately renewed the claim of the Ormond family to those tithes, and was at the last assizes, after a long hearing of six hours, nonsuited. The living of Clonmel is one of the largest, and yet the poorest parishes in this kingdom; being upon the whole (including the valuation of the houses) scarce worth one hundred pounds a year; out of which, a curate assistant being absolutely necessary on account of its extent, a salary of forty pounds must be paid.

My lord, your lordship's family has been always distinguished for their favour and protection to the established church, under her greatest persecutions; nor have you, in the universal opinion, ever degenerated from them. Those tithes in and about Clonmel are very inconsiderable, having never been let for above twenty-four pounds a year, made up of very small pittances collected from a great number of the poorest people; so that the recovery of them by an expensive law-suit, if it could be effected, would not be worth attempting.

Mr Moore is recommended to me by several persons of great worth (as I have already observed) and I hope I have not hitherto forfeited the credit I had with you.

My humble request therefore to your lordship is, that the minister of Clonmel may, without disturbance, enjoy that small addition to his support, which the king and your grandfather intended for him.

I have always understood and believed, that the duke your brother's retiring has not lessened your fortune, but increased it : and as to his grace, unless all our intelligence be false, he is as easy as he desires to be. I heard of several persons who have ventured to wait on him abroad, and it is agreed that his grace is perfectly easy in his mind and fortune.

Upon the whole, I do earnestly desire your lordship to resign those poor scraps of tithes in and about Clonmel to Mr Moore and his successors, in a legal form, for ever. Your loss will be at most but twenty-four pounds a year, and that with a thousand difficulties infinitely below your generosity and quality.

I am, &c.   Jon. Swift.

TO MR FAULKNER.

Dec. 4. 1739.

Sir,

I cannot find a manuscript I wrote, called, " Directions for Servants," which I thought was very useful, as well as humorous. I believe, you have both seen and read it. I wish you could give me some intelligence of it, because my memory is quite gone; therefore let me know all you can conjecture about it.

I am, Sir,
Your very humble servant,
Jon. Swift.

FROM THE REV. MR THROP *.

Dec. 10, 1739.

REV. SIR,

THE many professions of kindness you have made, and friendship you have shown, to my mother and her family, particularly in declaring your abhorrence and detestation of the cruel and inhuman behaviour of that monster———† to my unfortunate and innocent brother, induced my mother to trouble you with a few of the narratives of that case, to disperse among such members of the House of Commons as were of your acquaintance. The reason of our troubling you to do this, is because we intend presenting a petition to the members of the House of Commons, this session, to oblige ——— to wave his privilege, every other attempt we have tried since my brother's death proving fruitless.

---

* Son of Mr Thomas Throp, a merchant in Dublin, and brother to the Rev. Roger Throp, a clergyman, who suffered a series of persecution, under which his health finally gave way, at the hands of Colonel John Waller, who, in consequence of Mr Throp's declining a simoniacal compromise of his tithes, became, from being his patron, his bitter and vindictive enemy. At least such is the account of the transactions between them given in the narrative of his case, published in 1739, and referred to in the following letter; and if the tenth part of what is there stated be true, Colonel Waller must have been one of the most cruel and tyrannical wretches who ever existed. The injured and unfortunate clergyman, after being driven from his living, fell into a rapid consumption, of which he died, 23d January 1736. His brother, acting for his family, petitioned parliament, of which Colonel Waller was a member, to oblige Colonel Waller to wave his privilege, without which it was impossible to obtain justice against him.

† Mr Faulkner fills the blank with " Mr Wilson," most in-

Your appearing, Sir, in this affair, will not only make * —— the more ready to do justice, but prevent others from supporting him in his villanies, which will be of infinite service to my mother and her family.

The bearer carries you a dozen of cases; and if you should have occasion for any more, they shall be sent you by, Reverend Sir, your most obliged and obedient humble servant,

ROBERT THROP.

I have written the names of several persons mentioned in the narrative at length upon the back of the title-page:

TO MRS WHITEWAY.

Dec. 31, 1739.

MADAM,

IT is impossible to have health in such desperate weather : but you are worse used than others. Every creature of either sex are uneasy; for our kingdom is turned to be a Muscovy, or worse. Even I cannot do any good by walking : Is not warmth good against rheumatic pains? I hope Deane Swift † will be able to assist you both. I wish for a happy turn in the weather. I am doubly

---

accurately. The name of Colonel Waller of Castleton, the persecutor of the deceased Mr Roger Thorp, is that which is omitted.

* We must supply *parliament*.

† Then married to Mrs Harrison.——D. S.

desolate, and wish I could sleep until the sun would comfort us. Would neither your son or daughter save you the pains of writing on your back? You are much more friendly to me than a thousand of them. Adieu.

I am ever yours,

JON. SWIFT.

TO THE SAME.

DEAR MADAM,

I AM truly and heartily glad that you are a little mended, and can lie on your belly, or side, not altogether on your back. You are much in the right not to stir, and so was Croker* not to suffer you. I am not yet worse for the cold weather, but am angry at it. I am heartily sorry for yourself and daughter; but Mr Swift dares not be sick, for his chief business is to look after you and your daughter. I walk only in my bedchamber and closet, which has also a fire. I am ever yours,

JON. SWIFT.

New-Year's-day, 1739-40.

I wish you may have many, and all healthy ones.

---

* An eminent apothecary of great humanity and skill.——D. S.

CERTIFICATE TO A DISCARDED SERVANT.*

Deanery-house, Jan. 9, 1739-40.

WHEREAS the bearer served me the space of one year, during which time he was an idler and a

---

* The history of this certificate is related in the third volume of Mrs Pilkington's Memoirs. " Dean Swift discharged a servant, only for rejecting the petition of a poor old woman; she was very ancient, and, on a cold morning, sat at the Deanery steps a considerable time, during which the Dean saw her through a window, and no doubt commiserated her desolate condition. His footman happened to come to the door; and the poor creature besought him, in a piteous tone, to give that paper to his Reverence. The servant read it; and told her, with infinite scorn, " His master had something else to mind than her petition."—" What is that you say, fellow?" said the Dean, looking out at the window. " Come up here." The man tremblingly obeyed him.—He also desired the poor woman to come before him, made her sit down, and ordered her some bread and wine. After which, he turned to the man, and said, " At what time, sir, did I order you to open a paper directed to me, or to refuse a letter from any one? Hark ye, sirrah, you have been admonished by me, for drunkenness, idling, and other faults; but since I have discovered your inhuman disposition, I must dismiss you from my service: so pull off my clothes, take your wages, and let me hear no more of you." The fellow did so; and, having vainly solicited a discharge, was compelled to go to sea, where he continued five years; at the end of which time, finding that life far different from the ease and luxury of his former occupation, he returned, and, humbly confessing in a petition to the Dean his former manifold crimes, assured him of his sincere reformation, which the dangers he had undergone at sea had happily wrought; and begged the Dean would give him some sort of discharge, since the honour of having lived with him would certainly procure him a place. Accordingly the Dean called for pen, ink, and paper; and gave him a dismission, with which, and no other fortune, he set out for London,

drunkard, I then discharged him as such ; but how far his having been five years at sea may have mended his manners, I leave to the penetration of those who may hereafter choose to employ him.

JON. SWIFT.

TO MRS WHITEWAY.

Jan. 18, 1739-40.

DEAR MADAM,

I HAVE been many days heartily concerned for your ill health ; it is now twenty-five days since we have found nothing but frost and misery, and they may continue for as many more. This day is yet the coldest of them all. Dr Wilson* and I are both very uneasy to find no better message from you. I received, as I was going to dinner, the enclosed letter from your beloved of ———, which I shall make you happy with. It will show you the goodness, the wisdom, the gratitude, the truth, the civility, of that excellent divine, adorned with an orthography (spel-

---

Among others, he applied to me, who had known him at his late master's, and produced his certificate ; which, for its singularity, I transcribed. I advised him to go to Mr Pope, who, on seeing the Dean's handwriting, which he well knew, told the man, " If he could produce any credible person, who could attest that he was the servant the Dean meant, he would hire him." On this occasion he applied to me ; and I gave him a letter to Mr Pope, assuring him, that I knew the man to have been footman to the Dean. Upon this, Mr Pope took him into his service ; in which he continued till the death of his master."

* Dr Wilson, prebendary of Kilmactolway, was at this time resident in the Dean's house. They parted soon afterwards after a disgraceful fracas, and on the worst possible terms.

ling) fit for himself.   Pray read it a hundred times,
but return it after you have read it a hundred times.
My love and service to your son and daughter; let
them both read the enclosed.

I would not lose your lover's letter for 100l.   It
must be sent back by the bearer.   Let me know the
exact number of lies that are in it; but I fear that
that will take up your time too much.

I am ever yours,

JON. SWIFT.

FROM LORD CASTLEDURROW.

Dublin, Feb. 2, 1739-40.

SIR,

SINCE I am forbidden your presence, I think I
should be more explicit in my reason of thanks to
you for Dr Delany's obliging present, than I can
be in a verbal, crude, ill-delivered message by a
servant.   As I am not acquainted with the doctor,
I at first imagined his boundless generosity distributed his book among the lords, and that it was
sent me, as a member, though an unworthy one,
of that august body. I soon found myself mistaken;
and as all presents are enhanced in value proportion-
able to their manner of distribution, I thought it
incumbent on me to thank him by letter, for having
so obligingly distinguished me.   He has honoured
me with an answer to it, which highly elates me;
for weak minds are easily made vain; but whose
would not be so, on the compliment he makes me,
on having read some of my letters to you? They
were writ, (as most of mine are) in the wanton-

ness of fancy, without aiming at pomp of expression, or dress of words, lucky methods of gilding nonsense; yet, that he should approve, I will not wonder when I consider the benignity of your friendship. Oh! is it not sometimes too strong bias even for your judgment, that prompted you to think them worth his perusal? What am I now to do? I ought not to be silent; yet must I risk depreciating a favourable opinion he has conceived of me, by making myself farther known to him! Why, in prudence, no; in civility, yes. Under this dilemma give me your advice, as you are the origin of this favour. Or will you yield to what I suggest may not be improper? Take me under your protection (as soon as the weather will permit) in a warm hackney coach, which I shall take care to provide. Let us jumble together to his little paradise, which I long much to see, as well as to pay my debt due to his benevolence.

I am already alarmed with your excuse of deafness and dizziness. Yielding to such a complaint, always strengthens it; exerting against it, generally lessens it. Do not immerge in the sole enjoyment of yourself. Is not a friend the medicine of life? I am sure it is the comfort of it. And I hope you still admit such companions as are capable of administering it. In that number I know I am unworthy of rank: however, my best wishes shall attend you.

I have enclosed some verses. The Latin I believe will please you; one of the translations may have the same fortune, the other cannot. The verses written in the lady's book is, A Lamentable Hymn to Death, from a lover, inscribed to his mistress. I have made the author of it vain (who I am sure had never read Pope's Heloise to Abe-

lard) in telling him his six last lines seem a parody
oñ six of Pope's. They are on the other side, that
you may not be at a loss.

Then too, when fate shall thy fair frame destroy,
That cause of all my guilt, and all my joy,
In trance extatic may thy pangs be drown'd,
Bright clouds descend, and angels watch thee round ;
From opening skies may streaming glories shine,
And saints embrace thee with a love like mine.

I think the whole letter the most passionate I
ever read, except Heloise's own, on the subject of
love. I am equally struck with Cadenus to Vanessa. I have often soothed my love with both,
when I have been in a fit.

I will conclude with the above wish, and assuring you I am, with great sincerity, as well as esteem, Sir,
        Your most faithful
        ~ affectionate humble servant,
                        CASTLEDURROW.

My boy sends you his respects, and would fain pay
them in person to you.

TO MRS WHITEWAY.

February 3, 1739-40.

THE bad account I had of your health for many
days or rather weeks, has made me continually uneasy to the last degree ; and Mr Swift, who was with
me so long yesterday, could not in conscience give
me any comfort : but your kind letter has raised my
spirits in some measure. I hope we have almost

done with this cursed weather, yet still my garden is all in white. I read your letter to Dr Wilson, who is somewhat better, and he resolves to apply your medicine, I mean your improvements of what you prescribe to add to his surgeon's method.

I am ever, dear Madam, entirely yours,

JON. SWIFT.

FROM MRS WHITEWAY TO MR RICHARDSON.

March 25, 1740.

DEAR SIR,

ONCE I thought I could never receive a letter from, or answer one to you, without pleasure; and yet both has happened to me very lately. This is the third day I sat down to write to you, and as often tore my paper. I endeavoured to say something to alleviate your grief;——that would not do: Then I resolved to be silent on the occasion; but, alas! that was impossible for a friend. I will, therefore, for a moment, rather renew your grief by joining with you in it. Your trials have been most severe: the loss of two such valuable persons as Miss Richardson and Sir Joseph Eyles are irreparable; for, in a middle state of life, we have not time enough before us to make new friendships, were it possible to meet their equals. This is an unusual way of comforting a friend in trouble: Ought I not rather to persuade you to forget them, and call in Christianity to your aid? But I believe those expounders of it are mistaken in their notions, who would have us imagine this to be religion; for I am sure a just God will expect no more from us than to submit without repining. I am too much a fellow-sufferer in misfortunes of this nature not to feel for you. In a short time I lost a beloved husband and friend, an ingenious, a worthy son, and, what the world value as their chief happiness, some trifling conveniences. All these I have outlived, and am an instance that time will erase the blackest melancholy. I most sincerely wish, dear sir, this may be your case, and that it may be the last struggle of mind or tedious illness you will ever have to battle against.

You have conjured me by such a tie as the last request of dear Miss Richardson, that, as well as I am able, I will tell you what I guess the Dean may like. I know his candlesticks are the most indifferent of any of his plate, and therefore mention a pair of those : his snuffers are good*.

---

* The Dean used to say he was the richest man in Ireland who did not keep an equipage, the poorest who used a service of plate. The following list of the articles of which it consisted is copied from the original, in Swift's hand-writing, indorsed " An " account of the Dean's plate and prices." On the back *Esther Johnson* is twice written by the Dean's hand.

Account of D.'s Plate.

Soup dish,	L.16	7	8
Quart pot	8	0	10½
Tuns,	6	19	0
Sauce-pan,	6	12	8
6 spoons,	5	12	8
6 plates,	33	16	10
2 little cups,	3	13	3
Ladle,	2	5	0
Tobacco candlestick,	1	14	0
2 English candlesticks,	4	5	0
2 salvers,	4	0	0
3 casters,	12	0	0

Surely I was not such a beast as to forget mentioning the receipt of the papers you were so careful and obliging to send me : they came very safe. I entreat you to accept of my most humble thanks for this, and all your other most extraordinary favours.

The Dean of St Patrick's presents you his most affectionate love and service ; and commanded me to tell you he would have writ to you upon this late occasion, if he had not been too deeply affected with your grief.

Surely the two long months you have so often fixed for your return will be at an end ; and then I

Little tankard,	4	0	0
2 candlesticks,	5	0	10
Snuffers and dish,	3	11	0
2 cans,	5	2	10
4 salts,	4	1	9
Strainer,	1	4	3
Little sauce-pan,	2	12	6
Soup plates,	15	0	0
Platells, knives, &c.	15	0	0
Six tea-spoons,	1	4	0
Six silver plates,	34	18	1
A marrow-spoon,	1	2	0
Tundish,	0	7	6
Cup and save-all,	15	0	0
Six silver plates,	34	12	1
Six silver plates,	39	0	10
Six silver dishes,	73	17	3
Tundish,	0	7	6
Nutmeg grater,	0	9	0
Pepper-box,	1	0	0
Wax candlestick,	1	14	0

These particulars may gratify a minute antiquary. Swift's peculiar humour broke out even in these particulars. Mrs King, relict of the Reverend James King, rector of St Bridget's, Dublin, is possessed of a silver *save-all*, once the Dean's property, on which he had caused to be engraved the emphatic words, For Ireland.

shall have the opportunity of telling you from my mouth what I now give under my hand, that I am, with the highest respect and esteem, Dear Sir, your most obliged and most obedient humble servant,

MARTHA WHITEWAY.

My most obedient respects to Alderman Barber. Mr Swift and his wife beg you will accept of theirs.

MR NUGENT*, TO MRS WHITEWAY.

Bath, April 2, 1740.

MADAM,

I HAD not until very lately an opportunity of letting Mr Pope know his obligations to you ; of which he is very sensible, and has desired me to beg that you will remit to me, by a safe hand, whatever letters of his are now in your possession. I shall be in town next week ; so that you may be pleased to direct to me, by the first convenient opportunity, at my house in Dover-street, London. I am, Madam, with great esteem, your most humble and obedient servant, R. N.

My compliments to Mr and Mrs Swift. I shall say nothing of the picture †, because I am sure you remember it. I must beg that you will let Mr Bindon ‡ know I would have the picture no

---

* Afterward Lord Clare.——D. S.　　+ Of Dr Swift.——D. S.
‡ The greatest painter and architect of his time in these

more than a head upon a three quarter cloth, to match one which I now have of Mr Pope.

[MR POPE TO *SAMUEL GERRARD, ESQ.]

April 18, 1740.

Sir,

I was sorry not to be able to wait upon you, when you sent me Dr Swift's letter : I was at dinner, with my Lord Burlington, and a great deal of company at his table ; I could only reply, that as soon as I returned to London, I would receive the pleasure of seeing a friend of Dean Swift's.   In the mean time, I send this to my lodging to be delivered you, which is all I can do till my return from Windsor Forest ; and if you leave a line to acquaint me where you may be found, I will do myself that satisfaction in five or six days.

I am, with all respect,

Sir, your most humble servant,

A. Pope.

---

kingdoms.   On account of his age, and some little failure in his sight, he threw aside his pencil soon after the year 1750 ; and afterward lived to a good old age, greatly beloved and respected by all who had the happiness either of his friendship or acquaintance.   He died June 2, 1765.——D. S.

* The superscription is lost, but from a subsequent letter from Pope, dated 17th May, it appears to have been addressed to the same Mr Samuel Gerrard with whom the Dean had entertained a preceding correspondence respecting the purchase of land, and whom, as he entertained a high respect for him, he had furnished with an introduction to Pope.

TO MRS WHITEWAY.

April 29, 1740.

DEAR MADAM,

I FIND that you and I are fellow sufferers almost equally in our healths, although I am more than twenty years older. But I am and have been these two days in so miserable a way, and so cruelly tortured, that can hardly be conceived. The whole last night I was equally struck as if I had been in Phalaris's brazen bull, and roared as loud for eight or nine hours. I am at this instant unable to move without excessive pain, although not the one thousandth part of what I suffered all last night and this morning. This you will now style the gout. I continue still very deaf. Doctor Wilson's left eye is still disordered, and very uneasy. You have now your family at home: I desire to present them with my kind and hearty service.

I am ever entirely yours, &c.

JON. SWIFT.

MRS WHITEWAY TO MR RICHARDSON.

May 13, 1740.

DEAR SIR,

By the time this kisses your hand, I believe Mrs Richardson will not blush to be wished joy by a person you have done the honour to call a friend, and whose ambition it is to deserve some place in her esteem; and now that all insinuations in your favour are as needless as the formal ceremony between lovers, I shall take the liberty to tell her, it will be her own fault if she is not one of the happiest women in the world. This is an unusual way of recommending myself to a bride; nor should I do it to any but yours: yet surely when a lady is married to a gentleman with an easy fortune, good nature, and a man of honour, how little is required of her side toward mutual felicity, which can be comprised in two words, love and obey?

About a fortnight ago I dined at the Dean of St Patrick's in a mixed company; where one of the gentlemen told him you were married, or just going to be so, to a lady of fifteen, with a hundred thousand pound fortune, and a perfect beauty. I asked the person whether he had not that account from a woman! He said he had. The Dean inquired if I knew any thing of the affair. I answered yes; only with this difference, that she was at least fifty, and a most ungenteel disagreeable woman. The whole company looked upon me with contempt; and their countenances expressed they thought I drew my own picture whilst I enviously endeavoured to paint the lady's. The Dean only understood me; and, smiling, said he believed I was in the right. When we were alone, I let him know that you had commanded me to acquaint him with the affair; and I hoped, when I wrote to you next, he would add a postscript in my letter. He promised me to do it; and this day I intend to put him in mind of it.

I waited on Mr Hamilton yesterday to consult with him if it would not be proper to allow the servants board-wages from this time; and it was diverting enough to see us both keeping our distance about a secret the whole town has known these two months. However, at last we understood each other; and have agreed to give the coachman four shillings a week, and the maid three, until they go a shipboard.

There would have been no occasion to be so formal with a friend as to desire Mr Hamilton to give the servants money when you might have ordered me to do it, although I had not been in your debt; which, to my shame be it spoken, would be scandalous so long a time, if the fault were entirely mine. My son and daughter Swift present you and your lady their most obedient respects, and sincerest wishes. I am at a loss to express my obligations to her for the compliment she was pleased to remit to me; and I believe, when we meet, she will not be jealous that I dare give it under my hand to her, that I honour and esteem you more than any woman does except herself.

I am, Dear Sir,

Your most humble and most obedient servant,

MARTHA WHITEWAY.

TO MR RICHARDSON.

May 13, 1740.

DEAR SIR,

I could never believe Mrs Whiteway's gasconades in telling me of her acquaintance with you. But my age and perpetual disorders, and chiefly my vexatious deafness, with other infirmities, have completed the utter loss of my memory; so that I cannot recollect the names of those friends who come to see me twice or oftener every week. However, I remember to wish you a long lasting joy of being no longer a bachelor, especially because the teaser

at my elbow assures me that the lady is altogether
worthy to be your wife. I therefore command you
both (if I live so long) to attend me at the deanery
the day after you land; where Mrs Precipitate, alias
Whiteway, says I will give you a scandalous dinner. I suppose you will see your governor my old
friend John Barber, whom I heartily love; and so
you are to tell him.

I am, Dear Sir,
Your most obedient and obliged servant,
JON. SWIFT.

FROM MRS WHITEWAY TO MR POPE.

May 16, 1740.

SIR,

SHOULD I make an apology for writing to you,
I might be asked why I did so? If I have erred, my
design at least is good, both to you and the Dean of
St Patrick; for I write in relation to my friend, and
I write to his friend, which I hope will plead my
excuse. As I saw a letter of yours to him, wherein
I had the honour to be named, I take the liberty to
tell you (with grief of heart) his memory is so much
impaired, that in a few hours he forgot it; nor is
his judgment sound enough, had he many tracts by
him, to finish or correct them, as you have desired.
His health is as good as can be expected, free from
all the tortures of old age; and his deafness, lately
returned, is all the bodily uneasiness he has to complain of. A few years ago he burnt most of his

writings unprinted *, except a few loose papers,
which are in my possession, and which I promise
you (if I outlive him) shall never be made public
without your approbation.   There is one treatise in
his own keeping, called Advice to Servants, very
unfinished and incorrect, yet what is done of it, has
so much humour, that it may appear as a posthumous work.   The History of the Four Last Years
of Queen Anne's Reign I suppose you have seen with
Dr King, to whom he sent it some time ago, and, if
I am rightly informed, is the only piece of his (except Gulliver) which he ever proposed making money
by, and was given to Dr King with that design, if
it might be printed: I mention this to you, lest the
doctor should die, and his heirs imagine they have
a right to dispose of it.   I entreat, sir, you will not
take notice to any person of the hints I have given
you in this letter: they are only designed for yourself: to the Dean's friends in England they can only
give trouble, and to his enemies and starving wits
cause of triumph.   I enclose this to Alderman Barber, who I am sure will deliver it safe, yet knows
nothing more than its being a paper that belongs
to you.

The ceremony of answering women's letters, may
perhaps make you think it necessary to answer mine;
but I do not expect it, because your time either is or
ought to be better employed, unless it be in my
power to serve you in buying Irish linen, or any
other command you are pleased to lay on me, which
I shall execute to the best of my capacity, with the

---

* In resentment to the House of Commons of Ireland, who
sent Faulkner to Newgate for printing the satire on Quadrille.—
F.

greatest readiness, integrity, and secrecy; for whether it be my years, or a less degree of vanity in my composition than in some of my sex, I can receive such an honour from you without mentioning it. I should, some time past, have writ to you on this subject, had I not fancied that it glanced at the ambition of being thought a person of consequence, by interfering between you and the Dean; a character of all others which I dislike.

I have several of your letters to the Dean, which I will send by the first safe hand that I can get to deliver them to yourself; I believe it may be Mr M'Aulay, the gentleman the Dean recommended, through your friendship, to the Prince of Wales.

I believe this may be the only letter which you ever received without asking a favour, a compliment, extolling your genius, running in raptures on your poetry, or admiring your distinguishable virtue. I am, Sir, with very high respect, your most obedient and most humble servant,

MARTHA WHITEWAY.

Mr Swift, who waited on you last summer, is since that married to my daughter: he desires me to present you his most obedient respects and humble thanks for the particular honour conferred upon him in permitting him to spend a day with you at Twickenham; a favour he will always remember with gratitude.

MR POPE TO MR GERRARD.*

May 17, 1740.

Sir,

I am obliged to you for the notice of your intended return to Ireland, in order to what I desired, that
I might charge you with a letter to the Dean.   But
I had an opportunity, just after I saw you, of sending him a very long and full letter by a safe hand,
which leaves me nothing to tell him more, except
what I would always tell to the last day of my life;
and desire you to tell him and all mankind, that I
love, esteem, and respect him, and account it the
most pleasing circumstance of my fortune, to have
known him long, and experienced his friendship
through my life.

I am glad you found the benefit I promised myself you would from Dr Cheyne's care, to whom,
pray make my heartiest services.   There lives not
an honester man, nor a truer philosopher.   I wish
you a good journey, and am with respect,

   Sir,

  Your most obedient humble servant,

      A. Pope.

To Samuel Gerrard, Esq. at Mr
 Hencher's, apothecary, Cheap-
 Street, in Bath.

---

* See a preceding letter from Mr Pope to this gentleman, 18th
April preceding.

FROM MR PULTENEY.

London, June 3, 1740.

SIR,

I HAD, some time ago, a letter from Mr Stopford, who told me, that you enjoyed a better state of health last year than you had done for some time past. No one wishes you more sincerely than I do the continuance of it ; and since the gout has been your physic, I heartily hope you may have one good fit regularly every year, and all the rest of it perfect health and spirits.

I am persuaded you will do me the justice to believe, that if I have not writ to you for some time, it has proceeded from an unwillingness alone of engaging you in a very useless correspondence, and not from any want of a real regard and true esteem. Mr Pope can be my witness how constantly I inquire after you, and how pleased and happy I am, when he tells me that you have the goodness frequently to mention me in your letters to him.

I fear you have but little desire to come among us again. England has few things inviting in it at present. Three camps, near forty thousand troops, and sixteen kings*, and most of them such as are really fit to be kings in any part of the world. Four millions of money have been raised on the people this year, and in all probability nothing will be done. I have not the least notion, that even our expedition under Lord Cathcart † is intended to be sent any-

---

* Sixteen lords of the regency, the King being abroad.——B.
+ Against Carthagena. It went, and miscarried.——B.

where; and yet every minister we have (except Sir
Robert) very gravely affirms it will go; nay, and I
am afraid believes it too.   But our situation is very
extraordinary: Sir Robert will have an army, will
not have a war, and cannot have a peace; that is,
the people are so averse to it, that he dares not make
one. But in one year more, when, by the influence
of this army and our money, he has got a new parliament to his liking, then he will make peace, and get
it approved too, be it as it will.   After which I am
afraid we shall all grow tired of struggling any longer, and give up the game.

But I will trouble you with no more politics; and
if I can hear from you in two lines that you are well,
I promise you not to reply to it too soon. You must
give me leave to add to my letter a copy of verses at
the end of a declamation made by a boy at Westminster school on this theme,

Ridentem dicere verum,
Quid vetat?

Dulce decane, decus, flos optime gentis Hibernæ
  Nomine quique audis, ingenioque celer;
Dum lepido indulges risu, et mutaris in horas,
  Quô nova vis animi, materiesque rapit;
Nunc gravis astrologus, cœlo dominaris et astris,
  Filaque pro libitu Patrigiana secas.
Nunc populo speciosa hospes miracula promis,
  Gentesque æquoreas, aëriasque creas.
Seu plausum captat queruli persona draperi,
  Seu levis a vacuo fabula sumpta cado.
Mores egregius mira exprimis arte magister,
  Et vitam atque homines pagina quæque sapit.
Socraticæ minor est vis et sapientia chartæ,
  Nec tantum potuit grande Platonis opus.

Mrs Pulteney, knowing that I am writing to you,
charges me to present her services, when I assure
you that I am most faithfully and sincerely,

Your obedient humble servant,

W. PULTENEY.

MR POPE TO MRS WHITEWAY.

Twickenham, June 18, 1740.

I AM extremely sensible of the favour of your
letter, and very well see the kindness as well as honour which moved you to it.   I have no merit for
the one, but being (like yourself) a sincere friend
to the Dean, though much a less useful one ; for all
my friendship can only operate in wishes, yours in
good works. He has had the happiness to meet with
such in all the stages of his life ; and I hope in God
and in you, that he will not want one in the last.
Never imagine, madam, that I can do otherwise than
esteem that sex, which has furnished him with the
best friends.

The favour you offer me I accept with the utmost
thankfulness ; and I think no person more fit to con-
vey it to my hands than Mr M'Aulay, of whom I
know you have so good an opinion.   Indeed any
one whom you think worthy your trust, I shall think
deserves mine, in a point I am ever so tender of.

I wish the very small opportunity I had of showing Mr Swift, your son, my regards for him, had
been greater ; and I wish it now more, since he is
become so near to you, for whom my respect runs
hand in hand with my affection for the Dean ; and
I cannot wish well for the one without doing so for
the other.

I turn my mind all I can from the melancholy
subject of your letter. May God Almighty alleviate
your concern, and his complaints, as much as possible in this state of infirmities, while he lives ; and
may your tenderness, Madam, prevent any thing
after his death which may anywise depreciate his

memory. I dare say nothing of ill consequence can happen from the commission given to Dr King.

You see, Madam, I write to you with absolute freedom, as becomes me to the friend of my friend, and to a woman of sense and spirit. I will say no more, that you may find I treat you with the same delicacy that you do me (and for which I thank you) without the least compliment: and it is none when I add, that I am, with esteem, Madam, your most obliged and most obedient servant,

A. Pope.

FROM MR. POPE TO MR ALLEN.

My vexation about Dean Swift's proceeding has fretted and employed me a great deal, in writing to Ireland, and trying all the means possible to retard it; for it is put past preventing, by his having (without my consent, or so much as letting me see the book), printed most of it.—They at last promise me to send me the copy, and that I may correct and expunge what I will. This last would be of some use; but I dare not even do this, for they would say I revised it. And the bookseller writes, that he has been at great charge, &c. However, the Dean, upon all I have said and written about it, has ordered him to submit to any expunction I insist upon: this is all I can obtain, and I know not whether to make any use of it or not. But as to your apprehension, that any suspicion may arise of my being anywise consenting or concerned in it, I have the pleasure to tell you, the whole thing is so circumstanced and so plain, that it can never be the case. I shall be very desirous to see what the letters are at all events; and I thing that must determine my future measures; for till then I can judge nothing. The excessive earnestness the Dean has been in for publishing them, makes me hope they are castigated in some degree, or he must be totally deprived of his understanding. They now offer to send me the originals [which have been so long detained]; and I will accept of them, (though they have done their job,) that they may not have them to produce against me, in case there be any offensive passages in them. If you can give me any advice, do. I wish I could show you what the Dean's people, the women, and the bookseller, have done and writ, on my sending an absolute negative, and on the agency I have employed of some gentlemen to stop it, as well as threats of law, &c. The whole thing is too manifest to admit of any doubt in any man : how long this thing has been working ; how many tricks have been played with the Dean's papers, how they were secreted from him from time to time, while they feared his not complying with such a measure; and how, finding his weakness increase, they have at last made him the instrument himself for their private profit; whereas, I believe, before, they only intended to do this after his death.

TO MRS WHITEWAY.

I HAVE been very miserable all night, and to-day extremely deaf and full of pain. I am so stupid and confounded, that I cannot express the mortification I am under both in body and mind. All I can say is, That I am not in torture; but I daily and hourly expect it. Pray let me know how your health is and your family. I hardly understand one word I write. I am sure my days will be very few; few and miserable they must be.

I am, for those few days, yours entirely,
JON. SWIFT.

If I do not blunder, it is Saturday,
July 26, 1740.

If I live till Monday, I shall hope to see you, perhaps for the last time.

FROM THE EARL OF ORRERY.

Caledon, Dec. 17, 1740.

DEAR SIR,

GREAT men like you must expect numberless petitions, which, like Jupiter, you put to various uses; but wonder not, when there is a place vacant in your family, that every body is striving for the post. I mean your cathedral family; for we are told there is a vacancy in the choir. I am desired to recommend to you one James Colgan *, aged 25. His voice excellent, his behaviour good, his person indifferent, his recommendation to me irresistible. I beseech you, let Faulkner give me an answer; for neither he nor I, nor the choir of lords,

---

* One of the vicars-choral of Christ-church and St Patrick's cathedrals, remarkable for his fine manner of singing.—H

doctors,—commons, &c. are worth your while to give yourself one moment's uneasiness about, if you are not well, and I am more than afraid you are not; only I must be enabled to say, I have mentioned him to you. My frozen fingers will only serve me to present Lady Orrery's most humble service to you, and the best wishes, prayers, and acknowledgments of all this family. I am, dear Sir, your ever obliged and obedient humble servant,

ORRERY.

AN EXHORTATION

ADDRESSED TO THE SUB-DEAN AND CHAPTER OF ST PATRICK'S CATHEDRAL, DUBLIN. *

January 28, 1741.

WHEREAS my infirmities of age and ill health have prevented me to preside in the chapters held for the good order and government of my cathedral church of St Patrick, Dublin, in person: I have, by

---

* This curious document was copied from the original, found among the papers of the Rev. Dr James King, one of the Dean's executors, copies of which, so far as relating to Dean Swift, were in the most obliging manner given for this work by the Rev. Robert King, prebendary of Dunlavin. The original is in the Dean's hand-writing; and as it is a large copy-hand, and the paper seems to have been ruled, it seems probable, that in the weak state of his mind he might attach much consequence to the subject matter. The piece contains some flashes of his peculiar humour, although written in a state tending towards mental imbecility. The witnesses names are written in the Dean's own hand.

a legal commission, made and appointed the very reverend Doctor John Wynne, præcentor of the said cathedral, to be sub-dean in my stead and absence. I do hereby ratify and confirm all the powers delegated to the said Dr Wynne in the said commission.

And I do hereby require and request the very reverend sub-dean, not to permit any of the vicars-choral, choristers, or organists, to attend or assist at any publick musical performances, without my consent, or his consent, with the consent of the chapter first obtained.

And whereas it hath been reported, that I gave a licence to certain vicars to assist at a club of fiddlers in Fishamble Street, I do hereby declare that I remember no such licence to have been ever signed or sealed by me ; and that if ever such pretended licence should be produced, I do hereby annul and vocate the said licence.

Intreating my said sub-dean and chapter to punish such vicars as shall ever appear there, as songsters, fiddlers, pipers, trumpeters, drummers, drum-majors, or in any tonal quality, according to the flagitious aggravations of their respective disobedience, rebellion, perfidy, and ingratitude.

I require my said sub-dean to proceed to the extremity of expulsion, if the said vicars should be found ungovernable, impenitent, or self-sufficient, especially Taberner, Phipps, and Church, who, as I am informed, have, in violation of my sub-dean's and chapter's order in December last, at the instance of some obscure persons unknown, presumed to sing and fiddle at the club above mentioned.

My resolution is to preserve the dignity of my station, and the honour of my chapter ; and, gentlemen, it is incumbent upon you to aid me, and to

shew who and what the dean and chapter of Saint
Patrick's are.

Signed by me,

JONATHAN SWIFT,
Dean of St Patrick's.

Witness present,
James King.
Francis Wilson.

To the very Reverend Doctor John Wynne, sub-
dean of the cathedral church of Saint Patrick,
Dublin, and to the reverend dignitaries and pre-
bendaries of the same.

TO MRS WHITEWAY.

Jan. 13, 1740-41.

DEAR MADAM,

YOUR son,* who was with me yesterday, and
staid the whole afternoon till near ten o'clock, gave
me a very melancholy account of your ill health,
extremely to my grief.   I send a servant with this
letter, and you will please to employ Mr Swift to
answer it, because I am in very great pain about
you; for the weather is so extremely sharp, that it
must needs add to your disorders.   Pray let your
son or daughter write a few lines to give me some
sort of comfort.   My cold is now attended with a

----

* Mr Deane Swift.——D. S.

10

cough this bitter cold weather ; but I am impatient until your son or daughter gives me some hopes. I am ever your assured friend and most humble servant,

JON. SWIFT.

FROM THE EARL OF ORRERY.

Duke Street, Westminster, July 7, 1741.

THANKS to you, dear Sir, for your frequent remembrance of me by my great friend and patron master George Faulkner: thanks to you for the honours you have showed my wife : but above all, thanks to you for using exercise and taking care of your health. It is the strongest instance of affection your friends either desire or deserve. In mentioning your friends, I must particularize Mr Pope: he obeys your commands, and flings away much time upon me: *Nec deficit alter aureus;* doctor King does the same. Thus deities condescend to visit and converse with mortals.

Poor Lord Oxford is gone to those regions from whence travellers never return, unless in an airy visit to faithless lovers, as Margaret to William ; or to cities devoted to destruction, as Hector amidst the flames of Troy. The deceased earl has left behind him many books, many manuscripts, and no money: his lady brought him five hundred thousand pounds, four of which have been sacrificed to indolence, good-nature, and want of worldly-wisdom : and there will still remain, after proper sales, and right management, five thousand pounds a-year for his widow.

Mr Cæsar died about two months ago. Mrs Cæsar is still all tears and lamentations, although she certainly may be numbered *inter felices, sua si bona norint.*

Lord Bathurst is at Cirencester, erecting pillars and statues to Queen Anne. Lord Bolingbroke lives in France: posterity, it is to be hoped, may be the better for his retirement. The Duke of Argyll reigns or ought to reign in Scotland.—Such is the state of Europe; but our disappointment in America has cast a gloomy face over London and Westminster. The citizens have recourse to mum and tobacco, by which means they puff away care, and keep dismay at a proper distance. In the mean time, my friends the ducks and geese in the park cackle on, and join in chorus to the sounds of victory that are daily drummed forth on the parade, but reach no farther than the atmosphere of Whitehall.—— What news next? The weather—but you certainly know it is hot; for in truth, notwithstanding this letter comes from my heart, and is written in the pleasure of thinking of you, yet I sweat to assure you how much I am, dear Sir,

Your ever obliged and obedient humble servant,
ORRERY.

FROM THE EARL OF ORRERY TO DEANE SWIFT, ESQ.

Marston, Dec. 4, 1742.

Sir,

I AM much obliged to you for the full, though melancholy, account you have sent me of my ever honoured friend. It is the more melancholy to me, as I have heard him often lament the particular misfortune incident to human nature, of an utter deprivation of senses many years before a deprivation of life. I have heard him describe persons in that condition, with a liveliness and a horror, that on this late occasion have recalled to me his very words. Our litany, methinks, should have an addition of a particular prayer against this most dreadful misfortune. I am sure mine shall. The bite of a mad dog (a most tremendous evil) ends soon in death; but the effects of his loss of memory may last even to the longest age of man; therefore I own my friendship for him has now changed my thoughts and wishes into the very reverse of what they were, I rejoice to hear he grows lean. I am sorry to hear his appetite is good. I was glad when there seemed an approaching mortification in his eyelid. In one word, the man I wished to live the longest I wish the soonest dead. It is the only blessing that can now befall him. His reason will never return; or if it should, it will only be to show him the misery of having lost it. I am impatient for his going where imperfection ceases, and where perfection begins; where Wilsons cannot break in and steal, and where envy, hatred, and malice have no influence or power. While he continues to breathe, he is an example, stronger and more piercing than he or any other divine could preach, against pride, conceit, and vain-glory.   Good God! Doctor Swift beaten and marked with stripes by a beast in human shape, one Wilson. *   But he is not only an example against presumption and haughtiness, but in reality an incitement to marriage.   Men in years ought always

---

* Dr Francis Wilson was prebendary of Kilmactolway, and rector of Clondalkin, in the diocese of Dublin, the great tithes of which belong to the deanery of St Patrick's. Dr Wilson, who lived in the centre of this prebend and parish, and was well acquainted with the country, farmed these tithes of Dr Swift on very reasonable terms, greatly to his own advantage.   When the Dean was much in the decline of life, he invited Dr Wilson to accept of apartments for himself and his wife in the deanery-house at Dublin: where they had very good lodgings, with the benefit of his servants and stables. Dr Swift's memory failing him greatly at this time, Wilson took the advantage of carrying him to his house at Newland, within four miles of Dublin, and endeavoured to intoxicate him with liquor, which he could not accomplish: and on their return to Dublin, solicited Dr Swift to make him sub-dean of St Patrick's, and turn out Dr Wynne, (See p. 358.) a very worthy and hospitable gentleman, which Dr Swift refused; on which, Dr Wilson, in a most outrageous manner, insulted the Dean, beat him very severely, took him by the throat, and would have choked him, had it not been for the Dean's footman and coachman, who rescued him out of the hands of Wilson.   This affair made a great noise; Wilson was forbidden the Dean's house, and died soon after.   To this same " beast in human shape," as Lord Orrery justly calls him, Dr Swift had bequeathed " the works of Plato in three folio volumes, the Earl of Clarendon's History in three folio volumes, and my best Bible, together with thirteen small Persian pictures in the drawing-room, and the small silver tankard given to me by the contribution of some friends whose names are engraved at the bottom of the said tankard."—F.   Such is Faulkner's account of this extraordinary transaction.   It is however but fair to observe, that it is positively contradicted upon oath, by Dr Wilson himself, as appears from the following affidavit, which was found among the papers of Dr King, mentioned a few pages before.

to secure a friend to take care of declining life, and
watch narrowly, as they fall, the last minute particles

THE AFFIDAVIT

OF DR FRANCIS WILSON, PREBENDARY OF KILMACTOLWAY, AND
RECTOR OF CLONDALKIN, IN THE DIOCESE OF DUBLIN, EXCUL-
PATING HIMSELF FROM THE CHARGE OF CRUELTY, &C. TO DR
SWIFT, DEAN OF ST PATRICK'S, DUBLIN.

*The Examination of the Reverend Francis Wilson, Doctor in
Divinity,*

Who being duly sworn on the holy evangelists, saith, That on
Monday the 14th of June last he made a visit to the Rev. Doctor
Swift, Dean of St Patrick's, who received the said Wilson with
his usual fondness, which was always very great: That he told
the said Wilson he would take the air that morning, and dine
with him at his house in the country : That he did call accordingly for his coach ; and one Mrs Ann Ridgeway, (who usually attends him,) but the coachman and she being both abroad, an
hackney coach was sent for, in which the said Doctor Swift and
Wilson arrived at Newlands, * the said Wilson's house, the said
Dean did dine, and, as this examinant believes, drink half a pint
of white wine.

That soon after dinner they again went into the coach, in order to return to Dublin : That for about the first two miles of
the road, the Dean treated the said Wilson with remarkable civility and love ; but that of a sudden, he cried out the said Wilson
was the devil, and bid him go to hell, which words he often repeated in a most astonishing rage ; but of which the said Wilson
took no other notice than by an endeavour to appease him in repeating some passages out of such authors as the Dean admired
most ; but that, instead of giving any attention to what he said
Wilson spoke, he struck him several times on the face, scratched
him, and tore off his wig, all which usage the said Wilson bore
in pity for the poor Dean's infirmities, and in love to his person,

---

* Newlands, now the country-seat of the Right Hon. George Ponsonby.
It formerly belonged to the lamented Lord Kilwarden; and it was coming
thence to town that that respected Judge fell a victim to popular licentious-
ness.

of the hour-glass. A bachelor will seldom find,
among all his kindred, so true a nurse, so faithful a
friend, so disinterested a companion, as one tied to
him by the double chain of duty and affection. A
wife could not be banished from his chamber, or his
unhappy hours of retirement; nor, had the Dean
felt a blow, or wanted a companion, had he been
married, or, in other words, had Stella lived. All
that a friend could do, has been done by Mrs Whiteway; all that a companion could persuade, has been
attempted by Mrs Ridgeway. The rest—but I
shall run on for ever, and I set out at first only with
an intention of thanking you for your letter, and
assuring you that

I am, Sir, your most obedient humble servant,

ORRERY.

P. S. I beg to hear from you from time to time, if
any new occurrence happens in the Dean's unhappy state.

---

when he thrust his fingers into the said Wilson's eyes; upon
which the said Wilson ordered the coach to stop; and on his back
with the natural expressions of resentment and indignation, declaring he would not again tamely suffer the greatest man on
earth to strike him. And the said Wilson further saith, that he
did not once attempt to strike, or in any sort to violate the
Dean's person, notwithstanding the provocation was as before set
forth.

FRANCIS WILSON.

Sworn before me this 15th of July ——
DAV. CRAIGHEAD.*

(A true copy.)

* This gentleman was a magistrate of the county of Dublin of great re-
spectability and fortune. He resided in Dawson Street, Dublin, after having
peer, and had been fined for not serving the office of Lord Mayor.

A Cantata

slow.

In harmony would

fast.

you ex.cell, Suit your words to your music well, mu_sic well,

mu_sic well, Suit your words to your mu_sic well, Suit your

words to your mu_sic well.   For Pe_ga_sus

slow.

run _ _ _ _ s, run _ _ _ _ _ ev_ery race By gal _ _ _

fast.

_ _ _ _ _ _ _ loping high or le_ _vel pace Or amb_ling or

slow.

MR FAULKNER TO MR BOWYER.

Dublin, Oct. 1, 1745.

Dear Sir,

THE bank note for one hundred guineas came safe to hand. Enclosed you have part of the "Advice to Servants." I wish I could get franks to send it in. Fix your day of publication, and I will wait until you are ready, that we may both come out the same day. I think the middle of November will do very well, as your city, as well as Dublin, will be full at that time. I shall finish the volume with a Cantata of the Dean's, set to music, which

---

Dr Beattie, after censuring the practice of what he calls illicit imitation, observes, that "this abuse of a noble art did not escape the satire of Swift; who, though deaf to the charms of music, was not blind to the absurdity of musicians. He recommended it to Dr Echlin, an ingenious gentleman of Ireland, to compose a cantata in ridicule of this puerile mimickry. Here we have motions imitated, which are the most inharmonious, and the least connected with human affections, as the trotting, ambling and galloping of Pegasus; and sounds the most unmusical, as cracking and snivelling, and rough roistering rustic roaring strains; the words high and deep, have high and deep notes set to them; a series of short notes of equal lengths are introduced, to imitate shivering and shaking; an irregular run of quick sounds, to express rumbling; a sudden rise of the voice, from a low to a high pitch, to denote flying above the sky; a ridiculous run of chromatic divisions on the words Celia dies; with other droll contrivances of a like nature. In a word, Swift's cantata may convince any person, that music uniformly imitative would be ridiculous. I observe, in passing, that the satire of this piece is levelled, not at absurd imitation only, but also at some other musical improprieties; such as the idle repetition of the same words, the running of long extravagant divisions upon one syllable, and the setting of words to music that have no meaning."

in my opinion, will have a greater run with the lovers of harmony than any of the Corelli's, Vivaldi's, Purcell's, or Handel's pieces. When Arne, the famous composer, was last in Ireland, he made application to me for this cantata (which I could not then procure), to set it to music: perhaps he may do it now, and bring it on the stage; which, if he does, will run more than the Beggar's Opera; and therefore I would have you get it engraved in folio, with scores for bass, &c., which will make it sell very well. I believe you might get something handsome for it from Rich, or the managers of Drurylane, for which I shall send you the original MS. I am thus particular, that you may have the profit to yourself, as you will have the trouble. I was in daily expectation, for six weeks, of going to London; but was prevented by many accidents—I cannot say business, for I never had less, as Mr Hitch well knows, having had no order from me for two months past. The "Advice to Servants" was never finished by the Dean, and is consequently very incorrect; I believe you may see some Irishisms in it; if so, pray correct them. The Dean's friends do not know the manner of an assignment, and desire you will send over the form. The story of the Injured Lady does not make above a sheet; and will vex your northern hardy neighbours more than the "Public Spirit of the Whigs," of which they complained to Queen Anne. As you are famous for writing prefaces, pray help me to one for "Advice to Servants," for which I have not yet printed the title. My best compliments to our friends, and should be obliged to Mr Dodsley for the two letters; which you may send, under cover to Samuel Bindon, Esq., at my house. I am whimsical, and send you the beginning of "Advice," &c. and the remainder to Mr Hitch, that you may print it immediately. I think it might be printed without the "Injured Lady," as your volume will make the better figure with original pieces : but this I submit to your better judgment.

I long much to see London, although I have no other business than to visit my friends, and do them any service in my power ; and if I can be useful to you in England or Ireland, pray let me know, and I will do it. I would not have you advertise until two or three days before you publish, in which I wish you all imaginable success ; and am, dear Sir, your faithful friend, and obliged humble servant,

GEORGE FAULKNER.

AN ACCOUNT OF A MONUMENT ERECTED TO THE MEMORY OF DR SWIFT, IN IRELAND.

TO MR GEORGE FAULKNER. *

Neale, Feb. 14, 1750.

SIR,

I HAVE at last finished, what you have often heard me wish I might be able to do, a monument for the greatest genius of our age, the late Dean of St Patrick's. The thing in itself is but a trifle ; but it is more than I should ever have attempted, had I not with indignation seen a country (so honoured by the birth of so great a man, and so faithfully

---

* By Sir John Browne, of the county of Mayo.—F.

served by him all his life) so long and so shamefully
negligent in erecting some monument of gratitude
to his memory. Countries are not wise in such neglect ; for they hurt themselves.   Men of genius
are encouraged to apply their talents to the service
of their country, when they see in it gratitude to the
memory of those who have deserved well of them.
The ingenious Pere Castle told me at Paris. that he
reckoned it the greatest misfortune to him that he
was not born an Englishman ; and, when he explain-
ed himself, it was only for this, that, after two hundred years, they had erected a monument to Shake-
speare ; and another to a modern, but to the greatest
of them, Sir Isaac Newton.   Great souls are very
disinterested in the affairs of life ; they look for
fame and immortality, scorning the mean paths of
interest and lucre: and, surely, in an age so mer-
cenary as ours, men should not be so sparing to give
public marks of their gratitude to men of such virtue, dead, however they may treat them living;
since in so doing, they bespeak, and almost insure
to themselves, a succession of such useful persons in
society.   It was with this view that I have determined to throw in my mite.

In a fine lawn below my house, I have planted a
hippodrome.   It is a circular plantation, consisting
of five walks ; the central of which is a horse-course,
and three rounds make exactly a mile.   All the
lines are so laid out,.that, from the centre, the six
rows of trees appear but one, and form 100 arches
round the field; in the centre of which I have
erected a mount, and placed a marble column on
its proper pedestal, with all the decorations of the
order; on the summit of which I have placed a
Pegasus, just seeming to take flight to the Heavens;
and, on the die of the pedestal I have engraved

the following inscription, written by an ingenious friend :

IN MEMORIAM JONATHAN SWIFT, S. T. P. VIRI SINE PARI.

AONIDVM FONTES APERIS, DIVINE POETA,
ARTE NOVA : ÆTHEREAS PROPRIIS, ET PEGASVS, ALIS
SCANDE DOMOS : ÆTERNVM ADDET TVA FAMA COLVMNÆ
HVIC MEMORI DECVS.   HIC, TANTI QVA POSSVMVS VMBRAM
NOMINIS IN MENTEM, SACRO REVOCARE QVOTANNIS
LVDORVM RITV IVVAT; HIC TIBI PARVVS HONORVM
OFFERTVR CVMVLVS : LAVDVM QVO FINE TVORVM
COPIA CLAVDATVR QVI QVÆRIT, GENTIS IERNÆ
PECTORA SCRVTETVR, LATVMQVE INTERROGET ORBEM.
MDCCL.

I have also appointed a small fund for annual premiums to be distributed in the celebration of games at the monument yearly.   The ceremony is to last three days, beginning the first of May yearly.   On this day, young maids and men in the neighbourhood are to assemble in the hippodrome, with their garlands and chaplets of flowers, and to dance round the monument, singing the praises of this ingenious patriot, and strewing with flowers all the place : after which they are to dance for a prize ; the best dancer among the maids is to be presented with a cap and ribbands ; and, after the dance, the young men are to run for a hat and gloves.

The second day, there is to be a large market upon the ground : and the girl who produces the finest hank of yarn, and the most regular reel and count, is to have a guinea premium ; and the person who buys the greatest quantity of yarn is to have a premium of two guineas.

The third day, the farmer who produces the best yearling calf of his own breed is to have two guineas premium ; and he that produces the fairest colt or filly, of his own breed likewise, not over two years

old, shall receive a premium of two guineas also.——
Thus the whole will not exceed ten pounds ; and all
these useful branches of our growth and manufac-
ture will be encouraged, in remembering the patron
who with so much care and tenderness recommended
them to others, and cherished them himself.   I am,
dear Sir,

Your humble servant,

J. B.

APPENDIX

TO THE

ORIGINAL CORRESPONDENCE

BETWEEN

DEAN SWIFT AND HIS FRIENDS.

[The letters which follow have reached the Editor too late to be regularly inserted in the order of their dates, but are, for the most part, too interesting to be suppressed. Only two of the number, it is believed, have been hitherto published. The two letters from Swift to Addison, and the twelve letters from the Dean to Mr Tickell, were communicated, in the most obliging and liberal manner possible, by Major Tickell, the descendant of the poet.]

APPENDIX

TO THE

ORIGINAL CORRESPONDENCE

BETWEEN

DEAN SWIFT AND HIS FRIENDS.

TO MR ADDISON.

Dublin, August 22, 1710.

SIR,

I LOOKED long enough at the wind to set you safe at the other side, and then * **** our conduct, very unwilling for fear you [*about two lines are effaced*] up to a post-horse, and hazard your limbs to be made a member. I believe you had the displeasure of much ill news almost as soon as you landed. Even the moderate Tories here are in pain at these revolutions, being what will certainly affect the Duke of Marlborough, and, consequently, the success of the war. My lord-lieutenant asked me yesterday when I intended for England. I said I had no business there now, since I suppose in a little time I should not have one friend left that had any credit; and his excellency was of my opinion. I never once began your [*task,*] since you [*left this*] being perpetually prevented by all the company I kept, and especially Captain Pratt, to whom I am almost a domestic upon your account. I am convinced, that whatever Government come over, you will find all marks of kindness from any Parliament here, with respect to your employment; the Tories contending with the Whigs which should speak best of you. Mr Pratt says, he has received such marks of your sincerity and friendship, as he never can forget; and, in short, if you will come over again, when you are at leisure, we will raise an army, and make you king of Ireland. Can you think so meanly of a kingdom, as not to be pleased that every creature in it, who hath one grain of worth, has a veneration for you. I know there is nothing in this to make you add any value to yourself; but it ought to put you on valuing them, and to convince you that they are not an undistinguishing people. On Thursday, the Bishop of Clogher, the two Pratts, and I, are to be as happy as Ireland will give us leave; we are to dine with Mr Paget at the Castle, and drink your health. The bishop shewed me the first volume of the small edition of the Tatler, where there is a very handsome compliment to me; but I can never pardon the printing the news of every Tatler—I think he might as well have printed the advertisements. I knew it was a bookseller's piece of craft, to increase the bulk and price of what he was sure would sell; but I utterly disapprove it. I beg you would freely tell me whether it will be of any account for me to come to England. I would not trouble you for advice, if I knew where else to ask it. We expect every day to hear of my lord-president's removal; if he were to continue, I might, perhaps, hope for some of his good offices. You ordered me to give you a memorial of what I had in my thoughts. There were two things, Dr So——th's prebend and sinecure, or the place of historiographer. But if things go on in the train they are now, I shall only beg you, when there is an account to be depended on for a new government here, that you will give me early notice to procure an addition to my fortunes. And with saying so, I take my leave of troubling you with myself.

I do not desire to hear from you till you are out of [*the*] hurry at Malmsbury. * I long till you have some good account of your Indian affairs, so as to make public business depend upon you, and not you upon that. I read your character in Mrs Manly's noble Memoirs of Europe. It seems to me, as if she had about two thousand epithets and fine words packed up in a bag; and that she pulled them out by handfuls, and strewed them on her paper, where about once in five hundred times they happen to be right.

My lord-lieutenant, we reckon, will leave us in a fortnight; I led him, by a question, to tell me he did not expect to continue in the government, nor would, when all his friends were out. Pray take some occasion to let my [*Lord*] Halifax know the sense I have of the favour he intended me.

I am with great respect, Sir, your most obedient
and most obliged humble servant,
J. Swift.

---

* For which borough Addison was then candidate, and afterwards member.

LETTER FROM SWIFT.

[The address and envelope of this letter have been lost. It was found among the records in Birmingham Tower, Dublin Castle, and obligingly copied for this work, by Edward Lawson, Esq. Barrister at Law, and Sub-Commissioner of Records in Ireland. It seems to have been addressed to some friend in Ireland during Swift's residence at Letcombe in Berkshire, after the dissolution of Oxford's administration. There is no signature nor place of date.]

July 29, 1714.

SIR,

I HAVE been these two months fifty miles from London, to avoid the storm that has happened at Court. The news will tell you a post or two before this of my Lord Ox.'s laying down; he was to do it yesterday. He has sent to desire I would stay some time with him at his house in Herefordshire, which I am not likely to refuse, though I may probably suffer a good deal in my little affairs in Ireland by my absence. This makes it necessary for me to desire you would please to renew my license of absence, which expires about the end of August. As soon as it's expired, I should hope so much from your friendship, that, though any accident might happen to prevent your timely notice, that you would do me such a favour whenever there is occasion. I had fixed my journey to Ireland to be on the second of August, when this incident changed it. I think it is about this time two years * that you came to my lodgings with Mr Pratt, to tell me the

---

* This is an odd mistake, Lord Godolphin went out of office in 1710, four years before the date of the letter.

news of Lord Godolphin's going out, which was as joyful to me as this is otherwise. I believe you will reckon me an ill courtier to follow a discarded statesman to his retirement, especially when I have been always well with those now in power, as I was with him. But to answer that would require talking, and I have already troubled you so much who are a man of business. I am Sir,

Your most obedient humble servant,

J. SWIFT.

Pray let the absence be general as before. I was very near wanting it some months ago with a witness.* I know not what alterations this change may make in the scheme for Irish promotions. I hear Dr Pratt and Ellwood are secure.

TO MR ADDISON.†

Dublin, July 9, 1717.

SIR,

I SHOULD be much concerned if I did not think you were a little angry with me for not congratulat-

---

* Alluding probably to the chance there was of his being obliged to fly on account of the offence taken at the " Public Spirit of the Whigs."

† This curious and valuable letter was found amongst the papers of Mr Tickell the poet. There is a very kind letter from Addison, dated 20th March, 1717-18. Vol. XVI. p. 327. But as it refers to some application made by the Dean in favour of friends, it must have been in reply to a subsequent letter from Swift, as that which is now given to the public contains no such passage.

ing you upon being Secretary. But I choose my time as I would to visit you, when all your company is gone. I am confident you have given ease of mind to many thousand people, who will never believe any ill can be intended to the constitution in church or state, while you are in so high a trust, and I should have been of the same opinion though I had not the happiness to know you.

I am extremely obliged for your kind remembrance some months ago, by the Bishop of Derry, and for your generous intentions, if you had come to Ireland, to have made party give way to friendship by continuing your acquaintance.

I examine my heart, and can find no other reason why I write to you now, beside that great love and esteem I have always had for you. I have nothing to ask you either for any friend or for myself. When I conversed among ministers, I boasted of your acquaintance, but I feel no vanity from being known to a secretary of state. I am only a little concerned to see you stand single ; for it is a prodigious singularity in any court to *owe* one's rise entirely to merit. I will venture to tell you a secret, that three or four more such choices, would gain more hearts in three weeks, than all the methods hitherto practised have been able to do in as many years.

It is now time for me to recollect that I am writing to a secretary of state, who has little time allowed him for trifles ; I therefore take my leave, with assurances of my being ever, with the truest respect, Sir,

Your most obedient
and most humble servant,
JONATH. SWIFT.

TO THE REV. DR ROBERT MOSSOM,
DEAN OF OSSORY, AT KILKENNY.*

Dublin, February 14, 1720-21.

SIR,

WHEN I had the favour of your's of the 8th instant, I was in very ill health, and am since but slowly recovering. About five years ago I had some disputes with my chapter, upon this occasion of my negatives, which was never contradicted before, nor did the members directly do it then, but by some side ways of arguing the ill consequences which might follow if it had no exceptions. This they were spirited to by the A. B. of Tuam, who incited the A. B. of Dublin, and who said he had long entertained an opinion against my negative. Since that they never contradicted it : and the point is, as you say, perfectly absurd. I then writ to the Bishop of Rochester, and Dean of Sarum, who had been my old friends ; the former distinguished between deaneries of the old and new establishment, and both of them advised me to make as little stir as I could. † The Dean of Sarum said positively that he had no more power in the chapter than a senior prebendary ; that when he was absent, the next senior presided of course, and had only a vote. In this case, without doubt, [time] hath made it, that things may be

---

* The original of this letter is in the possession of Leonard Macnally, Esq. Barrister at law, Dublin. It refers to a controversy upon a point of ecclesiastical jurisdiction, upon which Swift also consulted Atterbury.

† See Swift's correspondence with Atterbury on this subject, Vol. XVI. p. 266.

[*done*] by the Dean and chapter, whether the former consents or no.   But you are to understand, that the privileges and powers of the Dean of St Patrick depend upon subsequent grants and confirmations of Popes, parliaments, kings, and archbishops. Now, if your charter be much older than Edward IV.'s time, for ought I know you may be on the foot of St Patrick's, as that was upon the foot of Sarum, before the subsequent * * [*some words illegible.*] There is a French act of Parliament, Edward IV. where it is recited, that whereas the Dean of St Patrick is ordinary, &c. and has such and such privileges, &c. so that then they were known.   This deanery is 503 years old, and several of the Dean's powers were granted in the first, second, and third century after ; and the error of my opponents lay in thinking this deanery was like that of Sarum, without considering what came after : I believe your best argument will be, to insist, in general, that you copy after St Patrick's, and if they allow that, I will provide you with power and privilege enough.   It is an infallible maxim, that not one thing here is done without the Dean's consent.   If he proposeth, it is then left to the majority ; because his proposal is his consent.   This is as much as I can send you at present, from a giddy aking head.   If you command any further particulars from me, of my practice here, or any other point wherein I can do you service, you shall find me ready to obey ; and I think there are few older acquaintances than you and I. . . . Believe, with great truth, Sir,

Your most obedient
humble servant,
JONATH. SWIFT.

TO MR TICKELL.

Deanery-House, July 11, 1724.

SIR,

I SHALL wait on you at the time and place you appoint, although it is hard that you last comers and lodgers should invite us old housekeepers, which I would have you to know I am, and can bring you half-a-dozen men in gowns to depose it. I shall therefore attend you only on this condition, that you will be ready to fix a day for dining at the deanery with Lord Forbes and Mr Sheridan, because the latter has been heard to boast that you will condescend to suffer him.

I am, with great respect, Sir,

Your most obedient humble servant,

JONATH. SWIFT.

TO THE SAME.

Deanery-House, August 3, 1724.

SIR,

I SHOULD have waited on you before now, if I had not been tormented with an old vexatious disorder of a deafness and noise in my ears, which has returned, after having left me above two years, and makes me unsupportable to others and myself.

I now make bold to trouble in an affair which goes very near my heart. Mr Proby, Surgeon-General, my old friend, and most generally beloved of any man in this kingdom, lies under a great misfortune at present. His eldest son, a captain in Lord Tirawly's regiment, hath been accused at Galloway for discovering an inclination to popery, and several affidavits have been made against him. The young man desires nothing but a fair trial. The accusation is generally judged malicious and false: But that concerns you not. He is to be tried in a few days, * but the matter must first go before the Lords-Justices. Mr Proby being utterly unknown to you, desires the favour to wait upon you either this afternoon or evening, or early to-morrow morning. He does not intend this as a solicitor for his son, he has too much discretion; but because the business will first come before the Lords-Justices, he thinks it will be proper for him to wait on you, and say or ask what is convenient, and thought that my recommendation will facilitate his access. Therefore, pray Sir mistake me not. I am not at all making you an advocate, but only desiring that he may not see you wholly as a stranger.

You will please to signify by one of your servants what hour you will permit Mr Proby to attend you.

I am, with great respect, Sir,

Your most obedient humble servant,

JONATH. SWIFT.

---

* Swift also interceded in behalf of this young gentleman with Lord Carteret, then lord-lieutenant. See Vol. XVI. p. 473.

TO THE SAME.

Deanery-House, Sept. 4, 1724.

Sir,

I DESIRE you will please to send the inclosed. I beg your pardon for so often troubling you, but I owed his excellency a letter.* I am pretty well eased of my troublous disorder, and intend to wait on you soon, and hope you will make some appointment with those you like best, that we may meet at the Deanery.

I am, Sir,

Your most obedient humble servant,

J. SWIFT.

TO THE SAME.

Deanery-House, Oct. 24, 1724.

Sir,

I DID not design to attend my lord-lieutenant, till his hurry of visits and ceremony were over ; but I fear it will be long before I can have that honour, for I am so cruelly persecuted with the return of my deafness, that I am fit for nothing but to moap in my chamber. I therefore humbly entreat your favour, to present my most humble duty to his excellency,

---

* The inclosure appears to have been the letter to Lord Carteret, dated 3d September 1724, upon the subject chiefly of Dr Berkeley's expedition to Bermudas. See Vol. XVI. p. 467.

and to let him know the unlucky cause that hinders me from waiting on him, which I apprehend will yet continue some weeks. I have already had but too much cause to complain of a disorder which hath so long deprived me of the happiness of your company.

I conclude you are now a busy man ; and therefore shall only add, that I am, with great esteem,

Sir, your most obedient humble servant,

J. SWIFT.

TO MR STAFFORD LIGHTBURNE.*

Quilca, April 22, 1725.

SIR,

YOUR letter was sent hither to me. I have been so ill with a giddiness and deafness, that I thought it best to retire far into the country, where I now am, in a wild place belonging to Mr Sheridan, seven miles from Kells. I am very glad of your good success in England, for I always believed you had justice on your side ; at the same time, I am grieved at the difficulties your adversary's family must be under by their own wrong proceedings, and should be more so, if that puppy, who is heir, had not so behaved himself, as to forfeit all regard or pity. Mr Worrall has the remaining bonds of Laracor, &c. and a power from me to receive the money, which I much

* The original is in the possession of General Lightburne : the transcript was obligingly furnished by Mr Theophilus Swift.

want, having half ruined myself by building a wall, which is as bad as a law-suit.   I desire Mr Proudfoot may, with his payments, give the names of every tenant, and the sums they paid, and take receipts from Mr Worrall.   Present my service to my cousin.   I hope this journey has contributed to her health, as well as her fortune.

I am your most humble servant,
J. SWIFT.

The postman tells me that a letter directed to me at Mr Latimer's at Kells, and put into the bye-bag at Trim, will be sent to me ; so that if you have any occasion to write, you may take that way.   I have desired Mr Wallis to appear for me at the visitation.

Feb. 23, 1727-8.

I have received from Mr Stafford Lightburne, L. 32 Sterling, in full of all interest, and all dues and demands whatsoever, to the day of the date hereof.   I say, received by me,

L. 32. JONATH. SWIFT.

TO MR TICKELL.

July 19, 1725.

SIR,

YOUR whole behaviour, with relation to myself, ever since I had the honour to be known to you, hath tended maliciously to hinder me from writing or speaking any thing that could deserve to be read or heard.   I can no sooner hint my desire of a favour to a friend, but you immediately grant it, on purpose to load me, so as to put it out of my power to express my gratitude ; and against your conscience you put compliments upon the letter I write, where the subject is only to beg a favour, on purpose to make me write worse, or not at all, for the future. I remember some faint strokes of this unjust proceeding in myself, when I had a little credit in the world, but in no comparison with yours, which have filled up the measure of iniquity.

I have often thought it a monstrous folly in us, who are tied to this kingdom, to have any friendship with *vous autres*, who are birds of passage, while we are sure to be forsaken like young wenches who are seduced by soldiers that quarter among them for a few months. Therefore I prudently resolved to make no other use of you, than for my present satisfaction, by improving myself from your conversation, or making use of your interest to the advantage of my friends. But when you leave us, I will, for my own quiet, send as few sighs after you as I can. For, when Gods used to come down to earth to converse with females, it was true judgment in the lady who chose rather to marry an earthly lover than Apollo, who would be always gambling to heaven, and, besides, would be young when she was old.

And, to shew I am serious in my resolutions, I now entreat another good office from you, in behalf of a young gentleman, Mr James Stopford, a fellow of the college. He is a man of birth and fortune, but the latter a little *engaged* by travelling ; and having now as strong temptations to travel again with great advantage, as governor to a young person, he desires the honour of being admitted to my lord-lieutenant by your means, with no other view but the credit that such a reception would give him, only whispering me, (as all men have base ends,) that he forsees his excellency, being about his own age, will be always of so great a consequence in England, as, many years hence, he may find his account in his lordship's protection and countenance.

He is reckoned the best scholar of his age among us, and abounds in every amiable quality, without any circumstance to detract from them, except one, which I hope his travels will put an end to, and that is, love.

In the letter directed to Dr Delany, there is one to Mr Stopford, who is soon expected in town, and therein I let him know what I write to you, and direct him to attend you, for which I humbly desire pardon, as well as for the trouble of sending the packet to Dr Delany, and for teasing you with so long a letter; which I will conclude with the sincerest profession of being ever, with great respect,

Your most obedient and obliged servant,
J. SWIFT.

The ladies present their best service and thanks to you for your remembrance. Mrs Johnson has blunted her pick-axe* with work.

---

* In a letter to Dr Sheridan, 25th January 1724-5, the Dean informs him, that Mrs Johnson " is so pleased with her pick-axe, that she wears it fastened to her girdle, on her left side, in balance with her watch." Vol. XVII. p. 1.

TO THE SAME.

Sep. 18, 1725.

Sir,

You court people have found out the way of vexing me in all my privacy and monkish manner of living. Here is Mr Sheridan perpetually teasing me with complaints, directly in the style I have often met among state letters, of loss of favour by misrepresentation, and envy and malice, and secret enemies, and the rest of that jargon. I have had share of it myself, and so I believe have you, and may have more in the course of your fortune. The worst evil is, that when ill opinions are instilled into great men, they never think it worth their while to be undeceived, and so a little man is ruined without the least tincture of guilt. And therefore, the last time I was in the world, I refused to deal with a chief minister, till he promised me, upon his honour, never to be influenced by any ill story of me, till he told it me plainly, and heard my defence; after which, if I cleared myself, it should pass for nothing, and he kept his word, and I was never once in pain. I was the person who recommended Mr Sheridan;* but the Bishop of Elphin took upon him to do it in form, and give it a sanction, and was seconded by two other bishops, all principled according to your heart's desire, and therefore his excellency hath nothing to answer for. I do believe Mr Sheridan hath been formerly reckoned a Tory, but no otherwise than hundreds among your favourites, who, perhaps, grew converts with more zeal, noise, and

---

* To be chaplain to the lord-lieutenant. See the vindication of Lord Carteret, Vol. VII. p. 489.

cunning, but with less decency.   And I hope a man
may be a convert, without being a renegado; and
however the practice is contrary, I know which of
them I should most favour.   It is most infallible, by
all sorts of reason, that Mr Sheridan is altogether innocent in that accusation of preaching, but, as he is
a creature without cunning, so he hath not overmuch
advertency.*   His books, his mathematics, the pres-
sures of his fortune, his laborious calling, and some
natural disposition or indisposition, give him an
egarement d'esprit, as you cannot but observe; but
he hath other good qualities enough to make up
that defect.   Truth, candour, good-nature, pleasant-
ness of humour, and very good learning; and it was
upon these regards I was bold to recommend him,
because I thought it was for the general good that
he should have some encouragement to go on in his
drudgery.   But if it be determined that party must
lay her talons upon him, there is no more to be said.
My lord-lieutenant hath too many great affairs, to
allow time for examining into every little business,
and yet it is hard that even a beggar should suffer
who is wholly innocent.   I heard King William say,
that if the people of Ireland could be believed in what
they said of each other, there was not an honest man
in the kingdom.   And if Mr Sheridan guesses right
of the person who is his chief accuser, there is no
man who is not altogether drunk and mad with party,
would value the accusation.   If, by the clatter made
upon this occasion, it should be thought most proper

---

* Swift refers to Sheridan's blunder, who chose for his text,
upon the anniversary of the Hanover accession, the memorable
verse, " Sufficient for the day is the evil thereof."   See the story
at length, Vol. XVII. p. 30.

for Mr Sheridan not to appear about the Castle at this juncture, I believe he will content himself, but not that he should lose any degree of favour with his excellency; and, if this be the case, I hope you will so order that my lord will condescend to signify so much to him, for I know too well how often princes themselves are obliged to act against their judgment, amidst the rage of factions.   Upon the whole, the good treatment you have given me, hath produced an ill effect, encouraging me to farther requests, that you will endeavour to make Mr Sheridan easy.   None but converts are afraid of shewing favour to those who lie under suspicion in point of principles; and that was Mr Addison's argument, in openly continuing his friendship to me to the very hour of his death.   And your case is the same, and the same I shall expect from you in a proper degree, both towards Mr Sheridan and myself.

Whether you are in Parliament or no, I am sensible you are too busy at this time to bear such an interruption as I have given you, and yet I have not said half what I had a mind; my excuse is, that I have title to your favour, as you were Mr Addison's friend, and, in the most honourable part, his heir;* and if he had thought of your coming to this kingdom, he would have bequeathed me to you.

I am ever, with true esteem and respect,

Your most obedient, and most humble servant,

JONATH. SWIFT.

---

* Addison loved Tickell with the affection of a father, and left him his literary executor.   Accordingly, he published the collected works of his friend, with an elegy, equally sublime and pathetic, by which he silenced the invidious critics, who had ascribed the beauties of his former productions to the secret assistance of Addison.

TO THE SAME.

Deanery-House, November 12, 1725.

Sir,

I HAVE got slowly out of a feverish disorder, that hath confined me these ten days. I shall dine to-morrow at home, after a sort, *en famille* with the two ladies my nurses. And if you please to be a fourth, I shall take care that no unacceptable fifth be of the company : And pray let me know to night or to-morrow morning, for as to Sunday, I look on you as a guest when you please.

I am, your most obedient,

J. SWIFT.

TO THE SAME.

[*London*,] April 16, 1726.

Sir,

THOUGH I am to desire a favour of you, yet I was glad it gave me an opportunity of paying you my respects. I am here now a month picking up the remnant of my old acquaintance and descending to take new ones. Your people are very civil to me, and I meet a thousand times better usage from them than from that denomination in Ireland.

This night I saw the wild boy, whose arrival here hath been the subject of half our talk this fortnight.*

---

* Peter the wild Boy, as he was called, caught in the forests of Hanover. Swift made him the subject of a *jeu d'esprit*, entitled,

He is in the keeping of Dr Arbuthnot, but the king and court were so entertained with him, that the princess could [*not*] get him till now. I can hardly think him wild in the sense they respect him. Mr Arundel is made surveyor of the works, which I suppose you will hear before you read this.

I hope I am to give you joy, and I am sure I wish it you ; the reason I trouble you with the enclosed, is, because it contains a bill of lading for a picture I have from France, and am afraid it might miscarry.

You will please to send one of your servants to the person it is directed to ; and accept my excuses.

     I am, with true respect, Sir,

        Your most obedient humble servant,

                  J. SWIFT.

TO THE SAME.

London, July 7, 1726.

SIR,

I HAVE led so restless, and visiting, and travelling, and vexatious a life, since I had the honour of your letter, that I never had humour enough to acknowledge it, though I carried it wrapped up safely in my pocket. You are now so old a married man, that I shall not congratulate with you, but pray God you may long congratulate with yourself, and that your situation will make you a tolerable Irish-

---

" It cannot rain but it pours, or London strowed with Rarities," which was published in the Miscellanies, and occurs in this Edition, Vol. XIII. p. 199.

man, at least till you can make the lady a good
Englishwoman, which, however, I hope will be
late. I cannot complain of any want of civility in
your friends, the Whigs; and I will tell you freely,
that most of them agree with me in quarrelling about
the same things. I have lived these two months
past for the most part in the country, either at
Twitenham with Mr Pope, or rambling with him
and Mr Gay for a fortnight together. Yesterday
my Lord Bolingbroke and Mr Congreve made up
five at dinner at Twitenham. I have been very
little more than a witness of any pleasantries you
may have seen from London. I am in no sedentary way for speculations of any kind, neither do I
find them so ready to occur at this late time of my
life. The thing you mention, which no friend
would publish, was written fourteen years ago, at
Windsor,* and shews how indiscreet it is to leave
any one master of what cannot without the least
consequence be shewn to the world. Folly, malice,
negligence, and the incontinence in keeping secrets,
(for which we want a word,) ought to caution men
to keep the key of their cabinets.

As to what you mention of an imaginary treatise,
I can only answer that I have a great quantity of
papers somewhere or other, of which none would
please you, partly because they are very incorrect,
but chiefly because they wholly disagree with your
notions of persons and things ; neither do I believe it
would be possible for you to find out my treasury
of waste papers, without searching nine houses, and
then sending to me for the key.

I find the ladies make the deanery their villa. I
have been told that Mrs Johnson's health has given

* This must have been the Windsor Prophecy.

her friends bad apprehensions; and I have heard but twice from them.* But their secretary, Dr Sheridan, just tells me she is much better, to my great satisfaction. I wonder how you could expect to see her in a morning, which I, her oldest acquaintance, have not done these dozen years, except once or twice in a journey. I desire to present my most humble service to Mrs Tickell.

I shall return in a few days to Twitenham, and there continue till August, at the latter end of which month I propose to wait on you at the Castle of Dublin, for I am weary of being among ministers whom I cannot govern, who are all rank Tories in government, and worse than Whigs in church; whereas I was the first man who taught and practised the direct contrary principle.

I am, Sir, with sincere respect,

Your most obedient humble servant,

JONATH. SWIFT.

TO THE SAME.

Deanery-House, April 7, 1727.

SIR,

I HUMBLY desire the favour of you to order one of your clerks to prepare a license for me to go to England for six months. I wish it might be finished by to-morrow, or at least the order got, after which I find I may set out legally. I am told the

---

* See letter to Dr Sheridan, 8th July 1726. Vol. XVII. p. 7.

veesel I go in will set out to-morrow, or on Sunday morning.

. I would desire that instead of England it might be expressed *partes transmarinas,* because it is probable my health may force me to Aix la Chapelle. I suppose the Bishop of Ferne's licence, when he went to France, ran in some such style. *

I have been so embroiled in my private affairs by the knavery of agents, that I have not had time to wait on you.   I am, with true respect,

Sir, your most obedient humble servant,
                                        JONATH. SWIFT.

I desire my most humble service to Mrs Tickell.

TO SAMUEL GERRARD, ESQ. NAVAN.

Dublin, Jan. 6, 1730. †

SIR,
    IT was with great concern that I first heard a dubious, and then a certain account of the death of

---

* Swift went to England in summer 1727, with the intention of proceeding from thence to the Continent.   But the news of the death of George I., put a stop to his purpose, as he hoped, through the interest of Mr Howard, to negociate an exchange betwixt his Irish preferment, and one which should place him among his English friends. See Vol. XVIII. p. 130.

    † This letter, which does so much honour to the Dean's friendly and benevolent disposition, was copied from the original, which is in the possession of Miss Cusack, grand-daughter of the gentleman whose loss he laments. They were a Catholic family. Tradition, which fondly preserves the most minute particulars of Swift's life, has recorded, that one day passing through the town of Navan, with the purpose of dining at Mr Cusack's, he recol-

our common friend Mr Cusack, whom, in an acquaintance of many years, I never found otherwise than a gentleman of honour, sincerity, candour, and every other good quality that can recommend a man to the friendship and esteem of all worthy persons. He is a great example of the uncertainty of life, for except an aptness he complained of to take cold in his head, I have known few persons likelier to live long. I am but too sensible of his unhappy family's loss in him, and particularly of the condition of his lady, who I hope will not live under the tyranny of that odious old woman. To her, poor Mr Cusack owed that he never passed one happy day at home, while she was under his roof. I must needs condole with you particularly for your loss in so worthy a friend : a thing so scarce in the country of Ireland, where the neighbouring squires are usually the most disagreeable of all human creatures.

You know, Sir, that last year he let me have a little mare, which I have rode ever since. I have often desired him to let me know the value he put on her. He answered, it was a present to him, and should be so to me. I protested I would suffer no such thing; he likewise sent me another young mare, which he was breeding up for me. I hope

---

lected it was fast-day, and therefore purchased a leg of mutton, to secure his own commons. The son of Mr Metye, (grandfather of the Baron,) at whose house the mutton had been left while the Dean attended prayers, plunged it by way of jest into a pot which was boiling in the kitchen fire. When the Dean returned and discovered what had happened, his passion was outrageous. He redeemed the half-boiled leg of mutton, however, and carried it with him to Mr Cusack's. Such an anecdote is not worth mentioning, were it not to shew the consequence which the Irish have gratefully and justly attached to the minutest particulars of Swift's life.

she will be good when she is cured of her starting; and in the mean time is very proper for a servant. I desire you will give your judgment what they both are worth; and I will pay the money immediately to the unfortunate widow's order, who may perhaps have occasion for it under her present circumstances. I shall continue for some weeks in town, and then, if my health permits, wander for a month or two in the country to preserve it. I am much obliged to our poor friend for bringing me acquainted with you, and he was a good judge of men, as I find by the character he often gave me of you; and I hope you will never come to this town while I am in it, without doing me the favour of calling on me. I am Sir, with true esteem,

Your most faithful humble servant,
J. SWIFT.

A CASE SUBMITTED BY DEAN SWIFT
TO MR LINDSAY, COUNSELLOR AT LAW.

[From the original in the Dean's hand-writing, indorsed, " Queries for Mr Lindsay ;" and " 21st Nov. 1730, Mr Lindsay's opinion concerning Mr Gorman, in answer to my queries."]

A. B. agent for J. S. comes to desire J. S. to sign an assignment of a lease in order to be registered for the security of L. 38. J. S. asks A. B. to shew him the lease. A. B. says he left it at home. J. S. asks the said A. B. how many years of the lease are

unexpired? what rent the tenant pays, and how much below the rack value? and what number of acres there are upon the farm? To each of which questions the agent A. B. answers categoricall, that he cannot tell, and that he did not think J. would ask him such questions. The said A. B. was asked how he came two years after the lease was assigned, and not sooner, to have it registered. A. B. answers, that he could not sue till the assignment.
- Query, Whether the said agent A. B. made any one answer like a man of business?

[ANSWER.]
I have carefully perused and considered this case, and am clearly of opinion, that the agent has not made any one answer like a man of business, but has answered very much like a true agent.

ROBERT LINDSAY.
Nov. 21, 1730.

[This document is from Dr Lyon's papers, and forms a curious instance of the Dean's strongly characteristic turn of humour.]

TO MR TICKELL.

Deanery-House, July 20, 1731.
SIR,
AFTER frequent reading with as much care as I could, I found but the three remarks above mentioned * that I could possibly make. Only I would

---

* The remarks are in this edition subjoined.

sink nine of the ten thousand fathom, and call it *a thousand.* I desire you will please to finish it. I have been riding out to-day, as well as yesterday, for my health, but find myself much disordered. If I grow better, I will wait on you to-morrow, if not, I will send the paper by a safe hand. *

I am, Sir, your, &c.

I have marked the figures 1, 2, 3, in your original.

1. For *when*, I would advise *where*.
2. I do not well understand this line.
3. I see what *this* and *that* refer to. But in the line just before, there are two words, *present* and *past,* and in the next line above *viscus,* and *leach,* which will make some difficulty to a common reader.

TO THE REV. THE DEAN OF ARMAGH,

AT KNOCHTOGHER, IN THE COUNTY OF KILKENNY †.

Dublin, June 30, 1732.

SIR,

IF you are not an excellent philosopher, I allow you personate one perfectly well ; and if you believe yourself, I heartily envy you, for I never yet saw in

---

* From this letter it would seem that the Dean had been engaged in revising some of Tickell's poetry.

† This remarkable letter is copied from the original in the hands of the Rev. Edward Maugin, translator of the Life of Malesherbes. It differs in some slight particulars from the copy inserted in Dr Barrett's Life of Swift, where Dr Brandreth, the clergyman to whom it is addressed, is called dean of Emly, to which benefice he was not promoted until three or four years afterwards.

Ireland a spot of earth two feet wide, that had not
in it something to displease.   I think I once saw in
that county of Tipperary, which is, like the rest of
the whole kingdom, a bare face of nature, without
houses or plantations,—filthy cabins, miserable, tat-
tered, half-starved creatures, scarce in human shape;
one insolent ignorant oppressive squire to be found
in twenty miles riding; a parish church to be only
found in a summer's day's journey, in comparison
of which, an English farmer's barn is a cathedral;
a bog fifteen miles round; every meadow a slough,
and every hill a mixture of rock, heath, marsh; and
every male and female, from the farmer, inclusive
to the day labourer, infallibly a thief, and consequently a beggar, which in this island are terms con-
vertible.   The Shannon is rather a lake than a river,
and has not the sixth part of the stream that runs
under London bridge.   There is not an acre of land
in Ireland turned at to half its advantage, yet it is
better improved than the people; and all these evils
are effects of English tyranny, so your sons and
grandchildren will find it to their sorrow.   Cork indeed was a place of trade, but for some years past is
gone to decay, and instead of being merchants, the
wretched dealers are dwindled to pedlars and cheats.
I desire you will not write such accounts of your
friends in England.   Did you ever see one cheerful
countenance among our country vulgar?—unless
once a-year at a fair, or on a holiday, where some
poor rogue happened to get drunk, and starved the
whole week after.   You will give a very different
account of your winter campaign, when you cannot walk five yards from your door without being
mired to your knees, nor ride half a mile without
being in slough to your saddle skirts; where your
landlord must send twenty miles for yeast before he
can brew or bake, and the neighbours five miles

round must club to kill a mutton. Pray take care
of damps, and when you leave your bedchamber, let
a fire be made to last till night, and, after all, if a
stocking happens at night to fall off a chair, you may
wring it next morning. *I nunc et tecum versus me-
ditare canoros.* I have not said all this out of any
malicious intention, to put you out of conceit with
the scene where you are, but merely for your credit, because it is better to know you are miserable, than to betray an ill taste. I consult your honour, which is dearer than life; therefore I demand
that you shall not relish one bit of victuals, or drop
of drink, or the company of any human creature
within thirty miles round Knocktogher, during your
residence in those parts, and then I shall begin to
have a tolerable opinion of your understanding. My
lameness is very slowly recovering, and if it be well
when the year is out, I shall gladly compound.
Yet I make a shift to ride about ten miles a-day,
by virtue of certain implements called gambadoes,
where my foot stands firm as on a floor, and I generally dine alone, like a king or a hermit, and continue alone till I go to bed; for even my wine will
not purchase me company, and I begin to think
the lame are forsaken as much as the poor and blind.
Mr Jibb never calls at the deanery of late; perhaps
he hath found out that I like him, as a modest man,
and of very good understanding. This town is neither large nor full enough to furnish events for entertaining a country correspondent. A murder now
and then is all we have to trust to. Our fruit is all
destroyed with the spring north-east winds, and I
shall not have the tenth part of my last year's fruit,
Miss Hoadly hath been nine days in the small-pox.
which I never heard of till this minute; but they
say she is past danger. She would have been a terrible loss to the archbishop. Dr Felton of Oxford

hath writ a very large octavo about Revelations, &c. I know not his character. He sent over four copies to me, one of which was for Mr Tickell, two for the bishops of Cork and Waterford, and one to myself, by way of payment for sending the rest, I suppose, for he sent me no letter, and I know him not. Whenever you are in this town, I hope you will mend your usage of me, by coming oftener to a philosophic dinner at the deanery. This I pretend to expect, for the sake of our common Princess, Lady E. G *. to whom I owe the happiness of your acquaintance, and, on her account, I expect your justice to believe me to be, with truest esteem,

Your most obedient humble servant,

JN. SWIFT.

EXTRACTS OF LETTERS

BETWEEN

CHARLES FORD, ESQ. AND MR BURTON.

[In a letter from Mr Ford to the Dean, dated 23d December 1732. Vol. XVIII. p. 123, there occurs a blank supplied by asterisks. This probably refers to the dispute between Mr Burton and Mr Ford, and may have been accompanied by the following extracts from the angry letters which passed between these gentlemen. The extracts are in the Dean's hand-writing, and seem to have been made for the purpose of being shewn to mutual friends.]

The contents, as well as I † can recollect, of my answer to Mr Burton's letter of Nov. 1. 1732.

---

* Lady Elizabeth Germaine. † That is, Mr Ford.

I acknowledged the receipt of his letter. I lamented my misfortune in expressing myself so ill as not to be understood. I repeated the reasons I had often given before, why I could not sign his deed. I said, I would try to explain myself otherwise. I did so, and added words to this effect; that I would not fling away the * only weapon I had of defence, when I was not sure of not being attacked the next moment: That the sum mention'd between you and him was not L.1000, but 300: That though I thought it a very large one, yet I would comply in deference to the Dean's judgment: That if through ignorance I had exceeded my power, the damage could not be very great, because I had notice of it from him within a month or thereabouts, after his lease took effect: That those whose authority in points of law was of most weight here, thought I had not exceeded my power, and that his lease was good; but since others differed from them, and a doubt arose, I would voluntarily charge Benetstowne, &c. I begged I might not be again mistaken in this proposal ; I repeated it in other words, that I would charge, &c. upon this condition, that I had a strong clause inserted to secure me against any further demand from him or any person claiming by virtue of that lease. I said, that I did not see why he should desire to have a difference with me, since I was willing of myself to do more than all lawyers agreed the law would compel me to do, and more than all men of honour told me they thought I was obliged to in honour. That neither [of] us could get any thing by law, but a great deal of

---

* Benetstowne, which in all his deeds he had entailed upon himself.—*Mr Ford's note.*

trouble added to great expence. That I hoped to continue to be,

His most, &c.

This paragraph is word for word, and letter for letter, out of Mr Burton's long letter, Dec. 4, 1732.

I will try to explain myself otherwise if I can. Fear is one of the passions which has the least predominance over me, and I thank God he has given me a mind strengthened with resolution, which is not so tenacious as to exceed the bounds of reason. I have a real estate in fee simple, free from settlement or any other incumbrance, of as good yearly value to me as any of my neighbours within two or three miles about me, except Lord Shelburne, and out of my personal estate can, upon an emergency, spare a competency at any time, to defend me from injuries, in any part of the world. Costs, I believe, would be as greaveous to you as to me, for which, and other reasons, my intention was and is that extremes should be avoided, and matters reasonably adjusted. I know a gentleman older, and feebler than I am, who, in an affair much less conscionable and honourable than this is, went as far at least as from this to London, and did himself right in a legal way, and otherwise, in respect to an injury brought upon him.

My answer to the whole letter, word for word.

London, December 19, 1732.

SIR,

YESTERDAY I received your letter of the 9th, and concur with you that we have had a very troublesome paper correspondence, at least it has been so to me

In answer to the first material part of your letter, I can tell you that Mr Cooper and I had agreed matters in less than three minutes after our first meeting, and it was neither of our faults that that agreement has not been yet executed. Other affairs have hitherto deferred appointments never put off by me. However, the delay has prevented me from signing what I am convinced by one of the succeeding paragraphs, and by former observations, would have been the worst thing, except your lease, that I ever did or could set my hand to.

I must acquaint you, in return to the latter part of your letter, (the true meaning of which I should not indeed have understood without your explanation), that I am not afraid of you either in a legal way or otherwise; that, notwithstanding your great substance, I am now determined to seek for justice the first way; and whenever you, old and feeble as you are, shall think fit to come here to demand it otherwise, I, old and fat as I am, will give it you under my hand, that I will not remove to avoid you.

CHA. FORD.

TO EATON STANNARD, ESQ*.

Deanery-House, December, 1732.

SIR,

Mr SANDYS told me some days ago, that when he waited upon you for advice, upon some papers that

---

* Mr Stannard was a barrister of eminence. He was chosen Recorder of the city of Dublin in the year 1733, on the death of Mr Stoyte. The Dean's letter to the Mayor and Corporation on the choice of a recorder, was written upon that occasion. Vol. VII. p. 561. Mr Stannard was soon after made the King's Prime Sergeant at law.

concern the greatest part of my little fortune, you were pleased to tell him, that you would not take a fee if I were to pay it. I own myself extremely obliged by such an act of generosity and friendship, to which I never had the least pretension, further than the merit of always professing a true esteem for you; and if you intend to proceed by that rule, you will never be a farthing the better for any honest man, who may, as well as I, put in his claim with you to be *amicus curiæ*. However, as I may be probably pestered with law, and have few friends at the bar, I must, of necessity, depend upon your assistance, which I will sooner lose my cause than do upon the hard terms you offered by Mr Sandys.

Last night the deeds were read and signed by me, my creditors and his tenant; in the copy of which deeds Mr Sandys shewed me your corrections in his own hand; and I conclude all the rest was right; by which I shall be richer L. 120 a year; and thereby abler to give you a fee, and a friend a bottle of wine more than usual. It seems the expences and fees in these cases are paid by the mortgager. But my obligations to you are not the less, who was so rash as to declare against taking my money before you knew whether I were to pay it or no.

If I had not still continued (as I have been for three months) confined by deafness and giddiness, I would have waited on you with my acknowledgements for your favour and goodness. But I shall ever remain, what I have always been, with great esteem, Sir,

Your most obedient and
obliged humble servant,
JONATH. SWIFT.

TO MR TICKELL.*

Deanery-House, Tuesday morning.

Sir

As you have been very obliging to me on all occasions, gratitude would not suffer me to be careless

---

* This letter relates entirely to a production of the notorious
Matthew Pilkington, who was, for some time, though very unwor-
thily, under the patronage of the Dean. This person having received an order for a gratuity of fifty pounds from Lord Carteret, for an Ode on the King's Birth-day, chose to express the
sentiments with which so unusual an influx of riches affected
him, in a *jeu d'esprit*, entitled, " The Plague of Wealth, or the
Poet's Diary, in a letter to Dr Delany," in which he relates and
exaggerates his surprise and anxiety, on finding himself the subject of such extravagant bounty. Amongst other details he
indulges himself in some pleasantries upon Mr Tickell, secretary to the Lords-Justices, from whom he was to receive the
premium, by order of the Lord Lieutenant. In this attempt at
humour, where, as Swift remarks, he exhibits his own character as a very mean one, liable to be totally overwhelmed by the
wonderful benefaction of fifty pounds, he mentions having obtained an order for this sum upon Mr Tickell the secretary, and
then proceeds : " Went in high spirits to the secretary's (but, as
a drawback to my happiness), received the dispiriting account of
his being confined to his chamber; denied admittance.

" Memorand. His Excellency easier of access than his officer.

Tuesday, 17. [February.]
" The secretary still sick ; paid a visit to his street door about
twelve ; returned melancholy.
Wednesday, ditto.
Thursday, ditto.
Friday, ditto.
Saturday, ditto.
Sunday, ditto.
O ! 'twas a dreadful interval of time !

to any thing relating to your credit. The last time you were here, you mentioned a foolish scribble printed in Mrs Pilkington's Poems. When you were gone I immediately looked into the book, and as I had told you could not find it. I then sent to Mr Pilkington, who brought me an edition printed in London, where I found it at the end of the book. The story of the thing is this : When that money was ordered by my Lord Carteret, Pilkington, not used to such sums, told his patron, Dr Delany, all the particulars of his fear, joy, &c. on the matter, which so diverted the doctor, that he made the young man to write it down, that Lord Carteret might see it ; and when his Lordship went to England, he writ to the doctor to send him a copy, which his Lordship having shewn to several persons, was transcribed, and, by the impertinence of the bookseller, printed at the end of the Poems, against Pilkington's knowledge, and much to his vexation ; for the character he gives

---

Monday, 23.

" Ordered to wait again on Mr T———; but happening to be over eager to receive the sum, I hastened away too unseasonably about half an hour after twelve, and found him asleep.

" Mem. Admitted this morning to stand in the hall, and not at the door, as hath been slanderously and maliciously reported ; I presume, because it happened so at other times.

" Walked in the piazzas till after one, ruminating on the various hopes and fears with which my mind had been tormented this week past ; could not forbear repeating aloud the two lines of the libel, which accidentally are not more true of Mr Addison than his friend,

Who, grown a minister of state,
See Poets at his levee wait."

Mr Tickell seems to have taken this familiar jocularity in bad part, and Pilkington has recourse to the Dean's intercession to propitiate his displeasure.

5

himself in it is a very mean one, and must be remembered, and much to his disadvantage if ever he
rises in the world. As for your part in it, I must
declare my thoughts that it does not affect you in
the least. You are said to be sick, and could not
be seen, and the complaint is of the usual kind
made by all who attend at Courts. The young man
was sorry, as he had reason, to see it in print, lest
it might possibly offend a person of your reputation
and consequence. He appears to me to be a modest good-natured man. I know but little of him.
Dr Delany brought him to me first, and recommended him as one whom I might safely countenance. He is in the utmost pain at hearing that
you imagine there was the least design to affront you;
since, as it would be the basest thing in itself, so
such a treatment would be the surest method to ruin
his interests.

I could not forbear telling you this out of perfect
pity to the young man.

I desire to present my humble service to Mrs
Tickell, and am with great esteem, Sir,

Your most obedient humble servant,

JONATH. SWIFT.

I am just going out of town for a few weeks, but
I have ordered that Mrs Tickell shall have her annual tribute of peaches and nectarines, which will
be ripe in a few days, if the sun is favourable, and
thieves will spare them.

TO EATON STANNARD, ESQ.

Deanery-House, March 12, 1733-4.

Sir,

I am commanded by my Lady Howth to use the
utmost of that little credit I may possibly have with
you, in favour of her brother, Mr George, to whom
I am a perfect stranger ; neither do I know any other
lady whose commands I would not have disobeyed
on the like occasion, being perfectly indifferent how
Parliament elections go, unless I could have any
hope of a majority half so honest, or a tenth part so
able as yourself.   It seems the election comes on upon Thursday next.   Her ladyship called here yesterday, but I was abroad, and she left her desire that
I would write to you as soon as possible.

I am, with great esteem, Sir,

Your most obedient humble servant,

JONATH. SWIFT.

TO THE SAME.

Deanery-House, April 11, 1735.

Sir,

I believe you may possibly have heard from me,
or public report, of my resolution to leave my whole
fortune, except a few legacies, to build an hospital
for idiots and lunatics in this city, or the suburbs.
And, after long consideration, I have been so bold
to pitch upon you as my director in the methods I
ought to take for rendering my design effectual.   I

have known and seen the difficulties of any such attempt, by the negligence, or ignorance, or some worse dealing by executors and trustees. I have been so unfortunate, for want of some able friend of a public spirit, that I could never purchase one foot of land.

The neighbouring country always watching, like crows for a carcase, over every estate that was likely to be sold, and that kind of knowledge was quite out of the life I have led; which, in the strength of my days, chiefly past at courts, and among ministers of state, to my great vexation and disappointment, for which I now repent too late. I therefore humbly desire you will please to take me into your guardianship, as far as the weight of your business will permit. As the city hath agreed to give me a piece of land, my wish would be to make the lord mayor, recorder, and aldermen, my trustees, executors or governors, according as you shall please to advise. And out of these, committees may be appointed to meet at proper times. My thought is, that the city will be careful in an affair calculated wholly for the city's advantage. If you would favour me so much, as to fix any day during this vacation to dine at the Deanery, I shall be extremely obliged to you; and give you my very crude notions of my intentions.

I am, with great esteem, Sir,
Your most obedient and obliged servant,
JONATH. SWIFT.

SCROLL OF A LETTER TO A LADY.

[From the original in the Dean's handwriting, found among Mr
Steele's papers. It is without any address, and displays his usual
style of real kindness and politeness, under the mask of cyni-
cal rudeness.]

Tuesday, Oct. 12, 1736.

MADAM,

You are very captious; for, in my last letter, I only said in the beginning, Madam, you lie! I have a
great deal worse than that to say, when I write to
ladies; and my fault is, what my enemies give out,
that I use you too well. I send you some fruit of
my own planting; and, like a fool, I send you the
best, though you never give the bearer a farthing;
and, when you do, may you never be worth another.
Let me know perfectly the condition of your eldest
sister. I will wait on you soon, if health will permit
me. I am now tolerably; which is more than you
can pretend to. My humble service to the little
woman's little man.

J. S.

FROM ERASMUS LEWIS TO DEAN SWIFT.*

London, Aug. 4, 1737.

I ASSURE you, my dear Dean, 'twas matter of joy to me to receive a letter from you, and I hope 'tis an earnest of many more I may have hereafter, before you and I leave this world; though I must tell you, that if you and I revive our former correspondence, you must indulge me the liberty of making use of another hand; for whether it be owing to age, or writ-

---

* This letter, and that from Mr Lewis, on p. 218. now first published, throw important light upon the reasons for suppressing Swift's History of the Four last Years of Queen Anne. The Earl of Oxford appears to have been very anxious to prevent the publication until the work had been previously revised by himself and some family friends. This request he presses upon the Dean in his letter of 7th April 1737, p. 140; and as Swift, in his reply, 14th June, p. 158, seems rather to decline the proposal, his Lordship repeats it more anxiously in a letter of 4th June, p. 174. It was also enforced by the Dean's old friend, Erasmus Lewis, on 30th June, who renews their correspondence with the obvious purpose of preventing the publication if possible till some revision of the manuscript had taken place. In his answer of 23d June, Swift consents, with obvious reluctance, that the person who was in possession of the MS. (Dr King apparently) should read it to Lord Oxford and Mr Lewis, but without trusting it out of his own hands. This is the reply in which Lewis claims that promise; and in his subsequent letter, 8th April 1738, p. 218, the reader will find, that, upon perusal of the manuscript, the friends to whom it was exhibited, saw so much ground for alteration, that the idea of publishing the work was altogether laid aside. It is scarce necessary to remind the reader, that Lewis had been Under Secretary of State during Lord Oxford's administration.

B b

ing formerly whole nights by candle-light, or to both those causes, my sight is so far impaired, that I am not able, without much pain, to scratch out a letter.

I do not remember ever to have read your history. I own my memory is much decayed; but still I think I could not have forgotten a matter of so much consequence, and which must have given me so great a pleasure. It is fresh in my mind, that Lord Oxford and the Auditor desired you to confer with me upon the subject matter of it; that we accordingly did so; and that the conclusion was, you would bury every thing in oblivion. We reported this to those two, I mean to his Lordship and his uncle, and they acquiesced in it. Now I find you have finished that piece. I ask nothing but what you grant in your letter of July 23d, viz. That your friend shall read it to me, and forbear sending it to the press, till you have considered the objections, if any should be made. In the meantime, I shall only observe to you in general, that three and twenty years, for so long it is since the death of Queen Anne, have made a great alteration in the world, and that what was sense and reason then is not so now; besides, I am told you have treated some people's characters with a severity which the present times will not bear, and may possibly bring the author into much trouble, which would be matter of great uneasiness to his friends. I know very well it is your intention to do honour to the then treasurer. Lord Oxford knows it; all his family and friends know it; but it is to be done with great circumspection. It is now too late to publish a pamphlet, and too early to publish a history.

It was always my opinion, that the best way of doing honour to the treasurer, was to write a history of the peace of Utrecht, beginning with a short preamble concerning the calamitous state of our debt, and ending with the breaking our army and restoring the civil power ; that these great things were completed under the administration of the Earl of Oxford, and this should be his epitaph. Lord Bolingbroke is undoubtedly writing a history, but I believe will not live to finish it, because he takes it up too high, viz. from the Restoration. In all probability he'll cut and slash Lord Oxford. This is only my guess. I don't know it.

As to our private friends, I must tell you, I believe Mr Mash[am] to be a good young man without any shining qualities. Charles Ford's mistress is his bottle, to which he is so entirely given up, that he and I converse but little, though he is a man of honour, and as such to be respected. Pope is very kind to me and I am vain of it. We meet often, and always remember you. I did so yesterday with Mr Hare, now Sir Thomas Hare. Poor George Arbuthnot is miserable. He is splenetick to a degree of —— He is going to France to try whether that merry nation will cure him. Lord and Lady Oxford and Lord Masham send you their compliments. As you make a friendly inquiry after my health, I must tell you I feel all the infirmities of age, but less of deafness than of any other. I find some relief in cards, which, I believe, you despise, but they keep me from thinking, and that is a great benefit. Adieu, dear Dean, and believe me most affectionately yours,   E. L.

TO EATON STANNARD, ESQ. DUBLIN.

Deanery-House, June 8, 1741.

Sir,

I know the bearer, Mr William Swift, to be a deserving young gentleman, and I think he hath some learning, although he be just returned from the study of law.   He is my relation, and I desire you will please to present him to my lord chancellor.

I am, worthy Sir, with true esteem,

Your most obedient humble servant,

JONATHAN SWIFT.

TO MRS DRELINCOURT. *

Twitenham, August 7, 1727.

Madam,

Two days ago I received a letter, signed M. Earbery, (if I read it right), which name it seems belongs to the person recommended by your brother as a sufferer by the times, and desirous to help himself by the translation of an Italian book.   I shewed his letter to my friends here, who all agree that it

---

* This original letter was found in the repositories of Viscountess Primrose (the Miss Drelincourt mentioned in the letter), by her executrix, Mrs Lillias Waldie, and is now in the possession of Mrs Smith of Kelso.   Mrs Drelincourt was wife to Peter, Dean of Armagh, third son to Drelincourt, the author of " Consolations against the Fear of Death."   A short account of the family is in Watkins's Biographical Dictionary.

is an original in its kind, beyond what we have any-where met with, being a heap of strange insolence and scurrility, without the least provocation. What I desired you to tell him was, that I thought his ob-servations were too long, and that, in my opinion, it would be better to enlarge his notes. When I met Miss Drelincourt on the Mall, I likewise said, that I could not decently give public encouragement to such a work where Mr Pope was openly reflected on by name. As for a distressed person, and a clergy-man that hath suffered for his opinion, I should be very ready to contribute my mite, and have done it oftener than it was deserved from me ; but this same Mr Earbery would be countenanced as an *author* and a *genius*, whereof I am no judge, and therefore it would be more convenient for him to apply to others who are. But I think whoever he applies to for encouragement, he would not succeed the worse, if he thought fit to spare the method of threatening and ill language ; although I have been so long out of the world, that, perhaps, I may be mistaken, and that these are the new arts of purchas-ing favour. For the same reason, let me add one thing more, that being wholly a stranger to the pre-sent way of writing, the objection I made to his ob-servations may be altogether injudicious, for want of knowing the taste of the age, or of conversing with its productions. This you may please to tell the writer of the letter, and that I promise never to med-dle with his liberty of understanding, although what he means is past mine.

I am, with true respect,
Madam,
Your most obedient humble servant,
JONATH. SWIFT.

My humble service to Miss Drelincourt.   I assure you she makes a good figure on the Mall, and I could, in conscience, do no less than distinguish her.

I have desired Mr Gay to shew you the letter, writ to me by this Mr Earbury, and I have writ a word or two at the bottom for you to read.

CORRESPONDENCE

BETWEEN

SWIFT AND MISS VANHOMRIGH.

CORRESPONDENCE, &c.

[The reader is here presented with what public curiosity has
longed to see, and what will, after all, probably afford it less
gratification than might have been expected. It is said, that the
unfortunate Vanessa, on her death-bed, charged her executors
to make these letters public, and there has been probably some
foundation for so uniform an averment, although no such in-
junction appears in her will, as has been affirmed by most
of Swift's biographers. The originals of the letters are
said to have been destroyed by Bishop Berkeley ; but Judge
Marshal, the other executor, preserved copies, from which
several extracts have, at different times, found their way to
the public. The following transcript was made some years
since, by my learned and most obliging friend, the Reverend
Mr Berwick of Esher, near Leixlip, well known to the literary world by the light which his labours have thrown upon
many abstruse passages of ancient history. The internal evidence, and the high character of Mr Berwick, are a sufficient
warrant of the authenticity of these letters, although the editor is unable to state in whose hands the original copy of Marshal is now to be found. The want of dates has, in some
places, rendered it doubtful whether the letters are arranged
in proper order, but in one instance only the editor has ventured to depart from the order of the transcript, for the reason
given in a note. Two or three extracts from Swift's letters
to Vanessa were already printed in Vol. XVII. before the editor became possessed of the full transcript. They are reprinted entire in the following series, to save the reader the trouble
of reference. The letters, although there is here and there a
degree of affected mystery, in alluding to circumstances of
their intercourse, which taken alone, might appear suspicious,
do, upon the whole, answer the description given of them by
Delany, on the authority of Bishop Berkeley,—that Swift's
consisted chiefly of gallantry, excuses, apologies, &c. while
Miss Vanhomrigh's expressed the most deep and violent passion, but without the least hint of a criminal intercourse between them ; which could scarcely have been avoided in so
long a correspondence, had there been any foundation for it.
Delany's Remarks, p. 123.]

CORRESPONDENCE

BETWEEN

SWIFT AND MISS VANHOMRIGH.

DR SWIFT TO MRS ESTHER VANHOM-RIGH, Junior,

[At her lodgings over against Park-Place, in St James's Street, London. *]

Windsor Castle, Aug. 15, 1712.

I THOUGHT to have written to little Miss-essy by the colonel, but at last I did not approve of him as a messenger. Mr Ford began your health last night under the name of the Jilt, for which I desire you will reproach him. I do neither study nor exercise so much here as I do in town. The colonel † will intercept all the news I have to tell you, of my fine

---

* This fatal correspondence seems to have commenced with Swift's residence in Windsor, in autumn 1712, while drawing together materials for his History of the Peace of Utrecht. It is not therefore wonderful that, about the same time, we find him apologizing to Stella for the slackness of his correspondence. Vol. III. p. 101.

† Vanessa's brother, who seems to have been in the army; he is sometimes called the Captain.

snuff-box, * and my being at a ball, and my losing my money at ombre with the Duke and Duchess of Shrewsbury. I cannot imagine how you pass your time in our absence, unless by lying a-bed till twelve, and then having your followers about you till dinner. We have dispatches to-day from Lord Bolingbroke; † all is admirably well, and a cessation of arms will be declared with France in London, on Tuesday next. I dined with the Duke of Shrewsbury to-day, and sat an hour by Mrs Warburton, teaching her when she played wrong at ombre, and I cannot see her defects; either my eyes fail me, or they are partial. But Mrs Touchet is an ugly awkward slut. What do you do all the afternoon? How come you to make it a secret to me, that you all design to come to Windsor? If you were never here, I think you all cannot do better than come for three or four days; five pounds will maintain you, and pay for your coach backwards and forwards. I suppose the Captain will go down with you now, for want of better company. I will steal to town one of these days and catch you napping. I desire you and Moll ‡ will walk as often as you can in the Park, and do not sit moping at home, you that can neither work, nor read, nor play, nor care for company. I long to drink a dish of coffee in the sluttery, and hear you dun me for Socrete, and " Drink

---

* Presented to Swift by General Hill, Governor of Dunkirk, See Vol. III. p. 105, for his celebrated repartee to Lord Oxford, upon the subject of the snail and the goose, which were enchased on this snuff-box. Mr Theophilus Swift describes this celebrated box as being of agate, richly mounted with gold. The goose and snail are still visible upon the lid.

† Then at Paris.

‡ Miss Mary Vanhomrigh, whom he afterwards calls Molkin.

your coffee.—Why don't you drink your coffee?"
My humble service to your mother, and Moll, and
the Colonel.—Adieu !

TO THE SAME,
[Whom he calls *Messheshinage.*]

Friday, at Mr Lewis's Office, [no date.]

Miss Hessy is not to believe a word Mr Lewis
says in his letter. I would have writ to you sooner,
if I had not been busy, and idle, and out of humour,
and did not know how to send to you, without the
help of Mr Lewis, my mortal enemy. I am so
weary of this place, that I am resolved to leave it in
two days, and not return in three weeks. I will
come as early on Monday as I can find opportunity, and will take a little Grub-street lodging, pretty
near where I did before, and dine with you thrice
a-week, and will tell you a thousand secrets, provided you will have no quarrels to me. Adieu !

Don't remember me to Moll, but humble service
to your mother.

TO THE SAME,
[Whom he calls *Missessy.*]

Sunday, nine, [no date.]

I DID not forget the coffee, for I thought you
should not be robbed of it. John does not go to

Oxford, so I send back the book as you desire. I would not see you for a thousand pounds if I could; but I am now in my night-gown, writing a dozen letters, and packing up papers. Why, then, you should not have come ;. and I know that as well as you.

My service to your mother. I doubt you do wrong to go to Oxford, but now that is past, since you cannot be in London to-night ; and if I * do not inquire for acquaintance, but let somebody in the inn go about with you among the colleges, perhaps you will not be known. Adieu.

John presents his humble service to you.
The fellow has been long coming.

FROM THE SAME TO THE SAME,

[Whom he calls *Little Misessy*.]

I HAVE writ three or four lies in as many lines. Pray seal up the letter to Mrs L.†, and let nobody read it but yourself. I suppose this packet will lie two or three hours till you awake. And pray let

---

* This probably should be read, " if *you* do not inquire," &c. It does not seem that Swift was to meet them at Oxford. Mrs Vanhomrigh, whose affairs were embarrassed, might have creditors at Oxford.

† Perhaps to Mrs Long, who was an intimate of the Vanhomrigh family. See a letter of hers to Swift, Vol. XV. p. 458, in which Miss Hessy is particularly mentioned. But if this conjecture be accurate, the letter should have been placed first of the series, for Mrs Long died December 1711. Ibid. p. 464. She was then retired to Lynne for fear of her creditors, which may be a reason for the precaution observed in addressing her.

the outside starched letter to you be seen, after you
have sealed that to Mrs L.   See what arts people
must [use,] though they mean ever so well.   Now
are you and Puppy lying at your ease, without
dreaming any thing of all this.   Adieu, till we meet
over a pot of coffee, or an orange and sugar, in the
sluttery, which I have so often found to be the most
agreeable chamber in the world.

FROM MISS ESTHER VANHOMRIGH TO DR SWIFT.

London, Sept. the 1st, 1712.

HAD I a correspondent in China, I might have
had an answer by this time.   I never could think till
now, that London was so far off in your thoughts,
and that twenty miles were, by your computation,
equal to some thousands.   I thought it a piece of
charity to undeceive you in this point, and to let
you know, if you give yourself the trouble to write,
I may probably receive your letter in a day : 'twas
that made me venture to take pen in hand the third
time.   Sure you'll not let it be to no purpose.   You
must needs be extremely happy where you are, to
forget your absent friends ; and I believe you have
formed a new system, and think there is no more of
this world, passing your sensible horizon.   If this
be your notion, I must excuse you ; if not, you can
plead no other excuse ; and, if it be, Sir, I must
reckon myself of another world ; but I shall have
much ado to be persuaded, till you send me some
convincing arguments of it.   Don't dally in a thing

of this consequence, but demonstrate that 'tis possible to keep up a correspondence between friends, though in different worlds, and assure one another, as I do you, that I am your most obedient

and most humble servant,

E. VANHOMRIGH.

FROM THE SAME TO THE SAME.

London, Sept. the 2d, 1712.

MR Lewis tells me you have made a solemn resolution to leave Windsor the moment we come there; 'tis a noble res. * pray keep to it. Now, that I may be noways accessory to your breaking it, I design to send Mr Lewis word to a minute when we shall leave London, that he may tell you. And might I advise you, it should be to set out from Windsor just at the same time that we leave London, and if there be a by-way you had better take it, for I very much apprehend, that, seeing us will make you break through all, at least I am sure it would make you heartily repent; and I would not for the world, could I avoid it, give any uneasiness upon this score, because I must infallibly upon another. For when Mr Lewis told me what you had done, (which I must needs say, was not in so soft a manner as he ought, both out of friendship to you, and compassion to me,) I immediately swore, that, to be revenged of you, I would stay in Windsor as long as Mrs H———e did,

---

* Resolution.

and, if that was not long enough to teaze you, I would follow her to Hampton Court, and then I should see which will give you most vexation, seeing me but sometimes, or not seeing her at all. Besides, Mr Lewis has promised me to intercept all your letters to her, and her's to you ; at least he says I shall read them *en passant*, and, for sealing them again, let him look to that.   I think your ruin is amply contrived, for which don't blame me, but yourself, for 'twas your rashness prompted to this malice, which I should never else have thought of.

FROM DR SWIFT TO MRS ESTHER VAN-HOMRIGH,

[The Younger, at her lodgings over against Park-Place, in St James's Street, London.   Carriage paid.]

Windsor Castle, Sept. 3. 1712.

I send this haunch of venison to your mother, not to you, and this letter to you, not your mother.   I had your last, and your bill, and know your reasons.   I have ordered Barber to send you the overplus sealed up : I am full of business and ill humour.   Some end or other shall soon be put to both. *   I thought you would have been here yesterday : Is your journey hither quite off? †   I hope

----

* About this time the business of his preferment was in agitation.   See the Journal, 15th September 1712.

† The visit of the Vamhomrigh family to Windsor did take place, as is afterwards intimated.

Moll is recovered of her illness, and then you may
come.   Have you 'scaped your share in this new
fever?* I have hitherto, though of late I am not
very well in my head.

You rally very well : Mr Lewis allows you to do
so.†

I read your letter to him.   I have not time to
answer, the coach and venison being just ready to
go.

Pray eat half an ounce at least of the venison,
and present my humble service to your mother,
Moll, and the Colonel.

I had his letter, and will talk to him about it when
he comes.

This letter, I doubt, will smell of the venison.
I wish the hang-dog coachman may not spoil the
haunch in the carriage.   Je suis a vous, &c.

TO THE SAME.

End of May 1712.

I PROMISED to write to you, and I have let you
know that it is impossible for any body to have
more acknowledgments at heart for all your kindness and generosity to me.   I hope this journey

---

* Journal, August 7, 1712. "We have a fever both here and
at Windsor, which hardly any body misses.   But it lasts not
above three or four days, and kills nobody.   The Queen has forty servants down in it at once." The new fever is again mentioned, 9th October.   Vol. III. pages 100, 109.

† This alludes to Vanessa's last letter.

will restore my health. I will ride but little every day, and I will write a common letter to you all from some of my stages, but directed to you. I could not get here till ten this night. Pray be merry, and eat, and walk, and be good; and send me your commands, whatever Mr L. shall think proper to advise you. I have hardly time to put my pen to paper, but I would make good my promise, Pray God preserve you, and make you happy and easy; and so adieu brat.

Service to mother and Molkin.

Mrs B.'s house, eleven at night, company *weighting* * who come to take leave of me.

TO MRS VANHOMRIGH, SENIOR.

[Addressed to Madam Van, at the sign of the three Widows in Pom-roy Ally. With care and speed. *Present.*]

Chester, June 6th, 1713.

MADAM,

You heard of me from Dunstable, by the way of Hessy. I have had a sad time since. If Moll's even so had been there, she would have none left. Now Hessy grumbles that I talk of Moll. I have resolved upon the direction of my letter already, for I reckon Hessy and Moll are widows as well as you, or at least half widows. D'Avila † goes off rarely now. I have often wished for a little of your rats-

---

* Waiting.
† It would appear, that, under Swift's tuition, Vanessa was engaged in reading Davila's Civil Wars of France.

bane; * what I met on the road does not deserve the name of ratsbane. I have told Mr Lewis the circumstances of my journey, and the curious may consult him upon it. Who will Hessy get now to chide, or Moll to tell her stories, and bring her sugar-plumbs? We never know any thing enough till we want it. I design to send Hessy a letter in print from Ireland, because she cannot read writing-hand, except from Mr Partington. I hope you have heard again from the Colonel, and that he is fully cured of ————, I dont know what, I forget. It was under cover to Mr Lewis that I wrote to you from Dunstable. I writ to Hessy, by Barber, from St Albans. I left London without taking leave of Sir John. I fear a person of his civility will never pardon me. I met no adventures in all my travels, only my horse fell under me, for which reason I will not ride him to Holyhead, I can assure him that. I could not see any marks in the chimney at Dunstable, of the coffee Hessy spilt there, and I had no diamond-ring about me, to write any of your names in the windows. But I saw written, *Dearest Lady Betty Hamilton*, and hard by, *Middleton Walker*, whom I take to be an Irish manmidwife, which was a plain omen of her getting a husband. I hear Moor, the handsome parson, came over with the A. B. of Dublin. Did he not marry one Mrs Devenish? Lord Lanesborough has been here lately in his way to Ireland, and has got the good-will of all the folks in our town. He had something to say to every little boy he met in the streets. Well, he is the courteousest man, and nothing is so fine in the quality as to be courteous.

---

* *Coffee*, probably.

Now Moll laughs because I speak wisely, and now Hessy murmurs again. Well : I had a charming handsome cousin here twenty years ago. I was to see her to-night, and, in my conscience, she is not handsome at all; I wonder how it comes about; but she is very good-natured, and you know, Moll, good-nature is better than beauty. I desire you will let me know what fellows Hessy has got to come to her bed-side in a morning,* and when you design again to hobble to Chelsea, if you did not tell me a lie, as I must suspect. My head is something better, though not so well as I expected by my journey. I think I have said enough for a poor weary traveller. I will conclude without ceremony, and go to bed. And, if you cannot guess who is the writer, consult your pillow, and the first fine gentleman you dream of is the man.

So adieu.

FROM MISS VANHOMRIGH TO DR SWIFT.

London, June 6th, 1713.

Sir,

Now you are good beyond expression, in sending me that dear voluntary from St Albans. It gives me more happiness than you can imagine, or I describe, to find that your head is so much better already. I do assure you all my wishes are employed for the continuance of it. I hope the next will tell me they have been of force. Had I the power

---

* The French custom of ladies' receiving visits at the toilette or ruelle was then general.

I want, every day that did not add as much to your health, till it was quite established, as Monday last, should be struck out of the kalendar as useless ones. I believe you little thought to have been teazed by me so soon ; but when Mr Lewis told me if I would write to you, that he would take care of my letter, I must needs own I had not self-denial enough to forbear. Pray why did not you remember me at Dunstable, as well as Moll ? Lord ! what a monster is Moll grown since. But nothing of poor Hess, except that the mark will be in the same place of Davila where you left it. Indeed, it is not much advanced yet, for I have been studying of Rochefoucault to see if he described as much of love as I found in myself a Sunday, and I find he falls very short of it. How does Bolingbroke * perform ? You have not kept your promise of riding but a little every day : thirty miles I take to be a very great journey. I am very impatient to hear from you at Chester. It is impossible to tell you how often I have wished you a cup of coffee and an orange at your inn.

FROM THE SAME.

June 1713, London.   [No day of the month.]

'Tis inexpressible the concern I am in ever since I heard from Mr Lewis, that your head is so much out of order. Who is your physician ? For God sake don't be persuaded to take many slops. Satisfy me so much as to tell me what medicines you

---

* Swift's horse, so called.

have taken, and do take. How did you find your-self while a ship-board ? I fear 'tis your voyage has discomposed you, and then so much business following so immediately before you had time to re-cruit ;—'twas too much. I beg you make all the haste imaginable to the country, for I firmly be-lieve that air and rest will do you more good than any thing in the world besides. If I talk imperti-nently, I know you have goodness enough to for-give me, when you consider how great an ease 'tis to me to ask these questions, though I know it will be a great while before I can be answered ;—I am sure I shall think it so. Oh ! what would I give to know how you do at this instant. My fortune is too hard, your absence was enough without this cruel addi-tion. Sure the powers above are envious of your thinking so well, which makes them at some times strive to interrupt you ; but I must confine my thoughts, or at least stop from telling them to you, or you'll chide, which will still add to my uneasi-ness. I have done all that was possible to hinder myself from writing to you, till I heard you were better, for fear of breaking my promise, * but 'tis all in vain, for had I vowed neither to touch pen, ink, nor paper, I certainly should have had some other invention ; therefore I beg you won't be angry with me, for doing what is not in my power to avoid. Pray make Parvisole write me word what. I desire to know, for I would not for the world have you hold down your head. I am impatient to the last degree to hear how you are. I hope I shall soon have you here.

---

* The reader must observe, that, at this early period of their af-fection, Swift seems to have imposed upon her the very same re-straints of which she afterwards complains so heavily.

FROM THE SAME.

London, June 1713.

Mr Lewis assures me that you are now well, but will not tell me what authority he has for it. I hope he is rightly informed. Though 'tis not my usual custom, when a thing of consequence is in doubt, to fix on what I earnestly wish, but I have already suffered so much by knowing that you were ill, and fearing that you were worse than you have been, that I will strive to change that thought, if possible, that I may have a little ease, and more, that I may not write you a splenetic letter. Pray, why would not you make Parvisol write me word how you did, when I begged it so much? and if you were able yourself, how could you be so cruel to defer telling me the thing of the which I wished the most to know? If you think I write too often, your only way is to tell me so, or at least to write to me again, that I may know you don't quite forget me ; for I very much fear that I never employ a thought of yours now, except when you are reading my letters, which makes me ply you with them : (Mr Lewis complains of you too.) If you are very happy, it is ill-natured of you not to tell me so, except 'tis what is inconsistent with mine. * But why don't you talk to me that you know will please me. I have often heard you say, that you would willingly suffer a little uneasiness, provided it gave another a vast deal of pleasure. Pray re-

---

* This is the only phrase in the whole correspondence which intimates jealousy on the part of Miss Vanhomrigh.

member this maxim, because it makes for me.
This is now the fourth letter I have wrote to you :
they could not miscarry, for they were all under
Mr Lewis's cover, nor could you avoid opening
them, for the same reason. Pray what have you
done about the two livings? Have you recovered
them or no?* You know I love law-business. I
have been with lawyers since I saw you, but have
not yet had their answers, therefore won't trouble.
you with what I have done, till I can tell you all.
Pray let me know when you design coming over;
for I must beg you to talk to Mr P. and settle some
affairs for me. Pray let me hear from you soon,
which will be an inexpressible joy to her that is
always ————

FROM THE SAME.

London, June 23, 1713.

HERE is now three long weeks passed since you
wrote to me. Oh! happy Dublin, that can employ
all your thoughts, and happy Mrs Emerson, that
could hear from you the moment you landed. Had
it not been for her, I should be yet more uneasy
than I am. I really believe, before you leave Ireland, I shall give you just reason to wish I did not
know my letters, or at least that I could not write;

* Laracor and Rathbeggan. The Dean, on his promotion,
talked of recommending Dr Raymond as his successor, in case of
his removal. He retained them, however. Vol. III. p. 104,
210.

and I had rather you should wish so than entirely forget me.   Confess; have you once thought of me since you wrote to my mother at Chester, which letter, I assure you, I take very ill?   My mother and I have counted the Molls and the Hessys; 'tis true, the number is equal; but you talk to Moll, and only say, *now Hessy grumbles.*   How can you, indeed, possibly be so ill-natured, to make me either quarrel or grumble when you are at so great a distance that 'tis impossible for me to gain by doing so?   Besides, you proposed the letter should be directed to me; but I'll say no more of that, but keep my temper till we meet.   Pray, have you received the letter I wrote you to Chester?   I hear you had a very quick passage.   I hope it was a pleasant one, and that you have no reason to complain of your health.   We have had a vast deal of thunder for this week past.   I wish you had been here last Thursday, I am sure you could have prevented the bills * being lost.   Are not you prodigiously surprised at Sir Thomas Hanmer and Lord Anglesey?   Lord! how much we differ from the ancients, who used to sacrifice everything for the good of the commonwealth; but now our greatest men will, at any time, give up their country out of pique, and that for nothing.   'Tis impossible to describe the rejoicings that are amongst the Whigs since that day, † and I fear the elections will add to them.   Lord-Trea-

---

* These bills referred to the 8th and 9th articles of the treaty of commerce with France.   They were opposed as prejudicial to the trade and manufactures of England, and lost 15th June 1712, by a majority of nine votes against ministry.   Sir Thomas Hanmer and Mr Francis Annesley, with many other Tories, voted with the opposition on this occasion.

† There were illuminations and public rejoicings in almost all the trading towns, and even in London and Westminster.

surer has been extremely to blame, for all his friends advised him to let it be dropt, by consent, till next session : but [he] would not, depending on the same success he had on the malt-tax. * I know you'll say, " What, does the slut mean to talk all this stuff to me ; if I was there, I had as lieve hear it as any thing they could say, but to pursue me with her nonsense is intolerable.—I'll read no more !—Will ! Go to the post-office and see if there be more letters for me ! What, will this packet on-ly serve to tease me ?" I can tell you, you'll have none from Lady Orkney by the post, whatever you may by any other carriage. † I have strictly ob-served your commands as to reading and walking. Mr Ford can witness the latter, for he has paddled with us several nights. (I have a vast deal to tell you about him when I see you.) Mr Lewis has given me " *Les Dialogues des Morts*," and I am so charmed with them, that I am resolved to quit my [*body*,] let the consequence be what it will, except you will talk to me, for I find no conversation on earth comparable but yours ; so, if you care I should stay, do but talk, and you will keep me with pleasure.

---

* The question of extending the malt-tax to Scotland, which excited violent opposition. Ministers gained the question by a very small majority.

† Lady Orkney was an old courtier, and probably did not care to commit herself by letters sent through the General Post-Office, which was then a suspicious channel of communication.

FROM DR SWIFT TO MISS VANHOM-RIGH. *

Laracor, July 8, 1713.

I STAYED but a fortnight in Dublin, very sick, and returned not one visit of a hundred that were made me ; but all to the Dean and none to the Doctor. I am riding here for life, and think I am something better, and hate the thoughts of Dublin, and prefer a field-bed and an earthen floor before the great house there which they say is mine. I had your last splenetic letter. I told you when I left England, I would endeavour to forget everything there, and would write as seldom as I could. I did, indeed, design one general round of letters to my friends, but my health has not yet suffered me. I design to pass the greatest part of the time I stay in Ireland here in the cabin where I am now writing ; neither will I leave the kingdom till I am sent for ; and if they have no further service for me, I will never see England again. At my first coming I thought I should have died with discontent, and was horribly melancholy while they were installing me ; but it begins to wear off, and change to dulness. My river walk is extremely

---

* This important letter has been already published in its most material part, and was printed, Vol. XVI. p. 73. before the editor was honoured with Mr Berwick's communication. But as the reader ought to see the singular correspondence of Swift and Vanessa in an uniform and correct state, it was thought advisable to reprint this and one or two other letters, which had been already partially inserted in the general correspondence.

pretty, and my canal in great beauty, and I see trout playing in it. I know not any thing in Dublin, but Mr Ford is very kind, and writes to me constantly what passes among you. I find you are likewise a good politician, and I will say so much to you that I verily think, if the thing you know of had been published just upon the peace, * the ministry might have avoided what hath since happened. But I am now fitter to look after willows, and to cut hedges, than to meddle with affairs of state. I must order one of the workmen to drive those cows out of my island, and make up the ditch again; a work much more proper for a country vicar, than driving out factions, and fencing against them. And I must go and take my bitter draught to cure my head, which is spoilt by the bitter draughts the public hath given me. † [How does Davila go on? Johnny Clark is chosen portrieve of our town of Trim, and we shall have the assizes there next week, and fine doings; and I must go and borrow a horse to meet the judges; and Joe Beaumont, and all the boys that can get horses will go too. Mr Warburton has but a thin school. Mr Percival has built up the other side of his house, but people whisper that it is but scurvily built. Mr Steers is come to live in Mr Melthorp's house, and 'tis thought the widow Melthorp will remove to Dublin. Nay, if you don't like this sort of news, I have no better,] so go to your Dukes and Duchesses, and leave me to Goodman Bumford, and Patrick Dollan of Glanduggan.—Adieu.

---

* The History of the Peace of Utrecht.
† The passage within crotchets is restored from Mr Berwick's copy, and has never been before printed.

FROM THE SAME. *

[To Mrs Esther Van-Homrigh, at her lodgings, over against the
Surgeons in Great Rider Street, near St James's Street.]

Upper Letcomb, near Wantage, in Berkshire,
June 8th, 1714.

You see I am better than my word, and write to
you before I have been a week settled in the house
where I am.   I have not much news to tell you
from hence, nor have I had one line from any body
since I left London, of which I am very glad.   But,
to say the truth, I believe I shall not stay here so
long as I intended.   I am at a clergyman's house,
an old friend and an acquaintance, whom I love
very well; but he is such a melancholy thoughtful
man, partly from nature, and partly by a solitary
life, that I shall soon catch the spleen from him.
Out of ease and complaisance, I desire him not to
alter any of his methods for me; so we dine exactly between twelve and one; at eight we have some
bread and butter, and a glass of ale, and at ten he
goes to bed.   Wine is a stranger, except a little I
sent him, of which, one evening in two, we have a
pint between us.   His wife has been this month
twenty miles off, at her father's, and will not return
these ten days.   I never saw her, and perhaps the

---

* This letter was written during Swift's secession to the
country, upon the breach between Oxford and Bolingbroke becoming open and irreconcilable.   It has been printed from
former editions of Swift, Vol. XVI. p. 141. but it is for the reasons expressed in the last note here reprinted entire from Mr
Berwick's manuscript.

house will be worse when she comes. I read all
day, or walk, and do not speak as many words as
I have now writ, in three days; so that, in short,
I have a mind to steal to Ireland, unless I feel myself take more to this way of living, so different, in
every circumstance, from what I left. This is the
first syllable I have writ to any body since you saw
me. I shall be glad to hear from you, not as you
are a Londoner, but a friend; for I care not three-
pence for news, nor have heard one syllable since I
came here. The Pretender, or Duke of Cambridge,
may both be landed, and I never the wiser. But if
this place were ten times worse, nothing shall make
me return to town while things are in the situation
I left them. I give a guinea a-week for my board,
and can eat any thing. I hope you are in good
health and humour. My service to Moll. My
cold is quite gone.

A vous, &c.

FROM THE SAME.

July 8, 1714.

I FIND you take heavily that touch upon your
shoulder.* I would not have writ to you so soon,

---

* Mrs Vanhomrigh was now dead, and her daughters were
left in embarrassment, if not in poverty, and even exposed to ar-
rest, as appears from the hint in the text, and the lordly pleasan-
try of Orrery, who assures us, "that the two daughters hastened in all secrecy back to Ireland, beginning their journey on a
Sunday, to avoid the interruption and importunities of a certain
fierce kind of animals called Bailiffs, who are not only sworn
foes to wit and gaiety, but whose tyranny, although it could not

if it were not to tell you, that, if you want to borrow any money, I would have you to send to Mr Barber, or Ben Tooke, which you please, and let them know it, and the sum, and that I will stand bound for it, and send them my bond. I did not know our posts went on Tuesday, else I would have writ two days ago to tell you this. I do not see how you can be uneasy when the year is out, for you can pay only what you receive;—you are answerable for no more, and I suppose you have not given bonds to pay your mother's debts. As for your L. 2, 5s. that you gave your note for, if that be all, it is a trifle, and your owning it with so much apology looks affected. If you have no more secret debts than that, I shall be glad. But still, I cannot understand how any of those creditors of your mother can give you any trouble, unless there be some circumstances that I do not know the bottom of. I believe I shall not stay here much longer, and, therefore, if you want to borrow money, I would have you do it soon, and of the two, rather of Ben Tooke; because I have just drawn a note upon Barber for thirty guineas for my own expences. I believe a bond had better be sent to me down to sign, and I will send it back to you, and you may give it Ben. You may speak freely to Ben of this, and if he has no money by him, we must apply to Barber. I am forced to conclude in haste, because the post-house is two miles off, and it will be late if I stay longer. Adieu.

My service to Molkin.

---

have reached the deified Vanessa, might have been very fatal to Esther Vanhomrigh." Orrery's Remarks on the Life and Writings of Swift, p. 68.

FROM THE SAME.

Aug. 1, 1714.

I HAVE had now two letters of yours to answer. I am pleased to see you piqued about my dearness to Ben and John. *   They are worthy subjects; there are some words I never use to some people, let that satisfy.   How many gentlemen, says you, and fine young gentlemen truly, would be proud to have you desire so much of them. †   Who told you I was going to Bath ? No such thing.   I had fixed to set out to-morrow for Ireland ; but poor Lord Oxford desires I will go with him to Herefordshire ; and I only expect his answer, whether I shall go there before, or meet him hereabouts, or go to Wimple, (his son's house,) and to go with him down ; and I expect to leave this in two or three days, one way or other.   I will stay with him till the Parliament meets agan, if he desires it.   I am not of your opinion about Lord Bolingbroke ; perhaps he may get the staff, but I cannot rely on his love to me.   He knew I had a mind to be historiographer, though I valued it not but for the public service, yet it is gone to a worthless rogue that nobody knows.   I am writ to earnestly by somebody to come to town, and join with these people now

---

* It would seem that the Dean, in addressing his printer and bookseller, had stiled them Dear Ben and Dear John.   Vanessa appears to have been jealous of a distinction never paid to her in the course of their correspondence, and the Dean gaily justifies himself.

† An imperfect extract from this letter, commencing at these words, is already printed, Vol. XVI. p. 202.

in power, but I will not do it.   Say nothing of this,
but guess the person.   I told Lord Oxford I would
go with him when he was out, and now he begs it
of me, and I cannot refuse him.   I meddle not with
his faults, as he was a minister of state; but you
know his personal kindness to me was excessive.
He distinguished and chose me above all other
men while he was great, and his letter to me
t'other day was the most moving imaginable. * [The
knife-handles should surely be done up in silver,
and strong.   I believe Brondeth, my toyman, in
Exchange Ally, would deal most honestly by me.
Barber knows him.   Where's your discretion in
desiring to travel with that body,† who, I believe,
would not do it for a thousand pounds, except it were
to Italy.   Pray God send you a good deliverance
through your accounts.   'Tis well you have been a
lawyer so long.   You will be two hours reading this
letter, it is writ so ill.]   When I am fixed anywhere,
perhaps I may be so gracious as to let you know :
but I will not promise.

Service to Moll.   Adieu.

---

* The passage within brackets is restored from Mr Berwick's
manuscript.
† Barber seems to be indicated.   He was a jacobite, and to
this the Dean probably alludes, in saying he would travel no-
where but to Italy.

z

FROM THE SAME. *

Aug. 12, 1714.

I HAD your letter last post ; and before you can send me another I shall set out for Ireland. I must go and take the oaths, and the sooner the better. [I think, since I have known you, I have drawn an old house upon my head. You should not have come by Wantage † for a thousand pounds. You used to brag you were very discreet : where is it gone ? It is probable I may not stay in Ireland long, but be back by the beginning of winter. When I am there, I will write to you as soon as I can conveniently, but it shall always be under a cover ; and if you write to me, let some other direct it ; and I beg you will write nothing that is particular, but what may be seen ; for I apprehend letters may be opened, and inconveniences will happen.] If you are in Ireland while I am there, I shall see you very seldom. It is not a place for any freedom, but where every thing is known in a week, and magnified a hundred degrees. These are rigorous laws that must be passed through ; but it is probable we may meet in London in winter, or, if not, leave all to fate, that seldom cares to humour our inclinations. I say all this out of the perfect esteem and friendship I have for you. These public misfortunes have altered all my measures,

---

* An extract from this letter occurs, Vol. XVI. p. 244. The parts within crotchets have never before appeared.

† In a subsequent letter he mentions the Berkshire surprise, which was probably an unexpected visit of Vanessa to Wantage.

and broke my spirits.   I shall, I hope, be on horse-back in a day after this comes to your hand.   I would not answer your questions for a million, nor can I think of them with any ease of mind. *
Adieu. † .

━━━━━━━━

FROM THE SAME. ‡

Philips-town, Nov. 5, 1714.

I MET your servant when I was a mile from Trim, and could send him no other answer than I did, for I was going abroad by appointment; besides, I would not have gone to Kildrohod § to see you for all the world.   I ever told you you wanted discretion.   I am going to a friend upon a promise, and shall stay with him about a fort-night, and then come to town, and I will call on you as soon as I can, supposing you lodge in Turn-stile Alley, as your servant told me, and that your neighbours can tell me whereabouts.   Your ser-

---

* The reference to these *questions* is a sort of cant expression, which repeatedly occurs afterwards. It would seem, Vanessa subjected her admirer to a sort of regular catechism, (it may be supposed to respect the state of his affections,) which must some-times have sufficiently embarrassed him.

† Swift left Letcombe, August 16, 1714, in order to go to Ire-land.

‡ The first and last sentence of this letter, which, taken apart from the rest, have almost an air of brutality, have found their way to the public. When the context is restored, it is merely an example of the Dean's playful rudeness.

§ Kildrohod, the Irish name of Celbridge, where Vanessa had her country residence.

vant said you would be in town on Monday; so that I suppose this will be ready to welcome you there. I fear you had a journey full of fatigues Pray take care of your health in this Irish air, to which you are a stranger. Does not Dublin look very dirty to you, and the country very miserable? Is Kildrohod as beautiful as Windsor, and as agreeable to you as the Prebend's lodgings * there? Is there any walk about you as pleasant as the avenue, and the Marlborough Lodge? I have rode a tedious journey to-day, and can say no more. Nor shall you know where I am till I come, and then I will see you. A fig for your letters and messages. Adieu.

[Thus directed:—To Mrs Vanhomrigh, at her lodgings in Turn-stile Alley, near College Green, Dublin.]

FROM MISS VANHOMRIGH.

Dublin, 1714.

You cannot but be sensible (at least in some degree) of the many uneasinesses I am slave to: a wretch of a brother, cunning executors, and importunate creditors of my mother's, things I can no way avoid being subject to at present, and weighty enough to sink greater spirits than mine without some support. Once I had a friend that would see

---

* Where Swift lodged when at Windsor. " My lodgings," he writes to Stella, 7th August 1712, " look upon Eton and the Thames. I wish I was owner of them: they belong to a prebend." Vol. III. p. 100.

me sometimes, and either commend what I did, or advise me what to do, which banished all my uneasiness. But now when my misfortunes are increased by being in a disagreeable place, among strange prying deceitful people, whose company is so far from an amusement, that it is a very great punishment, you fly me, and give me no reason, but that we are amongst fools, and must submit. I am very well satisfied we are amongst such, but know no reason for having my happiness sacrificed to their caprice.* [You once had a maxim (which was, to act what was right, and not mind what the world said), I wish you would keep to it now. Pray what can be wrong in seeing and advising an unhappy young woman? I can't imagine. You can't but know that your frowns make my life unsupportable. You have taught me to distinguish, and then you leave me miserable. Now all I beg is, that you will for once counterfeit (since you can't otherwise) that indulgent friend you once were, till I get the better of these difficulties for my sister's sake ; for were not she involved, who, I know, is not able to manage them as I am, I have a nobler soul than sit struggling with misfortunes, when at the end I can't promise myself any real happiness. Forgive me; I beg you'll believe it is not in my power to avoid complaining as I do.

---

* The passage within crochets has been printed in former editions of Swift. The sense is greatly illustrated, and many sinister interpretations confuted by restoration of the contexts.

FROM THE SAME.

Dublin, 1714.

WELL ! now I plainly see how great a regard you have for me.* [You bid me be easy, and you'd see me as often as you could : you had better have said as often as you could get the better of your inclinations so much ; or as often as you remembered there was such a person in the world.   If you continue to treat me as you do, you will not be made uneasy by me long.   'Tis impossible to describe what I have suffered since I saw you last ; I am sure I could have born the rack much better than those killing, killing words of yours.   Sometimes I have resolved to die without seeing you more, but those resolves, to your misfortune, did not last long : for there is something in human nature that prompts one so to find relief in this world, I must give way to it, and beg you'd see me, and speak kindly to me, for I am sure you would not condemn any one to suffer what I have done, could you but know it.   The reason I write to you is, because I cannot tell it you, should I see you ; for when I begin to complain, then you are angry, and there is something in your look so awful, that it strikes me dumb.   Oh ! that you may but have so much regard for me left, that this complaint may touch your soul with pity.   I say as little as ever I can.   Did you but know what I thought, I am sure it would move you.   Forgive me, and believe I cannot help telling you this, and live.

---

* This letter has been published in former editions, excepting only the first sentence.

TO MISS VANHOMRIGH.

Monday morning.

I WILL see you in a day or two, and believe me it goes to my soul not to see you oftener. I will give you the best advice, countenance, and assistance I can. I would have been with you sooner if a thousand impediments had not prevented me. I did not imagine you had been under difficulties. I am sure my whole fortune should go to remove them. I cannot see you, I fear, to-day, having affairs of my place to do : but pray think it not want of friendship or tenderness, which I will always continue to the utmost.

FROM MISS VANHOMRIGH.*

No date.

Is it possible that again you will do the very same thing I warned you of so lately ? I believe you thought I only rallied when I told you the other night that I would pester you with letters. [Did not I know you very well, I should think you knew but little of the world, to imagine that a woman would not keep her word whenever she promised

---

* An extract from this letter has been printed in former editions, with the date of the year 1720. The passages restored from Mr Berwick's manuscript, are inclosed in crotchets.

any thing that was malicious. Had not you better
a thousand times throw away one hour at some time
or other of the day, than to be interrupted in your
business at this rate : (for I know 'tis as impossible
for you to burn my letters without reading them, as
'tis for me to avoid reproving you, when you behave yourself wrong.) Once more I advise you, if
you have any regard for your own quiet, to alter
your behaviour quickly, for I do assure you, I have
too much spirit to sit down contented with this treatment. Because I love darkness extremely, I here
tell you now, that I have determined to try all manner of human arts to reclaim you ; and if all these
fail, I am resolved to have recourse to the black
one, which [*it*] is said never does. Now see what
inconveniencies you will bring both me and yourself into. Pray think calmly of it! Is it not better
to come of yourself, than to be brought by force,
and that perhaps at a time when you have the most
agreeable engagement in the world ; for when I undertake any thing, I don't love to do it by halves.
[But there is one thing falls out very luckily for you,
which is, that of all the passions, revenge hurries
me least, so that you have it yet in your power to
turn all this fury into good humour, and depend upon it, and more, I assure you. Come at what time
you please, you can never fail of being very well
received.]

TO MISS VANHOMRIGH.*

IF you write as you do, I shall come the seldomer, on purpose to be pleased with your letters, which I never look into without wondering how a brat who cannot read can possibly write so well. You are mistaken. Send me a letter without your hand on the outside, and I hold you a crown I shall not read it. But raillery apart; I think it inconvenient for a hundred reasons, that I should make your house a sort of constant dwelling-place. I will certainly come as often as I conveniently can, but my health, and the perpetual run of ill-weather hinders me from going out in the morning; and my afternoons are taken up, I know not how, that I am in rebellion with a dozen people, beside yourself, for not seeing them. For the rest, you need make use of no other black art besides your ink. 'Tis a pity your eyes are not black, or I would have said the same of them: but you are a white witch, and can do no mischief. If you have employed any of your art on the black scarf, I defy it for one reason; Guess. Adieu,—for Dr P. is come in to see me.

Directed to Miss Hessy Vanhom.

* This has been printed in former editions.

TO MISS VANHOMRIGH.*

Monday morning, 10 o'clock.

I RECEIVED your letter when some company was with me on Saturday night ; and it put me in such confusion that I could not tell what to do. I here send the paper you left me. This morning a wo-man who does business for me, told me she heard was in ——— † with one ——— naming you, and twen-ty particulars, that little master and I visited you, and that the A. B. ‡ did so, and that you had abun-dance of wit, &c.—I ever feared the tattle of this nasty town, and told you so, and that was the rea-son why I said to you long ago, that I would see you seldom when you were in Ireland, and I must beg you to be easy, if for some time I visit you seldomer, and not in so particular a manner. I will see you at the latter end of the week if possible.

These are accidents in life that are necessary, and must be submitted to, and tattle, by the help of dis-cretion, will wear off.

TO THE SAME.

I AM now writing on Wednesday night, when you are hardly settled at home, and it is the first hour of

---

* This letter has been printed.
† Supply Love.
‡ Archbishop.

leisure I have had, and it may be Saturday before you have it, and then there will be Governor Huff, * and to make you more so, I here enclose a letter to poor Molkin, which I will command her not to show you, because it is a love-letter. I reckon by this time, the groves and fields and purling streams have made Vanessa romantic, provided poor Molkin be well. Your friend † sent me the verses he promised, which I here transcribe.

> Nymph, would you learn the only art,
> To keep a worthy lover's heart :
> First, to adorn your person well,
> In utmost cleanliness excel :
> And though you must the fashions take,
> Observe them, but for fashion's sake :
> The strongest reason will submit
> To virtue, honour, sense, and wit :
> To such a nymph, the wise and good,
> Cannot be faithless, if they would,
> For vices all have different ends,
> But virtue still to virtue tends ;
> And when your lover is not true,
> 'Tis virtue fails in him, or you :
> And either he deserves disdain,
> Or you without a cause complain ;
> But here Vanessa cannot err,
> Nor are those rules applied to her :
> For who could such a nymph forsake,
> Except a blockhead, or a rake ;
> Or how could she her heart bestow,
> Except where wit and virtue grow.

In my opinion, these lines are too grave, and

---

* This cant expression, which often occurs, and sometimes in very puzzling passages, refers to Vanessa's desire of having things her own way, in which she was but seldom indulged.
† That is Swift himself, under the character of Cadenus. He often speaks in his mysterious manner of Cadenus as a different person from himself.

herefore, may fit you, who, I fear, are in the spleen;
but that is not fit either for yourself, or the person
you tend, * to whom you ought to read diverting
things. Here is an epigram that concerns you not:

> Dorinda dreams of dress a-bed,
>   Tis all her thought and art;
> Her lace hath got within her head,
>   Her stays stick to her heart.

If you do not like these things, what must I say?
This town yields no better. The questions which
you were used to ask me, you may suppose to be
all answered, just as they used to be after half an
hour's debate† ; " Entendez vous cela ?" You are to
have a number of parsons in your neighbourhood,
but not one that you love, for your age of loving
parsons is not yet arrived. What this letter wants in
length, it will have in difficulty, for I believe you
cannot read it. I will write plainer to Molkin, because she is not much used to my hand. I hold a
wager, there are some lines in this letter you will
not understand, though you can read them; so drink
your coffee, and remember you are a desperate chip,
and that the lady who calls you bastard, will be
ready to answer all your questions. It is now Sunday night before I could finish this.

---

* Her sister.
† See p. 418, Note.

TO THE SAME. *

IF you knew how many little difficulties there are in sending letters to you, it would remove five parts in six of your quarrel ; but since you lay hold of my promises, and are so exact to the day, I shall promise you no more, and rather choose to be better than my word than worse. I am confident you came chiding into the world, and will continue so while you are in it. I was in great apprehension that poor Molkin was worse, and till I could be satisfied in that particular, I would not write again : but I little expected to have heard of your own ill health, and those who saw you since made no mention to me of it. I wonder what Molkin meant by shewing you my letter ; I will write to her no more, since she can keep secrets no better.

It was the first love-letter I have writ these dozen years, and since I have such ill success, I will write no more. Never was a *belle passion* so defeated, but the Governor † I hear is jealous, and upon your word you have a vast deal to say to me about it. Mind your nurse-keeping, do your duty, and leave off your huffing. One would imagine you were in love, by dating your letter August 29th, by which means I received it just a month before it was written. You do not find I answer your questions to your satisfaction : prove to me first that it was possible to answer anything to your satisfaction, so as that you would not grumble in half an hour. I am

---

* Some very imperfect extracts from this letter have already been published.

† See note on p. 426.

glad my writing puzzles you, for then your time will be employed in finding it out; and I am sure it cost me a great many. thoughts to make my letter difficult. Sure Glassheel * is come over, and gave me a message from J. B. † about the money on the jewels, which I will answer. Molkin will be so glad to see Glassheel; ay Molkin! Yesterday I was half way towards you, where I dined, and returned weary enough. I asked where that road to the left led? and they named the place. I wish your letters were as difficult as mine, for then they would be of no consequence if they were dropt by careless messengers. A stroke thus . . . . signifies everything that may be said to *Cad*, at the beginning or conclusion. It is I who ought to be in a huff, that any thing written by *Cad* should be difficult to *Skinage*. I must now leave off abruptly, for I intend to send this letter to-day, August 4.

To Miss Essy.

FROM MISS VANHOMRIGH.

Cell Bridge, 1720.

. . . . CAD— you are good beyond expression, and I will never quarrel again if I can help it; but,

---

* This seems a cant name; and there is no indication of the individual whom it designates: an Irish gentleman, of course, for his country-house is afterwards mentioned.

† John Barber, as afterwards appears. He had, at Swift's instance, assisted Miss Vanhomrigh in some pecuniary matters, and was now desirous of being repaid.

with submission, 'tis you that are so hard to be pleased, though you complain of me.   I thought the
last letter I wrote you, was obscure and constrained
enough.   I took pains to write it after your manner; it would have been much easier for me to have
wrote otherwise.   I am not so unreasonable as to
expect you should keep your word to a day, but six
or seven days are great odds.   Why should your
apprehensions for Molkin hinder you from writing
to me ? I think you should have wrote the sooner
to have comforted me.   Molkin is better, but in a
very weak way. Though those who saw me told you
nothing of my illness, I do assure you I was for
twenty-four hours as ill as 'twas possible to be, and
live. You wrong me when you say, I did not find that
you answered my questions to my satisfaction : what
I said was, I had asked those questions as you bid,
but could not find them answered to my satisfaction.   How could they be answered in absence,
since Somnus is not my friend ? We have had a vast
deal of thunder and lightning ;—where do you think I
wished to be then, and do you think that was the only time I wished so, since I saw you. I am sorry my
jealousy should hinder you from writing more love-
letters ; for I must chide sometimes, and I wish I
could gain by it at this instant, as I have done, and
hope to do.——Is my dating my letter wrong the only
sign of my being in love ? Pray tell me, did not you
wish to come where that road to the left would have
led you ? I am mightily pleased to hear you talk of
being in a huff ; 'tis the first time you ever told me so ;
I wish I could see you in one.   I am now as happy
as I can be without seeing . . . . CAD, I beg you
will continue happiness to your own Skinage.

FROM MISS VANHOMRIGH.

. . . . CAD, I am, and cannot avoid being in the spleen to the last degree. Every thing combines to make me so. Is it not very hard to have so good a fortune as I have? and yet no more command of that fortune, than if I had no title to it. One of the D——rs* is . . . . I don't know what to call him. He behaved himself so abominably to me the other day, that had I been a man he should have heard more of it. In short he does nothing but trifle and make excuses. I really believe he heartily repents that ever he undertook it, since he heard the counsel first plead, finding his friend more in the wrong than he imagined.—Here am I obliged to stay in this odious town, attending and losing my health and humour. Yet this and all other disappointments in life I can bear with ease, but that of being neglected by . . . . Cad. He has often told me that the best maxim in life, and always held by the wisest in all ages, is to seize the moments as they fly, but those happy moments always fly out of the reach of the unfortunate. Pray tell . . . . . Cad, I dont remember any angry passages in my letter, and I am very sorry if they appeared so to him. Spleen I cannot help, so you must excuse it. I do all I can to get the better of it ; and it is too strong for me. I have read more since I saw Cad, than I did in a great while passed, and chose those books that required most attention, on purpose to engage my

---

* Doctors perhaps. Some of her affairs were under reference ; and she was, it seems, discontented with the referees.

thoughts, but I find the more I think the more unhappy I am.

I had once a mind not to have wrote to you, for fear of making you uneasy to find me so dull, but I could not keep to that resolution, for the pleasure of writing to you. The satisfaction I have in your remembering me, when you read my letters, and the delight I have in expecting one from . . . . . Cad, makes me rather choose to give you some uneasiness, than to add to my own.

FROM DR SWIFT TO MISS VANHOMRIGH.*

May 12, 1719.

[On vous a trompé en vous disant que je suis parti pour trois jours; des affaires assez impertinentes m'ont tirée sitost, et je viens de quitter cette place pour aller voir quelques amis plus loin, purement pour le retablissement de ma santé.

Croyez moi, s'il y a chose croyable au monde, que je pense tout ce que vous pouvez souhaiter de moy, et que tous vos desirs seront obei, comme de commandmens qu'il sera impossible de violer. Je pretends de mettre cette lettre dans une ville de poste où je passeray. J'iray en peu de tems visiter un seigneur; mais je ne sçay encore le nom de sa maison, ni du pais où il demeure. Je vous conjure de prendre guarde de votre santé. J'espere que vous

---

* An extract from the latter part of this letter has been printed. The passages marked with crotchets are restored.

passerez quelque part de cet eté dans votre maison
de campagne, et que vous promenerez à cheval autant que vous pouvez. Vous aurez vos vers à re-
voir quand j'aurai mes pensées et mon tems libre ;
la muse viendra. Faites mes complimens à la me-
chante votre compagnone, qui aime les contes et le
Latin. J'espere que vos affaires de chicane sont en
un bon train.] Je vous fais des complimens sur
votre perfection dans la langue Françoise : il faut
vous connoître long-tems de connoître toutes vos
perfections ; toujours en vous voyant et entendant,
il en paroissent des nouvelles qui estoient auparavant
cachées. Il est honteux pour moy de ne savoir que
le Gascon et le patois au prix de vous. Il n'y rien
à redire dans l'ortographie, la proprieté, l'elegance, le douceur, et l'esprit, et que je suis sot, moy
de vous repondre en même langage, vous qui estes
incapable d'aucune sottise ; si ce n'est l'estime qu'il
vous plait d'avoir pour moy ; car il n y a point de
merite, ni aucune preuve de mon bon goût de trou-
ver en vous l'honneur, la vertue, le bon sens, l'esprit,
la douceur, l'agrement, et la fermeté d'ame, mais en
vous cachant comme vous faites, le monde ne vous
connoit pas, et vous perdez l'eloge des millions de
gens. Depuis que j'avois l'honneur de vous con-
noitre, j'ay toujours remarqué, que, ni en conversation particulière ne generale, aucun mot a echappé
de votre bouche que pouvoit etre mieux exprimé ;
et je vous jure, qu'en faisant souvent la plus severe
critique, je ne pouvois jamais trouvez aucun defaut
en vos actions, ni en vos parolles : la coquetrie,
l'affectation, la pruderie, sont des imperfections que
vous n'avois jamais connu.

- Et avec tout cela, croyez-vous qu'il est possible de
ne vous estimer au dessus du reste du genre humain ?
Quelles bestes en jûppes sont, le plus excellentes de

celles, que je vois semez dans le monde au prix de vous, en les voyant, en les entendant, je dis cent foix le jour,—ne parle, ne regarde, ne pense, ne fait rien comme ces miserables. Sont-ce du même sexe—de même espece de creatures? Quelle cruauté! de faire mepriser autant de gens, qui, sans songer de vous, seroient assez supportables. Mais il est tems de vous delasser, et dire adieu! avec tout le respecte, la sincerité, et la estime de monde, je suis, et seray toujours.

For Madame Hester Vanhomri.

FROM DR SWIFT TO MISS VANHOMRIGH.

August 12, 1720.

I APPREHENDED, on the return of the porter I sent with my last letter, that it would miscarry, because I saw the rogue was drunk; but your's made me easy. I must neither write to Molkin, nor not write to her. You are like Lord Pembroke, who would neither go nor stay. Glassheel talks of going to see you, and taking me with him, as he goes to his country house. I find you have company with you these two or three days; I hope they are diverting, at least to poor Molkin. Why should Cad's letters be difficult; I assure you ——'s are not all.

I am vexed that the weather hinders you from any pleasure in the country, because walking, I believe, would be of good use to you and Molkin. I reckon you will return a prodigious scholar, a most admirable nurse-keeper, a perfect housewife, and a great drinker of coffee.

I have asked, and am assured there is not one beech in all your groves to carve a name on, nor purling stream for love or money, except a great river * which sometimes roars, but never murmurs, just like Governor Huff.† We live here in a very dull town, every valuable creature absent, and Cad. says he is weary of it, and would rather drink his coffee on the barrenest mountain in Wales, than be king here.

> A fig for partridges and quails ;—
> Ye dainties, I know nothing of ye ;
> But on the highest mount in Wales
> Would choose in peace to drink my coffee.

And you know very well that coffee makes us severe, and grave, and philosophical. What would you give to have the history of Cad—— and ————, exactly written, through all its steps, from the beginning to this time ? ‡ I believe it would do well in verse, and be as long as the other. I hope it will be done. It ought to be an exact chronicle of twelve years from   , the time of spilling of coffee, § to drinking of coffee ; from Dunstable to Dublin, with every single passage since.

---

* The Liffey.

† A name which he gave to Vanessa when she was disposed to assume authority over him.

‡ The Dean never completed this second part of the poem of Cadenus and Vanessa.

§ Some jest is alluded to of Vanessa spilling coffee at Dunstable, mentioned in a letter to her mother, 6th June 1713. With respect to the other circumstances, they must be left chiefly to the charitable construction of the reader, a just penalty to the corres-

There would be the chapter of Madame going to Kensington; the chapter of the blister; the chapter of the colonel going to France; the chapter of the wedding, with the adventures of the lost key; of the sham; of the joyful return; two hundred chapters of madness; the chapter of long walks; the Berkshire surprise;* fifty chapters of little times; the chapter of Chelsey; the chapter of swallow and cluster; a hundred whole books of myself, &c.; the chapter of hide and whisper; the chapter of who made it so; my sister's money. Cad—— bids me tell you, that if you complain of difficult writing, he will give you enough of it. See how much I have written without saying one word of Molkin; and you will be whipt before you will deliver a message with honour. I shall write to J. Barber next post, and desire him to be in no pain about his money. I will take not one word of notice of his riches, on purpose to vex him. If heaven had looked upon riches to be a valuable thing, it would not have given them to such a scoundrel.† I delivered your letter, inclosed, to our friend,‡ who happened to be with me when I received it. I find you are very much in his good grace, for he said a million of fine

pondents who wrap up an innocent meaning in innuendos. But, if any less than innocence were implied, it appears impossible that Vanessa should have received with rapture (as she does in the next letter,) the proposal of Cadenus to immortalize these incidents of their intercourse.

* When Vanessa seems to have visited the Dean's retreat near Wantage. See his letter of 12th August 1714.

† This remarkable sentiment is the sting of Arbuthnot's celebrated epitaph on Chartres. It is applied by the Dean, in a moment of hasty peevishness, to his old friend Barber.

‡ Cadenus, to wit. See a preceding note.

things upon it, though he would let nobody read a word of it but himself, though I was so kind to shew him your's to me, as well as this, which he has laid a crown with me you will not understand, which is pretty odd for one that sets up for so high an opinion of your good sense. I am ever, with the greatest truth, your's, &c.

August 13.

FROM MISS VANHOMRIGH TO DR SWIFT.

Cell Bridge, 1720.

. . . . CAD, is it possible that you will come and see me? I beg for Godsake you will; I would give the world to see you here (and Molkin would be extremely happy). Do you think the time long since I saw you?

I did design seeing you this week, but will not stir in hopes of your coming here. I beg you'll write two or three words by the bearer, to let me know if you think you'll come this week. I shall have the note to-night. You make me happy beyond expression by your goodness. It would be too much once to hope for such a history; if you had laid a thousand pound that I should not understand your letter, you had lost it. Tell me sincerely did those circumstances crowd on you, or did you recollect them only to make me happy?

FROM DR SWIFT TO MISS VANHOMRIGH.

Thursday morn. 10.

I will see you to-morrow if possible.   You know it is not above five days since I saw you, and that I would ten times more if it were at all convenient, whether your Old Dragon come or no, whom I believe my people cannot tell what to make of, but take him for some conjuror.
Adieu.

FROM DR SWIFT TO MISS VANHOM-RIGH. *

October 15, 1720.

I sit down, with the first opportunity I have, to write to you, and the Lord knows when I can find conveniency to send the letter ; for all the mornings I am plagued with impertinent visits or impertinent business below any man of sense or honour to endure, if it were any way avoidable.   Dinners and afternoons and evenings are spent abroad, and in walking to ————— ; and to avoid spleen as far as I can : so that when I am not so good a correspondent as I could wish, you are not to quarrel and be Governor, but to impute it to my situation ; and to conclude infallibly that I have the same respect,

* About one half of this letter has been printed ; the passages within crotchets now appear for the first time.

esteem, and kindness for you I ever professed to have, and shall ever preserve, because you will always merit the utmost that can be given you, especially if you go on to read and still further improve your mind, and the talents that nature has given you. [I had a letter from your friend J. B. * in London, in answer to what I told you that Glassheel said about the money. J. B.'s answer is, that you are a person of honour; that you need give yourself no trouble about it; that you will pay when you are able, and he shall be content till then. These are his own words, and you see he talks in the style of a very rich man, which he says he yet is, though terribly pulled down by the fall of stocks. I am glad you did not sell your annuities, unless somebody were to manage and transfer them while stocks were high.] I am in much concern for poor Molkin, and the more, because I am sure you are so too. You ought to be as cheerful as you can for both your † sakes, and read pleasant things, that will make you laugh, and not sit moping with your elbows on your knees on a little stool by the fire. It is most infallible that riding would do Molkin more good than any other thing, provided fair days and warm clothes be provided; and so it would to you, and if you lose any skin, you know Job says, " Skin for skin will a man give for his life;" it is either Job or Satan says so, for ought you know. [Oct. 17. I had not a moment to finish this since I sat down to it. A person was with me just now, and interrupted me as I was going on, with telling me of

---

* John Barber.
† In former editions this is printed *our sakes*, a variation slight in sound, but important in sense.

great people here losing their places, and now some more are coming about business. So adieu, till by and by, or to-morrow.] Oct. 18.—I am getting an ill head in this cursed town for want of exercise. I wish I were to walk with you fifty times about the garden, and then —— drink your coffee. I was sitting last night with half a score of both sexes for an hour, and grew as weary as a dog. [Glassheel takes up abundance of my time in spight of my teeth.] Every body grows silly and disagreeable, or I grow monkish and splenetic, which is the same thing. Conversation is full of nothing but South Sea, and the ruin of the kingdom, and scarcity of money. [I had a thousand times hear the Governor chide two hours without reason.

Oct. 20.—The Governor was with me at six o'clock this morning, but did not stay two minutes, and deserves a chiding, which you must give when you drink your coffee next. I hope to send this letter to-morrow. I am a good deal out of order in my head, after a little journey I made ; ate too much I suppose, or travelling in a coach after it. I am now sitting at home alone, and will go write to Molkins. So adieu.]

FROM MISS VANHOMRIGH TO DR SWIFT.

Cell Bridge, 1720.

You had heard from me before, but that my messenger was not to be had till to-day, and now I have only time to thank you for your's, because he was going about his business this moment, which is very happy for you, or you would have had a long letter full of spleen. Never was human creature more distressed than I have been since I came. Poor Molkin has had two or three relapses, and is in so bad a way, that I fear she will never recover. Judge now what a way I am now in, absent from you, and loaded with melancholy on her score. I have been very ill with a stitch in my side, which is not very well yet.

FROM MISS VANHOMRIGH TO DR SWIFT.*

Cell Bridge, 1720.

BELIEVE me it is with the utmost regret that I now complain to you, because I know your good-nature such, that you cannot see any human creature miserable, without being sensibly touched, yet what can I do? I must either unload my heart, and tell you all its griefs, or sink under the inexpressible distress I now suffer by your prodigious neglect of me. 'Tis now ten long weeks since I saw you, and in all that time I have never received but one letter from you, and a little note with an excuse. Oh, how have you forgot me. You endeavour by severities to force me from you, nor can I blame you; for with the utmost distress and confusion, I behold myself the cause of uneasy reflections to you, yet I cannot comfort you, but here declare, that 'tis not in the power of time or accident to lessen the inexpressible passion which I have for . . . . .

Put my passion under the utmost restraint, send me as distant from you as the earth will allow, yet you cannot banish those charming ideas which will

* This letter has been already printed.

ever stick by me whilst I have the use of memory, Nor is the love I bear you only seated in my soul, for there is not a single atom of my frame that is not blended with it. Therefore, don't flatter yourself that separation will ever change my sentiments; for I find myself unquiet in the midst of silence, and my heart is at once pierced with sorrow and love. For Heaven's sake, tell me what has caused this prodigious change on you, which I have found of late If you have the least remains of pity for me left, tell me tenderly; No: Don't tell it, so that it may cause my present death, and don't suffer me to live a life like a languishing death, which is the only life I can lead, if you have lost any of your tenderness for me.

FROM MISS VANHOMRIGH TO DR SWIFT.*

TELL me sincerely, if you have once wished with earnestness to see me, since I wrote last to you. No, so far from that, you have not once pitied me, though I told you how I was distressed. Solitude is insupportable to a mind which is not at ease. I have worn on my days in sighing, and my nights with watching and thinking of . . . . who thinks not of me. How many letters must I send you before I shall receive an answer? Can you deny me in my misery the only comfort which I can expect at pre-

---

* This letter has been published with some literal and minute inaccuracies, which are here corrected from Mr Berwick's MS.

sent? Oh! that I could hope to see you here, or that I could go to you. I was born with violent passions, which terminate all in one, that inexpressible passion I have for you. Consider the killing emotions which I feel from your neglect, and shew some tenderness for me, or I shall lose my senses. Sure you cannot possibly be so much taken up, but you might command a moment to write to me, and force your inclinations to do so great a charity. I firmly believe, could I know your thoughts, which no human creature is capable of guessing at, (because never any one living thought like you,) I should find you have often in a rage wished me religious, hoping then I should have paid my devotions to Heaven; but that would not spare you,—for was I an enthusiast, still you'd be the deity I should worship. What marks are there of a deity, but what you are to be known by;—you are at present everywhere; your dear image is always before mine eyes. Sometimes you strike me with that prodigious awe, I tremble with fear; at other times a charming compassion shines through your countenance, which revives my soul. Is it not more reasonable to adore a radiant form one has seen, than one only described?

FROM DR SWIFT TO MISS VANHOMRIGH.

Four o'Clock.

I DINED with the provost, and told him I was coming here, because I must be at prayers at six. He said you had been with him, and would not be at home this day, and went to Cellbridge to-morrow.

I said I could however go try. I fancy you told him so, that he might not come to-night; if he comes, you must piece it up as you can, else he will think it was on purpose to meet me, and I hate any thing that looks like a secret.

I cannot possibly call after prayers : I therefore came here in the afternoon while people were in church, hoping certainly to find you. I am truly affected for poor Moll, who is a girl of infinite value, and I am sure you will take all possible care of her, and I hope to live to see the sincerest friendship in the world long between you. I pray God of Heaven protect you both, and am, entièrement.

FROM DR SWIFT TO MISS VANHOMRIGH.

Monday.

I AM surprised and grieved beyond what I can express. I read your letter twice before I knew what it meant, nor can I yet well believe my eyes. Is that poor good creature dead ?* I observed she looked a little ghastly on Saturday, but it is against the usual way for one in her case to die so sudden. For God's sake get your friends about you to advise, and to order every thing in the forms. It is all you have to do. I want comfort myself in this case, and can give little. Time alone must give it you. Nothing now is your part but decency. I was wholly unprepared against so sudden an event, and pity you most of all creatures at present.

---

* Miss Mary Vanhomrigh.

FROM DR SWIFT TO MISS VANHOMRIGH.*

Gallstown, near Kinnegad, July 5, 1721.

IT was not convenient, hardly possible to write to you before now, though I had more than ordinary mind to do it, considering the disposition I found you in last, though I hope I left you in a better. I must here beg you to take more care of your health by company and exercise, or else the spleen will get the better of you, than which there is not a more foolish or troublesome disease, and what you have no pretences in the world to, if all the advantages in life can be any defence against it. Cad. assures me, he continues to esteem, and love, and value you above all things, and so will do to the end of his life, but at the same time entreats that you would not make yourself or him unhappy by imaginations. The wisest men in all ages have thought it the best course to seize the minutes as they fly, and to make every innocent action an amusement. If you knew how I struggle for a little health ; what uneasiness I am at in riding and walking, and refraining from every thing agreeable to my taste, you would think it but a small thing to take a coach now and then, and converse with fools and impertinents, to avoid spleen and sickness. Without health you will lose all desire of drinking your coffee, and [become] so low as to have no spirits. [I answer all your questions that you were used to ask Cad. and he protests he answers them in the affirmative. How go your law

---

* All this letter has appeared excepting a short passage within crotchets.

affairs ? you were once a good lawyer, but Cad. hath spoiled you. I had a weary journey in an Irish stage coach, but am pretty well since.] Pray write to me cheerfully, without complaints or expostulation, or else Cad. shall know it and punish you. What is this world without being as easy in it as prudence and fortune can make it. I find it every day more silly and insignificant, and I conform myself to it for my own ease. I am here as deep employed in other folks plantations and ditchings as if they were my own concern ; and think of my absent friends with delight, and hopes of seeing them happy, and of being happy with them.

Shall you, who have so much honour and good sense, act otherwise to make Cad. and yourself miserable. Settle your affairs and quit this scoundrel island, and things will be as you desire.

I can say no more, being called away ; mais soyez assurée que jamais personne du monde a été aimée, honorée, estimée, adorée par votre ami que vous. I drank no coffee since I left you, nor intend till I see you again : there is none worth drinking but yours, if myself may be the judge. Adieu !

FROM DR SWIFT TO MISS VANHOMRIGH.*

Clogher, June 1, 1722.

[This is the first time I have set pen to paper since I left Dublin, having not been in any settled

---

* An extract from this letter has been published ; the passages restored are marked with crotchets.

place till ten days ago, and I missed one post by ignorance, and that has stopt me five days. Before that time I was much out of order by the usual consequences of wet weather and change of drink, neither am I yet established, though much better than I was.] The weather has been so constantly bad, that I have wanted all the healthy advantages of the country, and it seems likely to continue so. It would have been infinitely better once a week to have met Kendall, and so forth, where one might pass three or four hours in drinking coffee in the morning, or dining tête-a-tête, and drinking coffee again till seven. I answer all the questions you can ask me in the affirmative. I remember your detesting and despising the conversation of the world. I have been so mortified with a man and his lady here two days, that it has made me as peevish as, (I want a comparison). I hope you are gone, or going to your country-seat, though I think you have a term upon your hands. I shall be here long enough to receive your answer, and perhaps to write to you again; but then I shall go farther off, (if my health continues,) and shall let you know my stages. I have been for some days as splenetic as ever you was in your life, which is a bold word. Remember I still enjoin you reading and exercise for the improvement of your mind, and health of your body, and grow less romantic, and talk and act like a man of this world. It is the saying of the world, and I believe you often say, I love myself, but I am so low, I cannot say it, though your new acquaintance were with you, which I heartily wish for the sake of you and myself.] God send you through your law and your reference; and remember that riches are nine parts in ten of all that is good in life, and health is the tenth; drinking coffee comes long after, and yet it is the eleventh, but without the two former you cannot drink it right; and remember the china in the old house, and Rider Street, and the Colonel's journey to France, and the London wedding, and the sick lady at Kensington, and the indisposition at Windsor, and the strain by the box of books at London. Last year I writ you civilities, and you were angry; this year I will write you none, and you will be angry; yet my thoughts were still the same, [and I give you leave to be ———, and will be answerable for them. I hope you will let me have some of your money when I see you, which I will pay honestly you again. Repondez moy si vous entendez bien tout cela,] et croyez que je seray toujours tout ce que vous desirez. Adieu.

FROM DR SWIFT TO MISS VANHOMRIGH.[*]

Lochgall, county of Armagh, July 13, 1722.

[I HAVE received your's, and have changed places so often since, that I could not assign a place where I might expect an answer from; and if you be now in the country, and this letter does not reach you in the due time after the date, I shall not expect to hear from you, because I leave this place the beginning of August.] I am well pleased with the account of your visit, and the behaviour of the ladies. I see every day as silly things among both sexes,

---

* Extracts from this letter have appeared. The restored passages are marked with crotchets.

1

and yet endure them for the sake of amusement.
The worst thing in you and me is, that we are too
hard to please, and, whether we have not made ourselves so, is the question ; at least I believe we have
the same reason.   One thing that I differ from you
in, that I do not quarrel with my best friends.   I
believe you have ten angry passages in your letter,
and every one of them enough to spoil two days
a-piece of riding and walking.   We differ prodigiously in one point,—I fly from the spleen to the
world's end, you run out of your way to meet it.
I doubt the bad weather has hindered you much
from the diversions of your country-house, and put
you upon thinking in your chamber.

The use I have made of it was to read I know
not how many diverting books of history and travels.   I wish you would get yourself a horse, and
have always two servants to attend you, and visit
your neighbours,—the worse the better.   There is a
pleasure in being reverenced, and that is always in
your power, by your superiority of sense, and an
easy fortune.   The best maxim I know in life is,
to drink your coffee when you can, and when you
cannot, to be easy without it ; while you continue
to be splenetic, count upon it, I will always preach.
Thus much I sympathize with you, that I am not
cheerful enough to write, for, I believe, coffee once
a-week is necessary to that.   I can sincerely answer
all your questions, as I used to do, but then I gave
all possible way to amusements, because they preserve my temper, as exercise does my health ; and
without health and good humour I had rather be a
dog.   I have shifted scenes oftener than I ever did
in my life, and I believe have lain in thirty beds
since I left the town ;—I always drew up the clothes
with my left hand, which is a superstition I have

learnt these ten years. [These country posts are always so capricious, that we are forced to send our letters at a call on a sudden, and mine is now demanded, though it goes not out till to-morrow. Be cheerful, and read, and ride, and laugh, as Cad—— used to advise you long ago. I hope your affairs are in some better settlement.] I long to see you in figure and equipage : pray do not lose that taste. Farewell.

FROM MISS VANHOMRIGH TO DR SWIFT.

. . . . CAD. . I thought you had quite forgot both me and your promise of writing to me. Was it not very unkind to be five weeks absent without sending me one line to let me know you were well, and remembered me. Besides, you have had such bad weather, that you could have no diversion abroad ; what then could you do, but write and read. I know you do not love cards, neither is this a time of year for that amusement. Since I saw you, I have gone more into the world than I did for some time past, because you commanded me, and I do protest here that I am more and more sick of it every day than another. One day this week I was to visit a great lady that has been a travelling for some time past, where I found a very great assembly of ladies and beaux, (dressed as I suppose to a nicety.) I hope you'll pardon me now I tell you that I heartily wished you a spectator, for I very much question if in your life you ever saw the like scene, or one more extraordinary. The lady's

behaviour was blended with so many different characters, I cannot possibly describe it without tiring
your patience. But the audience seemed to be a
creation of her own, they were, so very obsequious.
Their forms and gestures were very like those of ba-
boons and monkeys; they all grinned and chatter-
ed at the same time, and that of things I did not
understand. The rooms being hung with arras, in
which were trees very well described, just as I was
considering their beauty, and wishing myself in the
country with . . . . , one of these animals snatched my fan, and was so pleased with me, that it
seized me with such a panic that I apprehended
nothing less than being carried up to the top of the
house and served as a friend of yours was,* but in
this ———— one of their own species came in, upon which they all began to make their grimaces,
which opportunity I took and made my escape. I
have not made one single step in either law or reference since I saw you. I meet with nothing but
disappointments, yet am obliged to stay in town attending Mr P., &c. which is very hard. I do declare I have so little joy in life, that I don't care how
soon mine ends. For God's sake write to me soon,
and kindly, for in your absence, your letters are all
the joy I have on earth, and sure you are too good-
natured to grudge one hour in a week to make any
human creature happy. . . . Cad. think of me
and pity me.

---

* This passage plainly shews that Vanessa had read the manuscript of Gulliver's Travels, which were not published until
1746, about four years after her death.

1726

FROM DR SWIFT TO MISS VANHOM-
RIGH.*

I AM this moment leaving my present residence,
and if I fix any where, shall let you know it, [for I
would fain wait till I got a little good weather for
riding and walking, there never having been such a
season as this remembered ; though I doubt you
know nothing of it, but what you learn by sometimes looking out at your back window to call your
people. I had your last, with a splendid account of
your law affairs. You were once a better solicitor,
when you could contrive to make others desire your
consent to an act of Parliament against their own
interest to advance yours. Yet at present you neither want power nor skill, but disdain to exercise
either. When you are melancholy, read diverting
or amusing books : it is my receipt, and seldom
fails. Health, good humour, and fortune, are all
that is valuable in this life, and the last contributes
to the two former. I have not rode in all above poor
400 miles since I saw you, nor do I believe I shall
ride above 200 more till I see you again ; but I desire you will not venture to shake me by the hand,
for I am in mortal fear of the itch, and have no hope
left, but that some ugly vermin - called ticks have
got into my skin, of which I have pulled out some,
and must scratch out the rest. Is not this enough
to give me the spleen ? for I doubt no Christian family will receive me : and this is all a man gets by a

* A partial extract of the letter, dated 7th August 1722, has
been printed. The additions from Mr Berwick's MS. are marked as usual with crotchets.

5

northern journey.   It would be unhappy for me to
be as nice in my conversation and company as you
are, which is the only thing wherein you agree with
Glassheel, who declares there is not a conversible
creature in Ireland except Cad.   What would you
do in these parts, where politeness is as much a
stranger as cleanliness.   I am stopt, and this letter
is intended to travel with me; so adieu till the
next stage.   Aug. 8.

Yesterday I rode 29 miles without being weary,
and I wish little *Heskinage* could do as much.   Here
I leave this letter to travel one one way while I go
another, but where I do not know, nor what cabins
or bogs are in my way.   I see you this moment as
you are visible at ten in the morning, and now you
are asking your questions round, and I am answering them with a great deal of affected delays, and
the same scene has passed forty times as well as
the other, from two till seven, longer than the first
by two hours, yet each its *ses agremens particuliers.*]
A long vacation. Law lies asleep, and bad weather.
How do you wear away the time.   Is it among the
fields and groves of your country seat, or among
your cousins in town, or thinking in a train that
will be sure to vex you, and then reasoning and
forming teasing conclusions from mistaken thoughts?
The best company for you is a philosopher, whom
you would regard as much as a sermon.   I have
read more trash since I left you than would fill all
your shelves, and am abundantly the better for it,
though I scarce remember a syllable.   [Go over the
scenes of Windsor, Cleveland Row, Rider Street, St
James's Street, Kensington, the Sluttery, the Colonel in France, &c.   Cad. thinks often of these, es-

pecially on horseback,* as I am assured.]   What a
foolish thing is time, and how foolish is man, who
would be as angry if time stopt as if it passed.   But
I will not proceed at this rate ; for I am writing and
thinking myself fast into a spleen, which is the only thing that I would not compliment you by imi-
tating.   So adieu till the next place I fix in, [if I fix
at all till I return, and that I leave to fortune and
the weather.]

[As a supplement to this remarkable correspondence, I insert Miss
Vanhomrigh's last will, from a regular official extract.]

COPY OF THE WILL OF ESTHER VAN-
HOMRIGH,

FROM THE REGISTRY OF THE PREROGATIVE COURT IN IRELAND.

*Extracted from the Registry of his Majesty's Court of Prero-
gative in Ireland.*

In the name of God, Amen.——I Esther Vanhomrigh, one of the daughters of Bartholomew Vanhomrigh, late of the city of Dublin, Esq. deceased,
being of sound and disposing mind and memory,
do make and ordain this my last will and testament,
in manner and form following, that is to say :——First,

---

* Cadenus somewhat resembles Hotspur in this respect;

    " And when I am on horseback, I will swear
    - I love thee infinitely."

I recommend my soul into the hands of Almighty God, and my body I commit to the earth, to be buried at the discretion of my executors hereinafter named.   In the next place, I give and devise all my worldly substance, whether in lands, tenements, hereditaments, or trusts, and all my real and personal estate, of what nature or kind soever, unto the Reverend Doctor George Berkly, one of the Fellows of Trinity College, Dublin, and Robert Marshall of Clonmell, Esq. their heirs, executors, and administrators, chargeable nevertheless with, and subject and liable to the payment of all such debts of my own contracting, as I shall owe at the time of my death, as also unto the payment of the several legacies hereinafter bequeathed, or which shall hereafter be bequeathed by any codicil to be annexed to this my last will and testament: *Item*, I give and bequeath unto Erasmus Lewis of London, Esq. the sum of twenty-five pounds sterling, to buy a ring: *Item*: I give and bequeath unto Francis Annesly of the city of London, Esq. twenty-five pounds sterling, to buy a ring: *Item*, I give and bequeath unto John Hooks, Esq. of Gaunts in Dorsetshire, twenty-five pounds sterling, to buy a ring: *Item*, I give unto the Right Reverend Father in God William King, Lord Archbishop of Dublin, twenty-five pounds sterling, to buy a ring: *Item*, I give and bequeath unto the Right Reverend Father in God Theop. Bolton, Lord Bishop of Clonfert, twenty-five pounds sterling, to buy a ring: *Item*, I give and bequeath unto Robert Lindsey of the city of Dublin, Esq. twenty-five pounds sterling, to buy a ring: *Item*, I give and bequeath unto Edmund Shuldam of the city of Dublin, Esq. twenty-five pounds sterling, to buy a ring: *Item*, I give and bequeath unto William Lingin of the castle of

Dublin, Esq. twenty-five pounds sterling, to buy a ring : *Item*, I give and bequeath unto the Rev. Mr John Antrobus, my cousin, the like sum of money, to buy a ring : *Item*, I give and bequeath unto Bryan Robinson, doctor of physic in the city of Dublin, fifteen pounds sterling, to buy a ring : *Item*, I give and bequeath unto Mr Edward Cloker of the city of Dublin, fifteen pounds sterling, to buy a ring : *Item*, I give and bequeath unto Mr William Marshall of the city of Dublin, fifteen pounds sterling, to buy a ring : *Item*, I give and bequeath unto John Finey, son of George Finey of Kildrought in the county of Kildare, and godson to my sister, the sum of twenty-five pounds sterling, to be paid him when he shall attain the age of twenty-one years : Also I give and bequeath to his mother, Mrs Mary Finey, the sum of ten pounds sterling, to buy mourning ; and to Mrs Ann Wakefield, her sister, of the parish of St Andrews in the city of Dublin, the like sum, to buy mourning : *Item*, I give and bequeath unto Ann Kindon, who is now my servant, the sum of five pounds sterling, to buy mourning ; and to her daughter, Ann Clinkskells, the like sum of money, to buy mourning : *Item*, I give and bequeath unto every servant that shall live with me at the time of my death half a year's wages ; and to the poor of the parish, where I shall happen to die, five pounds sterling : And I do hereby make, constitute, and appoint the said Dr George Berkly, and Robert Marshall, Esq. of Clonmel, sole executors of this my last will and testament : And I do hereby revoke and make void all former and other wills and testaments by me in any wise heretofore made, either in word or writing, and declare this to be my last will and testament. In witness whereof, I, the said Esther Vanhomrigh, have hereunto set my hand and seal, this first day of May, in the year of our Lord 1723.

E. VANHOMRIGH. (*Seal.*)

Signed, published, and declared by the said Esther Vanhomrigh, for and as her last will and testament, in presence of us, who attest the same by subscribing our names in the presence of her the said testatrix.

JAS. DOYLE. ED. THRUSH. DARBY GAFNY.

The last will and testament of Esther Vanhomrigh, late deceased (having, and so forth), was proved in common form of law, and probat granted by the most Reverend Father in God Thomas, and so forth, to the Reverend George Berkely and Robert Marshall, the executors, they being first sworn personally.—Dated the 6th of June 1723.

A true copy, which I attest,
JOHN HAWKINS, *Dep. Reg.*

[There is also before the editor a copy of a commission from the Archbishop of Canterbury to the Archbishop of Dublin, to grant a probate to Miss Vanhomrigh's executors, dated London, 26th November 1725.]

ERRATA.

Page 394, last line, *Socrete* read Secrete.

416, line 11, *Brondeth* read Brandeth.

The Colonel mentioned on p. 393, is conjectured in the note to have been Miss Vanhomrigh's brother; but I now incline to believe Colonel Godfrey is meant. See Journal to Stella, Vol. II. p. 353.

The letter p. 399, with a present of venison to Mrs Vanhomrigh, ought perhaps to have been dated 30th Sept. 1711, instead of 3d Sept. 1712. Of the former date, Swift writes to Stella, " I have sent a noble haunch of venison this afternoon to Mrs Vanhomrigh. I wish you had it sirrahs." See Vol. II. p. 314.

INDEX.

END OF VOLUME XIX.

Printed by George Ramsay & Co.
Edinburgh, 1814.

Im TheStory

personalised classic books

JANE
IN
WONDERLAND

LEWIS
CARROLL

"Beautiful gift.. lovely finish.
My Niece loves it, so precious!"

Helen R Brumfieldon

★★★★★

UNIQUE GIFT

FOR KIDS, PARTNERS
AND FRIENDS

Timeless books such as:

Kids

Alice in Wonderland · The Jungle Book · The Wonderful Wizard of Oz
Peter and Wendy · **Robin Hood** · The Prince and The Pauper
The Railway Children · Treasure Island · A Christmas Carol

Adults

Romeo and Juliet · Dracula

Highly Customizable

Change Books' Title

Replace Characters Names with yours

Upload Photo that in order page)

Add Inscriptions

Visit
Im TheStory .com

and order yours today!

CPSIA information can be obtained
at www.ICGtesting.com
Printed in the USA
BVHW082208110819
555624BV00020B/3025/P